T0305049

Directors' Duties and Shareholder Litigation in
the Wake of the Financial Crisis

CORPORATIONS, GLOBALISATION AND THE LAW

Series Editor*: Janet Dine, *Director, Centre for Commercial Law Studies, Queen Mary College, University of London, UK*

This uniquely positioned monograph series aims to draw together high quality research work from established and younger scholars on what is an intriguing and under – researched area of the law. The books will offer insights into a variety of legal issues that concern corporations operating on the global stage, including interaction with World Trade Organization (WTO), international financial institutions and nation states, in both developing and developed countries. While the underlying foundation of the series will be that of company law, broadly-defined, authors are encouraged to take an approach that draws on the work of other social sciences, such as politics, economics and development studies and to offer an international or comparative perspective where appropriate. Specific topics to be considered will include corporate governance, corporate responsibility, taxation and criminal liability, among others. The series will undoubtedly offer an important contribution to legal thinking and to the wider globalisation debate.

Titles in the series include:

Directors' Duties and Shareholder Litigation in the Wake of the Financial Crisis

Edited by

Joan Loughrey

Director of the Centre for Business Law and Practice, School of Law, University of Leeds, UK

CORPORATIONS, GLOBALISATION AND THE LAW

Edward Elgar

Cheltenham, UK • Northampton, MA, USA

Published by
Edward Elgar Publishing Limited
The Lypiatts
15 Lansdown Road
Cheltenham
Glos GL50 2JA
UK

Edward Elgar Publishing, Inc.
William Pratt House
9 Dewey Court
Northampton
Massachusetts 01060
USA

A catalogue record for this book
is available from the British Library

Library of Congress Control Number: 2012942514

ISBN 978 0 85793 965 4

Typeset by Columns Design XML Ltd, Reading
Printed and bound by MPG Books Group, UK

Contents

Contributors

Dr Folarin Akinbami, Lecturer in Commercial Law in the School of Law, Durham University, UK.

Mr Andrew Campbell, Director, Ashridge Strategic Management, London, UK.

Mr Robin Hollington QC, New Square Chambers, London, UK.

Professor Andrew Keay, Professor of Corporate and Commercial Law, Centre for Business Law and Practice, School of Law, University of Leeds, UK and Barrister, Kings Chambers, Leeds, and 13 Old Square, London, UK.

Professor Joan Loughrey, Professor of Law, Director of the Centre for Business Law and Practice, School of Law, University of Leeds, UK.

Professor Roman Tomasic, Dean of Law, University of South Australia, Visiting Professor of Company Law, Durham University, UK.

Professor Charlotte Villiers, Professor of Company Law, School of Law, University of Bristol, UK.

Abbreviations

ACCA	Association of Chartered Certified Accountants
ASB	Accounting Standards Board
BIS	Department for Business, Innovation and Skills
CDO	collateralized debt obligations
CLRSG	Company Law Review Steering Group
CPR	Civil Procedure Rules
DTI	Department of Trade and Industry
FRC	Financial Reporting Council
FRRP	Financial Reporting Review Panel
FSA	Financial Services Authority
OFR	Operating and Financial Review
WTO	World Trade Organization

Introduction

Joan Loughrey

This book brings together contributions from both academics and practitioners assessing the operation and efficacy of directors' duties and
shareholder litigation in the wake of the financial crisis and its aftermath.
It is striking that no significant litigation has yet emerged against the
directors of banks and financial institutions for breaching their duties,
despite the disastrous management that was uncovered by the crisis.
What could be the reason for this? Does it reveal inadequacies in the law
on directors' duties and shareholder litigation? During the period up to
and after the start of the financial crisis, the duties of directors, and the
right of shareholders to take action on the company's behalf against
directors for breach of their duties was governed by the common law. If
that was deficient then does the Companies Act 2006, which replaced the
common law with codified directors' duties and a new statutory derivative action, address those deficiencies? Given that sufficient time has
elapsed since the commencement of the crisis for shareholder litigation to
emerge, and given that enough is now known about the crisis in the UK
from various public reports, it seems timely to assess directors' duties
and shareholder litigation with these questions in mind. This is what the
contributions in this collection set out to do.

The story of the global financial crisis is well-known. The first signs of
trouble emerged in the US sub-prime markets but by early 2007 in the
UK the Bank of England and the Financial Services Authority (FSA)
were raising concerns about the possibility of liquidity problems in the
wholesale markets.[1] In September 2007 there was the first run on a
British bank for over 100 years at Northern Rock plc (Northern Rock). In
2008, in the US, Lehman Brothers went bankrupt, following which there
was a massive loss of confidence and the money markets froze world-
wide. In the UK, by the end of 2008, Northern Rock, Bradford and

---

[1] The House of Commons Treasury Committee, *The Run on the Rock* (HC
56–1) (January 2008) at 14.

Bingley plc, the Royal Bank of Scotland Group plc (RBS), Lloyds TSB Bank plc, and HBOS plc had been bailed out by the Government and entered full or part-public ownership.[2] HBOS plc was taken over by Lloyds TSB Bank plc in January 2009 while Alliance & Leicester disappeared in 2010, having been taken over by Santander plc, as were parts of Bradford and Bingley plc's business.[3] The problems that were initially confined to the financial sector ultimately had an impact on the real economy, ushering in the deepest recession in the UK for 70 years. At the time of writing many of the world's economies, including the UK's, remain weak and the future is uncertain.

The question of what caused the financial crisis has been extensively discussed and no consensus has been reached other than that it was the product of the interaction of different factors. It is generally accepted that macro-economic factors such as global imbalances played a significant part.[4] While countries such as the US, UK, Ireland and other countries had large current account deficits[5] others such as Japan and China had accumulated large current account surpluses and developed large foreign currency reserves which they sought to invest in, inter alia, overseas securities, particularly in the US and the UK. In the US this took the form of investment in government bonds or government-guaranteed bonds and in the UK, investment in mortgage-backed securities.[6] This resulted in large capital flows into both the UK and the US and allowed both countries to keep their interest rates at artificially low levels.[7] The low interest rates led to the availability of easy credit, the growth of the sub-prime market in the US and, in the UK, the extension of high-risk mortgages to low-income groups. As a result there was a property and credit bubble in both countries.[8] At the same time, the low rates of return

---

[2]   BBC, 'UK banks receive £37bn bail-out' (13 October 2008).

[3]   See discussion in the House of Commons Treasury Committee, *Banking Crisis: Dealing with the Failure of the UK Banks,* Seventh Report of Session 2008–09 (HC 416) (21 April 2009).

[4]   FSA, *The Turner Review: A Regulatory Response to the Global Banking Crisis* (March 2009) at 11; The House of Commons Treasury Committee, *Banking Crisis: Dealing with the Failure of the UK Banks,* Seventh Report of Session 2008–09 (HC 416) (21 April 2009) at 12–13.

[5]   FSA, *The Turner Review: A Regulatory Response to the Global Banking Crisis* (March 2009) at 33.

[6]   Ibid at 12, 32.

[7]   Ibid at 13.

[8]   Ibid at 13, 29–30.

on government bonds led investors to seek higher returns on riskier investments and this demand was met by new financial products.[9]

This financial innovation has been identified as a key factor in either causing or exacerbating the crisis for several reasons. First, the products became so complicated that the risks they presented were not understood.[10] Second, because executives erroneously believed that these products dispersed risks,[11] they took even greater risks than they might have otherwise taken. Third, because of globalization,[12] the products, and the unrecognized risks they carried, were exported across the global financial system through a complex chain of products and relationships. This interconnectedness exacerbated systemic risk, and ultimately led to the economic shock of the financial crisis being transmitted across the world from one economy to another.

Another key factor in the crisis was therefore the failure of risk management. In assessing the risk of complex financial products and the likelihood of adverse events, both regulators and the regulated placed undue reliance on faulty risk models containing erroneous or incomplete assumptions, and complex mathematical formulae that were not properly understood.[13] As a result there was a failure to recognize the extent of the risk retained by the institutions.[14]

---

[9]   Ibid at 14.

[10]   Though it may be that the lack of comprehension among market players of the real value of these products and the risks they presented has been over-stated. For example, the top CDO trader at Deutsche Bank is said to have referred to the assets underlying collateralized debt obligations as 'crap' and 'pigs': T. Braithwaite, F. Guerrera and J. Baer, 'Senate Report Says Goldman Misled Investors' *Financial Times*, 14 April 2011.

[11]   FSA, *The Turner Review: A Regulatory Response to the Global Banking Crisis* (March 2009) at 42.

[12]   Ibid at 36; M. Legg and J. Harris, 'How the American Dream Became a Global Nightmare: An Analysis of the Causes of the Global Financial Crisis' (2010) 32 *University of New South Wales Law Journal* 350 at 370.

[13]   FSA, *The Turner Review: A Regulatory Response to the Global Banking Crisis* (March 2009) at 22, 44; M. Legg and J. Harris, 'How the American Dream Became a Global Nightmare: An Analysis of the Causes of the Global Financial Crisis' (2010) 32 *University of New South Wales Law Journal* 350 at 362.

[14]   FSA, *The Turner Review: A Regulatory Response to the Global Banking Crisis* (March 2009) at 16, 43.

However, the crisis has also been blamed on: financial deregulation and regulatory failure,[15] in particular the failure of risk-based regulation,[16] and the failure to regulate the new financial products; political pressure to engage in 'light touch regulation' so that competitiveness was not impeded;[17] and gate-keeper failure, particularly that of the credit rating agencies, who awarded financial products the triple A rating that allowed public bodies to invest in them.[18] The crisis has also been blamed on inadequately capitalized financial institutions that were excessively lever-aged and that lacked a sufficient buffer to cope with the crisis;[19] irrational exuberance in the market followed by a collapse in confidence;[20] a mis-placed faith in the efficiency and rationality of capital markets and a mistaken belief that these would restrain excessive risk taking and winnow out harmful financial products, coupled with a presumption in favour of deregulation;[21] and executive remuneration policies that created perverse incentives to take undue risk.[22]

In addition, however, a number of policy-makers and commentators have blamed failings in corporate governance in banks and financial institutions,[23]

---

[15]   Ibid at 36–38, 43.

[16]   FSA, *The Failure of the Royal Bank of Scotland* (December 2011) at 253–294; M. Legg and J. Harris, 'How the American Dream Became a Global Nightmare: An Analysis of the Causes of the Global Financial Crisis' (2010) 32 *University of New South Wales Law Journal* 350 at 371–372.

[17]   FSA, *The Failure of the Royal Bank of Scotland* (December 2011) at para 672.

[18]   FSA, *The Turner Review: A Regulatory Response to the Global Banking Crisis* (March 2009) at 22; M. Legg and J. Harris, 'How the American Dream Became a Global Nightmare: An Analysis of the Causes of the Global Financial Crisis' (2010) 32 *University of New South Wales Law Journal* 350 at 376–378.

[19]   FSA, *The Turner Review: A Regulatory Response to the Global Banking Crisis* (March 2009) at 43; FSA, *The Failure of the Royal Bank of Scotland* (December 2011) at 64–93. Banks also had liquidity issues.

[20]   FSA, *The Turner Review: A Regulatory Response to the Global Banking Crisis* (March 2009) at 25.

[21]   Ibid at 39, 45, 49; R. Tomasic, 'Raising Corporate Governance Standards in Response to Corporate Rescue and Insolvency' (2009) *Corporate Rescue and Insolvency* 5.

[22]   FSA, *The Turner Review: A Regulatory Response to the Global Banking Crisis* (March 2009) at 47.

[23]   Ibid. See the review of the literature in H. Mehran, A. Morrison and J. Shapiro, 'Corporate Governance and the Banks: What Have We Learned from the Financial Crisis?' Federal Reserve Bank of New York Staff Report No 502 (June 2011) at http://www.newyorkfed.org/research/staff_reports/sr502.pdf (accessed 31 March 2012).

though this claim has been disputed.[24] The FSA, for example, concluded that there were no corporate governance failings at board level in RBS,[25] although closer scrutiny of its findings show that in making this assertion the FSA focused on processes and procedures, rather than the substantive effectiveness of those procedures. In fact, it found that there were questions raised over the board's effectiveness.[26] In any event it is not disputed that corporate governance problems were revealed by the crisis. Thus the Turner and Walker Reviews concluded that shareholders failed to act as a check on management[27] even when, as the FSA found in the case of the acquisition of ABN AMRO by RBS, they had significant reservations about the strategy adopted by the board,[28] and that boards themselves failed to identify and restrain excessive risk-taking.[29] Problems were also identified in relation to the performance of non-executive directors who lacked relevant industry experience,[30] failed to commit sufficient time to their role and failed to monitor and challenge the executive.[31] Boards also failed to exercise adequate oversight of remuneration policies for senior employees with the result that executive remuneration, including bonuses, was linked to short-term performance.[32]

---

[24] B. Cheffins, 'Did Corporate Governance "Fail" During the 2008 Stock Market Crisis? The Case of the Standard and Poor 500' (2009) 65 *Business Lawyer* 1.

[25] FSA, 'FSA closes supervisory investigation of RBS' (2 December 2010).

[26] FSA, *The Failure of the Royal Bank of Scotland* (December 2011) at paras 583–593.

[27] FSA, *The Turner Review: A Regulatory Response to the Global Banking Crisis* (March 2009) at 46. See also D. Walker, *A Review of Corporate Governance in UK Banks and Other Financial Industry Entities: Final Recommendations* (26 November 2009) at 12.

[28] FSA, *The Failure of the Royal Bank of Scotland* (December 2011) at 166–167. Despite a number of shareholders, particularly hedge funds, having concerns, 94.5 per cent of shareholders supported the ABN AMRO acquisition.

[29] FSA, *The Turner Review: A Regulatory Response to the Global Banking Crisis* (March 2009) at 92; D. Walker, *A Review of Corporate Governance in UK Banks and Other Financial Industry Entities: Final Recommendations* (26 November 2009) at 220, 225–226, 231.

[30] Although Northern Rock's board included an experienced fund manager, the former CEO of a bank and a former member of the Court of the Bank of England: F. Guerrera and P. Thal-Larsen 'Gone by the Board: Why the Directors of Big Banks Failed to Spot Credit Risks' *Financial Times*, 26 June 2008.

[31] D. Walker, *A Review of Corporate Governance in UK Banks and Other Financial Industry Entities: Final Recommendations* (26 November 2009) at 234.

[32] Ibid at para 1.14. FSA, *The Failure of the Royal Bank of Scotland* (December 2011) at 225–226; T. Kirchmaier, 'Inject Governance and Not Just

In the light of these failings this book considers what lessons can be drawn from the financial crisis regarding the operation of directors' duties and shareholder litigation more generally. It might be suggested that such a project overlooks the fact that banks are quite different from other types of commercial company. The nature of their business means that they are likely to be more highly leveraged than other types of business and more vulnerable.[33] Because they play a central role in the economy, bank crises are far more significant for the real economy and for the taxpayer than other kinds of corporate collapses.[34] Banks and financial institutions may therefore need to be more strictly regulated and have governance arrangements that go beyond those normally required of other types of company.[35] Consequently, one needs to be cautious about drawing conclusions from the banks' experience during the financial crisis and attempting to apply these more widely.

Nevertheless, the financial crisis has highlighted issues that have ramifications beyond the financial sector. The Walker Review itself concluded that some of its findings and recommendations were equally applicable to other types of UK company, particularly regarding the lack of institutional shareholder engagement and the need to enhance this to facilitate greater monitoring and disciplining of management.[36] The UK Code of Corporate Governance was amended in the light of the Walker Review. It stipulates, inter alia, that all boards need to have a balance of skills, experience, independence and knowledge of the company,[37] that directors should have appropriate knowledge of the company and access to its staff,[38] that non-executive directors should constructively challenge executives,[39] that risk management should be addressed and boards should be responsible for determining the nature and extent of the risks

---

Cash: Some Thoughts on the Governance of Banks and the Likely Failure of More Banking Regulation' (27 October 2008) at 5–6 at http://ssrn.com/abstract= 130320 (accessed 16 January 2012).

[33]   D. Walker, *A Review of Corporate Governance in UK Banks and Other Financial Industry Entities: Final Recommendations* (26 November 2009) at para 1.4.

[34]   FSA, *The Turner Review: A Regulatory Response to the Global Banking Crisis* (March 2009) at 42.

[35]   D. Walker, *A Review of Corporate Governance in UK Banks and Other Financial Industry Entities: Final Recommendations* (26 November 2009) at para 1.6.

[36]   Ibid at 6.

[37]   FRC, The UK Code of Corporate Governance (June 2010), Principle B1.

[38]   Ibid, Principle B4.

[39]   Ibid, Principle A4.

that the company should undertake.[40] These responses point to concerns about the role of boards, non-executive directors and institutional shareholders that are common to both banks and other types of company.

Moreover, the law's capacity to respond to the failings identified in the performance of bank directors in the run up to and during the crisis holds lessons that go wider than the financial crisis and the banks. Given the level of shareholder anger at the scale of the losses incurred by institutions during the crisis, and given that various inquiries into the crisis identified missteps by bank directors, then arguably if ever there was going to be shareholder litigation against directors for breaching their duties to their companies, it would have materialized against the directors of banks. Generally though, this has not occurred. Instead, shareholders have attacked on other fronts, including a claim against the Government by the shareholders of Northern Rock in respect of the compulsory acquisition of their shares during nationalization,[41] litigation or threatened litigation against various institutions for making false and misleading statements in prospectuses preceding rights issues in troubled entities, and claims by investors against banks over the mis-selling of financial products.[42] Thus although Lloyds directors faced action by shareholders in the US and threatened litigation in the UK, these actions related to the making of misleading statements to shareholders in relation to the takeover of HBOS plc by Lloyds plc, and non-disclosure by Lloyds plc and its directors of the fact that HBOS plc had received emergency liquidity funding from the Bank of England.[43] In contrast, there has been no litigation by institutions, or by shareholders on their institutions' behalf, against bank directors for breaching their duties in the run up to and during the crisis. If, even in such extreme circumstances, and with such huge losses, a claim against bank directors was not viable, either because nothing that bank boards did or failed to do amounted to an

---

[40] Ibid, Principle C2.

[41] The shareholders' claim was dismissed by the Court of Appeal: *R (on the application of SRM Global Master Fund LP) v Treasury Commissioner* [2009] EWCA Civ 788; [2010] BCC 558. See discussion in Chapter 4 of this book.

[42] These claims have, in turn, generally been unsuccessful see: *Titan Steel Wheels Ltd v Royal Bank of Scotland* [2010] EWHC 211 (Comm); *Camerata Property Inc v Credit Suisse Securities (Europe) Ltd* [2011] EWHC 479 (Comm); [2011] 1 CLC 627; *Camerata Property Inc v Credit Suisse Securities (Europe) Ltd* [2012] EWHC 7 (Comm). RBS shareholders are bringing a similar action in respect of a 2008 rights issue: H. Wilson, 'Fred Goodwin: we weren't at fault in RBS failure' *The Telegraph* 26 June 2012.

[43] 'Lloyds faces lawsuit from US investors' *The Financial Times*, 1 January 2012.

actionable breach of duty, or because the obstacles facing shareholders wishing to bring litigation were too high, or due to problems with the very concept of shareholders as effective monitors, then this has ramifications that go well beyond the financial sector. It raises far broader questions about the efficacy of the law on directors' duties and shareholder litigation as a means of holding directors to account, particularly in the context of dispersed share-ownership companies.

The purpose of this book is to consider these issues. Although any action against bank directors would be for breach of their common law duties, the book is forward-looking and considers how effective the present law under the Companies Act 2006 would be at addressing the problems flagged up by the financial crisis.

ORGANIZATION OF THE BOOK

The discussion in the book falls broadly into three sections. The first is devoted to directors and directors' duties. The second part focuses on shareholder litigation and the third part draws together both themes and concludes.

The first section focuses on two duties that are particularly relevant in the context of the financial crisis, namely the directors' duty of care and skill now contained in the Companies Act 2006 s.174, and the duty to promote the success of the company for the benefit of its members as whole contained in the Companies Act 2006 s.172. As for the first, given the poor quality of board decisions as revealed, for example, in the FSA's reports into Northern Rock and RBS, it seems self-evident that directors would be vulnerable to claims that they breached their duties of care and skill. Therefore, in Chapter 1 Loughrey examines the directors' duty of care and skill at common law and under s.174. Through an analysis of the case law, and the various public reports into the crisis, she identifies the obstacles to successful claims against bank directors for breach of their duties of care and skill.

In Chapter 2 Keay analyses the duty under the Companies Act 2006 s.172 which had been heralded as introducing a new model for corporate decision-making based on 'enlightened shareholder value', and questions whether it is fit for purpose. The financial crisis highlighted in an extreme fashion the costs to society of reckless corporate behaviour that focuses on the promotion of shareholder value in the short-term and disregards the costs of corporate behaviour to other stakeholders. Keay considers whether s.172 will be successful in discouraging short-term behaviour and in encouraging boards to take a more inclusive approach.

He also considers the prospects for successful claims for breach of the s.172 duty where boards take decisions that do not promote the success of the company.

In the third chapter Villiers turns to the related issue of the obligation under the Companies Act 2006 s.417 for companies and their boards to provide a business review and the manner in which companies are complying with their reporting obligations. Both Villiers and Keay point out that s.417 is closely related to s.172, as the reporting obligations under the former are designed to allow shareholders to assess how directors are performing their duty to promote the success of the company under the latter. It is key therefore to facilitating shareholder monitoring and to promoting the concept of enlightened shareholder value. Villiers assesses the extent to which the reporting obligations under s.417 contribute to these goals, and thus to the success or otherwise, of s.172 and to the objective of more informed shareholder engagement.

While some have argued that the crisis was the product of moral failure and greed,[44] there is evidence that behavioural factors were at work in leading to the short-termist and reckless behaviour exhibited by bank boards. Thus the Walker Review claimed that

'the principal deficiencies in [bank] boards related much more to patterns of behaviour than to organization'[45]

and that behavioural changes were required from boards and senior managers.[46] Campbell's chapter examines the kinds of cognitive failure that could cause senior managers to make bad decisions and suggests safeguards that could be put in place to reduce the impact of these sub-conscious influences on decision-making. As explained in the Conclusion his arguments give us a different way of thinking about s.172 and its potential to alter directors' behaviour.

In Chapter 5 the book turns to examine the shareholder role in more detail, with a review by Tomasic and Akinbami of the factors contributing to a lack of shareholder activism in the UK. These factors explain in part the very low levels of litigation involving shareholders in public companies that Tomasic and Akinbami detected in their survey of shareholder

---

[44] A. Kling, 'The Financial Crisis: Moral Failure or Cognitive Failure?' (2010) 33 *Harvard Journal of Law and Policy* 507.

[45] D. Walker, *A Review of Corporate Governance in UK Banks and Other Financial Industry Entities: Final Recommendations* (26 November 2009) at 12.

[46] Ibid at 9–10.

litigation in England and Wales between 2000 and 2010. Tomasic and Akinbami also examine one of the few significant shareholder actions that have resulted so far from the crisis, namely the unsuccessful litigation by the Northern Rock shareholders against the Government arising out of the compulsory acquisition of their shares.[47]

In Chapter 6 Hollington provides a rare example of successful shareholder litigation that has arisen as a direct result of the financial crisis, namely the use of the remedy for just and equitable winding up by members of open-ended investment funds in the Cayman Islands and the British Virgin Islands. The remedy for just and equitable winding up is rarely used now in the UK owing to the availability of the unfair prejudice remedy, but Hollington's chapter provides an opportunity to consider how an established shareholder remedy can be utilized imaginatively by shareholders to obtain effective redress, provided that they are faced with cooperative courts.

Subsequently in Chapter 7 Loughrey and Keay examine the statutory derivative action under the Companies Act 2006, which replaced the derivative action at common law. The derivative action provides a remedy to the company for breaches by directors of their duties to the company. In the absence of litigation authorized by the company itself through the board, this would be the form of action that shareholders would have to utilize to pursue claims against bank directors on their company's behalf. However after issuing the claim form shareholders must seek the court's permission to continue with the claim. Consequently the utility of the derivative action as a remedy for breaches of directors' duties is contingent on the manner in which the courts perform this gatekeeper function. Loughrey and Keay consider the case law on applications for permission under s.261 and s.263 of the Companies Act 2006 and assess the approach the courts have adopted to date. This chapter was previously published in the *Journal of Business Law* in 2010[48] and has been updated to incorporate discussion of the later decisions of *Stainer v Lee*,[49]

---

[47]   *SRM Global Master Fund LP v Commissioners of HM Treasury* [2009] EWCA Civ 788; [2010] BCC 558.

[48]   J. Loughrey and A. Keay, 'Derivative Proceedings in a Brave New World for Company Management and Shareholders' (2010) 3 *Journal of Business Law* 151.

[49]   [2010] EWHC 1539 (Ch); [2011] BCC 134.

Langley Ward Ltd v Trevor,[50] *Kleanthous v Paphitis*[51] and *Parry v Bartlett*.[52]

To accurately assess the impact of the law and to identify any weaknesses, it is necessary to understand how it operates in practice. Chapter 8 therefore features a debate between academic and practitioner experts regarding, amongst other matters, the efficacy and impact of s.172 Companies Act 2006 and the derivative action in practice. It provides a valuable insight into the practitioner approach to these issues, a matter that will be returned to in the Conclusion.

Finally, the Conclusion draws together the various themes that emerge during the course of the book.

Thanks are due to the contributors to this collection for their patience, to Professor Janet Dine for her encouragement, to my colleagues in the Centre for Business Law and Practice at Leeds for their support and assistance, particularly Michael Galanis and Professor Andrew Keay, to those who contributed to the debate in Chapter 8, and to the editor and publishers of the *Journal of Business Law* for granting permission to include Keay and Loughrey's material on the derivative action in Chapter 7. Professor Tomasic would also like to thank the British Academy for funding some data collection under the Stakeholders and Gatekeepers in Corporate Governance project funded under Co-Reach Project 64-033. They would also like to thank the Leverhulme Trust for funding on the Tipping Points project. The chapters are up to date as of June 2011, with some chapters incorporating limited consideration of later developments.

---

[50]   [2011] EWHC 1893 (Ch).
[51]   [2011] EWHC 2287 (Ch).
[52]   [2011] EWHC 3146 (Ch).

1 The director's duty of care and skill and the financial crisis

Joan Loughrey

I. INTRODUCTION

In December 2010 the Financial Services Authority (FSA) announced that the crisis at the Royal Bank of Scotland plc (RBS) could not be attributed to a lack of integrity or dishonest activity on the part of any individual at the bank. Rather, senior management had made a series of bad decisions, such as the aggressive acquisition of ABN AMRO and the expansion of the investment banking business. These matters went to competence rather than integrity.[1] The FSA's full report into the matter subsequently confirmed this position.[2] Similarly, the Treasury Committee concluded that at Northern Rock plc (Northern Rock) the directors had 'pursued a reckless business model'[3] featuring an aggressive expansionary lending policy combined with low holdings of retail deposits,[4] reliance on securitization and wholesale funding to maintain liquidity, and a lack of adequate insurance against liquidity problems.[5] It had continued to expand this funding model despite signs that this could cause problems if the markets became less liquid.[6] However, while this business strategy was described as 'fatally flawed', and the directors were

---

[1] FSA, 'FSA Closes Supervisory Investigation of RBS' (2 December 2010).

[2] FSA, *The Failure of the Royal Bank of Scotland* (December 2011).

[3] The House of Commons Treasury Committee, *The Run on the Rock* (HC 56–1) (January 2008) at 3.

[4] Ibid at 13–14.

[5] Ibid at 16.

[6] The risks had been identified by the Bank of England in its Financial Stability Report (April 2007) and by the FSA in its Financial Risk Outlook: ibid at 14. By March 2007 the board of Northern Rock plc itself had picked up signs of problems in the US sub-prime market: ibid at 15.

criticized as being the principal authors of the bank's difficulties,[7] there was no suggestion of fraud or bad faith on their part.

Given these conclusions, any claims against directors arising out of the financial crisis were likely to be based on breach of their duty of care rather than breach of fiduciary duty. Moreover if it is true that 'directors' mismanagement and incompetence were the primary causes of the crisis'[8] (something that is disputed),[9] one might have expected such claims to have materialized by now, brought either by new boards against past directors, or by shareholders in the form of a derivative action.[10] But this has not occurred. On the contrary, the new board of Northern Rock was advised that there were insufficient grounds to proceed with any legal action for negligence against its former directors and disclaimed any intention of bringing such an action.[11] Again, there was little sign that RBS intended to take any legal action against its former directors.[12]

While there may be many reasons for this, some of which are explored elsewhere in this book, this chapter focuses on the substantive content of the director's duty of care and skill and considers what obstacles a claim against directors for breach of this duty might face. Any claim against bank directors would be under the common law, given that this was applicable at the relevant time. However it is unlikely that there was much difference between the common law duty as it had developed immediately prior to the Companies Act 2006, and the statutory duty of care in the Companies Act 2006 s.174. Moreover recent case law on the common law duty of care is likely to remain relevant in interpreting the

---

[7] Ibid at 18.

[8] D. Arsalidou, 'The Banking Crisis: Rethinking and Refining the Accountability of Bank Directors' (2010) 5 *Journal of Business Law* 284 at 285.

[9] See for example: B. Cheffins, 'Did Corporate Governance "Fail" During the 2008 Stock Market Meltdown? The Case of the Standard & Poor 500' (2009) 65 *Business Lawyer* 1.

[10] Under the Companies Act 2006 s.260.

[11] 'No Legal Action Against Northern Rock Bosses' *The Independent*, 14 October 2008.

[12] There remains however the possibility of personal claims by shareholders: the RBS shareholders intended to commence an action based on misleading statements in the prospectus for the rights disclosure in April 2008 which they claimed failed to disclose the true financial situation of the bank. Similar actions are pending against Bradford & Bingley and against Lloyds TSB Bank plc (in respect of the takeover of HBOS plc): 'Lloyds Faces Lawsuit From US Investors' *The Financial Times*, 1 January 2012.

codified duty.[13] However, older case law must be approached with caution given the relaxed attitude to the duty of care and application of a purely subjective standard in many of the early decisions.[14] Given this, any conclusions about how the duty of care would have applied in the context of the financial crisis will throw light not just on the common law duty but also on the likely effect of the statutory duty.

The chapter is organized as follows: it first provides a brief overview of the nature and scope of the duty of care, skill and diligence and its development from what was thought to be a purely subjective standard to a more objective standard. It then considers the kinds of conduct by bank directors that may have breached that duty before focusing in more detail on the prospects of a successful claim against bank directors on four key grounds namely: that they failed to monitor and failed to ensure that adequate risk management systems were instituted; that they failed to keep themselves sufficiently informed about their company's business; that they placed undue reliance on executives and failed to supervise delegations of power; and that they took negligent decisions. Finally it considers the issue of causation, before concluding.

II. THE DEVELOPMENT OF THE DUTY OF CARE, SKILL AND DILIGENCE

Historically the duty of care and skill was undemanding. Following the leading case of *Re City Equitable Fire Insurance Co Ltd*[15] it was thought that directors would only be in breach of duty if they failed to exercise the care and skill that they in fact possessed. This may have been a misinterpretation of the case[16] but subsequent decisions continued to apply a low subjective standard. Then in *Norman v Theodore Goddard*[17]

---

[13]   Since the Companies Act 2006 s.170(4) states that the general duties in the Act shall be interpreted and applied in the same way as common law rules or equitable principles, and regard shall be had to the corresponding common law rules and equitable principles in interpreting and applying the general duties.

[14]   P.L. Davies, *Gower and Davies' Principles of Company Law*, 8th edn (Sweet and Maxwell, London, 2008) at 491.

[15]   [1925] Ch 407.

[16]   A. Hicks, 'Directors' Liability for Management Errors' (1994) 110 *Law Quarterly Review* 390 at 392; S. Worthington, 'The Duty to Monitor: A Modern View of the Director's Duty of Care' in F. Patfield (ed), *Perspectives on Company Law: 2* (London, Kluwer Law International, 1997) at 183–190.

[17]   [1992] BCC 14 at 16.

and *Re D'Jan of London Ltd*[18] Lord Hoffmann (then Justice and Lord Justice Hoffmann respectively) held that the standard of care required of directors was accurately set out in the Insolvency Act 1986 s.214(4). This required directors to show the skill and care of

> '… a reasonably diligent person having both (a) the general knowledge, skill and experience that may reasonably be expected of a person carrying out the same functions as are carried out by that director in relation to the company, and (b) the general knowledge, skill and experience that that director has.'

This imposed a mixed objective/subjective standard, with the former establishing a minimum standard expected of all directors and the latter raising the standard where the director possessed a special skill.[19] While this was thought to have replaced the purely subjective standard the matter remained unresolved[20] until the Companies Act 2006 was enacted.

The Companies Act 2006 s.174 provides that a director must exercise the care, skill and diligence that would be exercised by a reasonably diligent person with (a) the general knowledge, skill and experience that may reasonably be expected of a person carrying out the functions carried out by the director in relation to the company, and (b) the general knowledge, skill and experience that the director has. Thus a director will be measured against a minimum objective standard while the subjective element raises the bar so that if a director has special skills, knowledge or experience then he or she will breach their duty if they fail to exercise these.[21] This reflects the law as set out in *Re D'Jan of London Ltd* and *Norman v Theodore Goddard* and brings the tortious duty of care into

---

[18] [1993] BCC 646 at 648.

[19] D. Prentice, 'Corporate Personality, Limited Liability and the Protection of Creditors' in R Grantham and C. Rickett (eds), *Corporate Personality in the Twentieth Century* (Oxford, Hart Publishing, 1998) at 112. For explanations of the interaction between the subjective and objective standard in the context of s.214 Insolvency Act 1986 see *Re Brian D Pierson (Contractors) Ltd* [1999] BCC 26 at 49, 55.

[20] See the Law Commission, *Company Directors: Regulating Conflicts of Interest and Formulating a Statement of Duties* (Law Com, Report No 261, Cm 4436) (Scot Law Commission No 173) (London, Stationery Office, 1999) at paras 15.5 and 15.8.

[21] *Lexi Holdings Plc (in administration) v Luqman* [2008] EWHC 1639; [2008] 2 BCLC 725 at 738 per Briggs J; on appeal [2009] EWCA Civ 117; [2009] BCC 716 at 721 per Sir Andrew Morritt C.

line with the objective contractual duty of care owed by executive directors through their contract of employment.[22]

However although s.174 settles the debate around the standard of care, it leaves many other questions unanswered. For example, while the same standard applies to both executive and non-executive directors, what is expected of directors will vary, depending on the functions the director carries out for the company. This may reflect the fact that while all directors should display the same degree of care, the degree of skill that can be expected of them will vary depending on what skills they have or can be expected to have given their role in the company.[23] Thus there will be different expectations of finance directors, for example, compared with human resources directors, and of non-executive directors and executive directors.[24] It has been said that no particular skills are expected of non-executive directors and they will be assessed on the skills they bring to the job.[25]

Again while this is not explicit on the face of s.174, it is likely that the courts will take account of the size and nature of the company, the composition of the board and the manner in which functions are distributed in the company in determining what could be expected of a person in the director's position.[26] These were matters that were taken into account at common law[27] and the statutory duties are to be interpreted in the light of relevant case law.[28]

One problem in ascertaining what the duty of care requires is the absence of case law on the matter. Some guidance can be gleaned from the case law on the Insolvency Act 1986 s.214 and on directors' disqualification under the Company Directors Disqualification Act 1986 s.6, which requires the disqualification of unfit directors of insolvent companies. However in relation to the latter, in the absence of dishonesty, a high degree of incompetence is necessary before disqualification is

---

[22]   C. Riley, 'The Company Director's Duty of Care and Skill: the Case for an Onerous but Subjective Standard' (1999) 62 *Modern Law Review* 697 at 700.

[23]   A. Hicks, 'Directors' Liability for Management Errors' (1994) 110 *Law Quarterly Review* 390 at 393; A. Keay, *Directors' Duties* (Bristol, Jordan Publishing, 2009) at 215.

[24]   *Secretary of State for Trade and Industry v Baker (No 5)* [1999] 1 BCLC 433 at 484.

[25]   A. Keay, *Directors' Duties* (Bristol, Jordan Publishing, 2009) at 216.

[26]   Ibid at 187.

[27]   *Re City Equitable Fire Insurance Co Ltd* [1925] Ch 407 at 427.

[28]   Companies Act 2006 s.170(4).

warranted,[29] whereas it is not clear whether it is necessary to establish gross negligence in order to succeed in a claim based on a breach of the duty of care, skill and diligence.[30] If not, behaviour that does not attract the sanction of disqualification could nevertheless constitute a breach of the duty of care.

In fact one of the leading cases on the director's duty of care is a disqualification case. In *Secretary of State for Trade and Industry v Baker (No 5)* (*'Re Barings'*) Parker J stated that:

'Directors have, both collectively and individually, a continuing duty to acquire and maintain a sufficient knowledge and understanding of the company's business to enable them properly to discharge their duties as directors.'[31]

Without such information directors cannot effectively discharge their duty to monitor. Parker J went on to say:

'Whilst directors are entitled (subject to the articles of association of the company) to delegate particular functions to those below them in the management chain, and to trust their competence and integrity to a reasonable extent, the exercise of the power of delegation does not absolve a director from the duty to supervise the discharge of the delegated functions.'[32]

These statements apply as much to non-executive directors as to executive directors[33] but the extent of the latter's duty and whether it has been discharged depend on the facts of the case and the director's role in the company.[34]

---

[29] *Secretary of State for Trade and Industry v Baker (No 5)* [1999] 1 BCLC 433 at 483–484 and on appeal: *Re Secretary of State for Trade and Industry v Baker (No 6)* [2001] BCC 272 at 283.

[30] See *Dorchester Finance Co Ltd v Stebbing* [1989] BCLC 498 at 501–502. The director was found to have been grossly negligent. With the introduction of the objective standard in s.174 it is arguable that cases that suggest that gross negligence is required must be treated with caution.

[31] *Secretary of State for Trade and Industry v Baker (No 5)* [1999] 1 BCLC 433 at 489.

[32] Ibid and cited on appeal, *Re Secretary of State for Trade and Industry v Baker (No 6)* [2001] BCC 272 at 283 per Morritt LJ.

[33] *Equitable Life Assurance Society v Bowley* [2003] EWHC 2263 (Comm); [2003] BCC 829 at 836.

[34] *Secretary of State for Trade and Industry v Baker (No 5)* [1999] 1 BCLC 433 at 489.

It has also been suggested that, where the case law is silent, guidelines and soft law, such as the UK Code of Corporate Governance and reports such as the Turnbull Guidance,[35] indicate what could be expected of a reasonable director.[36] The Turnbull Guidance emphasizes that it is the board's responsibility to ensure that there is regular and systematic assessment of the risks facing its businesses and that internal control systems are instituted to manage risk.[37] In addition, the UK Code of Corporate Governance and its predecessor, the Combined Code, require non-executive directors to constructively challenge management.[38]

III. THE ALLEGATIONS AGAINST BANK DIRECTORS

Directors of banks and other financial institutions may have failed to meet the standards in the case law and corporate governance guidelines in a number of respects. Specifically, bank boards contained large numbers of non-executive directors with little experience in the financial services industry[39] and there is empirical evidence from the US that financial institutions with more independent non-executive directors fared

---

[35] FRC, *Internal Control: Revised Guidance for Directors on the Combined Code* (October 2005).

[36] P.L. Davies, *Gower and Davies' Principles of Company Law*, 8th edn (Sweet and Maxwell, London, 2008) 487 at 492–493.

[37] FRC, *Internal Control: Revised Guidance for Directors on the Combined Code* (October 2005) at 1. However it was not until 2010 that the UK Code of Corporate Governance explicitly made boards responsible for determining significant risks: see FRC, *UK Code of Corporate Governance* (June 2010), Principle C2.

[38] FRC, *Combined Code on Corporate Governance* (June 2008), Guiding Principle to Principle A1; FRC, *UK Code of Corporate Governance* (June 2010) Principle A4.

[39] The House of Commons Treasury Committee, *The Run on the Rock* (HC 56–1) (January 2008) at 33. House of Commons Treasury Committee, *Banking Crisis: Reforming Corporate Governance and Pay in the City* Ninth Report of Session 2008–09 (12 May 2009) (London, Stationery Office, 2009) at para 152 although as the report records there was no consensus on whether this was in fact a problem with Lord Turner for example, disagreeing that it was at para 146. Neither the Chairman of RBS nor HBOS had formal banking qualifications whereas both Barclays and HSBC had non-executives with significant banking experience: at paras 142–143.

worse than those with less.[40] The Walker Review was not alone in concluding that inadequate financial industry experience of non-executive directors was an element in the failures of individual bank boards to mitigate or avoid wider financial catastrophe.[41] It has been suggested that these independent directors lacked the expertise to properly understand the information provided to them about their bank's business models and processes including the complex securitization banks engaged in. It has been asserted that even those non-executive directors who had extensive relevant experience failed to devote sufficient time to their role to understand what was going on.[42] As a result non-executive directors were unable to monitor and challenge the executive effectively, and so act as a check on excesses.[43] Furthermore their lack of expertise may have led them to place too much reliance on management to explain what was going on.

The Walker Review also found that boards had failed to identify and give appropriate weight to risks[44] and recommended that if a proposed new product left the board risk committee uncomprehending or undecided, its launch should be delayed or abandoned. It is implicit in this suggestion that this was not occurring prior to the financial crisis.[45] Meanwhile the Turner Review found that

---

[40] R. Adams,'Governance and the Financial Crisis' ECGI Finance Working Paper No 248/2009 at http://papers.ssrn.com/sol3/papers.cfm?abstract_id=1398583 (accessed 23 April 2011) at 13.

[41] D. Walker, *A Review of Corporate Governance in UK Banks and Other Financial Industry Entities: Final Recommendations* (26 November 2009) ('The Walker Review) at paras 4.2 and 4.3.

[42] House of Commons Treasury Committee, *Banking Crisis: Reforming Corporate Governance and Pay in the City* Ninth Report of Session 2008–09 (12 May 2009) (London, Stationery Office, 2009) at paras 146, 151–152.

[43] The House of Commons Treasury Committee, *The Run on the Rock* (HC 56–1) (January 2008) at 19.

[44] D. Walker, *A Review of Corporate Governance in UK Banks and Other Financial Industry Entities: Final Recommendations* (26 November 2009) at para 6.10. See also FSA, *The Failure of the Royal Bank of Scotland* (December 2011) at 400–401.

[45] D. Walker, *A Review of Corporate Governance in UK Banks and Other Financial Industry Entities: Final Recommendations* (26 November 2009) at para 6.17.

'the very complexity of mathematics used to measure and manage risk ... made it increasingly difficult for top management and boards to assess and exercise judgment over the risks being taken.'[46]

This suggests that executive directors, as well as non-executive directors, failed to understand the complex products their institutions were creating or the risks these exposed their institutions to.[47]

However, not only may bank directors have failed to do that which they ought to have done, they also took decisions and committed their institutions to actions that turned out badly. These included RBS' acquisition of ABN AMRO which was criticized as a product of defective due diligence and judgment;[48] Bradford & Bingley plc's acquisition of Mortgage Express and its deal with General Motors Acceptance Corporation which increased the numbers of self-certification (and so high risk) mortgages on its books;[49] the aggressive expansion of HBOS plc's lending business and reliance on wholesale markets to fund this, even up to and after the appearance of warning signs in the market;[50] and the development of the high risk and ultimately disastrous business strategy at Northern Rock.[51] Again it has been argued that decisions taken by remuneration committees led to the perverse remuneration structures in banks and other financial institutions that encouraged excessive risk-taking by executives.[52]

---

[46] FSA, *The Turner Review: A Regulatory Response to the Global Banking Crisis* (March 2009) at 22.

[47] See also The House of Commons Treasury Committee, *Banking Crisis: Dealing with the Failure of the UK Banks,* Seventh Report of Session 2008–09 (HC 416) (21 April 2009) at paras 78–79; FSA, *The Failure of the Royal Bank of Scotland* (December 2011) at 387.

[48] FSA, *The Failure of the Royal Bank of Scotland* (December 2011) at 177 and 410.

[49] The House of Commons Treasury Committee, *Banking Crisis: Dealing with the Failure of the UK Banks,* Seventh Report of Session 2008–09 (HC 416) (21 April 2009) at paras 22–27.

[50] Ibid at paras 41–44.

[51] For a detailed analysis of the problems at Northern Rock see R. Tomasic, 'Corporate Rescue, Governance and Risk Taking in Northern Rock: Part 2' (2008) 29 *Company Lawyer* 330.

[52] House of Commons Treasury Committee, *Banking Crisis: Reforming Corporate Governance and Pay in the City* Ninth Report of Session 2008–09 (12 May 2009) (London, Stationery Office, 2009) at paras 19–20; T. Kirchmaier, 'Inject Governance and Not Just Cash-Some Thoughts on the Governance of Banks and the Likely Failure of More Banking Regulation' (27 October 2008) at http://ssrn.com/abstract=130320 (accessed 16 January 2011) at 2 and 6;

For the purposes of this discussion it will be assumed that the various factual allegations that have been made against bank directors are true and the following discussion considers the feasibility of claims against directors for breach of their duty of care on the grounds detailed. Obviously for any action to succeed these allegations would need to be proven and the conclusions of, for example, the Treasury Committee as to whether this has been achieved may not necessarily coincide with those of a court.

(a)   Failure to Monitor/Failure to Institute Risk Management Systems

The duty to monitor has been described as one of the most crucial aspects of a director's duty of care.[53] The leading decision on the failure of directors to monitor and to ensure that adequate risk management systems are in place is the disqualification case of *Secretary of State for Trade and Industry v Baker (No 5) (Re Barings)*[54] and there appear to be some parallels between the events that led to ten Barings directors being disqualified and the events of the financial crisis. To briefly recap, Barings collapsed in 1995 with a loss of £827 million incurred through the activities of a rogue trader, Leeson. Three directors unsuccessfully contested their disqualification proceedings: Baker who was responsible for overseeing Leeson's activities; Tuckey who was, inter alia, the deputy chairman of the Barings Group and as a director of Barings Investment Bank ('BIB') had ultimate responsibility for Leeson's switching business; and Gamby who was Head of Settlements at BIB.[55]

Parker J found that all three had breached their duties by failing to monitor Leeson and failing to introduce systems that would have reduced, and perhaps eliminated, the risk he presented. The range of failings Parker J identified included that neither Tuckey, nor the management committee Tuckey chaired, checked that there were risk limits in

---

L. Bebchuk and H. Spamann, 'Regulating Bankers' Pay' (2010) 98 *Georgetown Law Journal* 247. Not everyone agrees: S. Bhagat and R. Romano, 'Reforming Executive Compensation: Simplicity, Transparency and Committing to the Long-term' (2010) 7 *European Company and Financial Law Review* 273 at fn 3 in that article.

[53]   S. Worthington, 'The Duty to Monitor: A Modern View of the Director's Duty of Care' in F. Patfield (ed.), *Perspectives on Company Law: 2* (London, Kluwer Law International, 1997) at 194.

[54]   *Secretary of State for Trade and Industry v Baker (No 5)* [1999] 1 BCLC 433.

[55]   Ibid at 497, 530–531 and 575.

place on Leeson's trading.[56] Parker J also found that Tuckey failed to respond to increasingly serious danger signals because he was pre-occupied with other company business.[57] In addition, Parker J found that Baker, who was directly responsible for Leeson, did not, in his own words, 'look in detail' at the way in which Leeson was trading to produce such extra-ordinary profits, knew that there were no risk limits placed on his trading, and failed to introduce systems to monitor Leeson's risk.[58] Indeed, he failed to exercise control over Leeson even when danger signs emerged, and simply took on trust what Leeson told him.[59] Parker J also found that neither Baker nor Gamby ensured that Leeson's trading and settlement roles were segregated;[60] and that Gamby failed to introduce appropriate systems for settlements throughout the group including systems that would have drawn problems to his attention.[61] As a result, Leeson was provided with large sums of money (at the time of the collapse amounting to £742 million, more than twice the reported capital of the Group) in the absence of any evidence that this corresponded with legitimate trading.[62]

If comparisons were to be drawn between this sorry catalogue of failings and the behaviour of bank boards prior to the crisis, these might include that, just as at Barings, so long as profits continued to flow, bank directors were not prepared to ask hard questions about the nature of the business their institutions were engaged in, did not understand exactly how profits were being made and did not understand the risk attached to those profits. Even if they did understand these matters, they failed to oversee the introduction of effective risk management systems.[63] For example, Hester, the new Chief Executive of RBS, accepted that, going

---

[56]   Ibid at 511.

[57]   Ibid at 522–526.

[58]   Ibid at 537 and 573.

[59]   Ibid at 539, 553–554 and 561.

[60]   Ibid at 574 and 595.

[61]   Ibid at 592 and 598–600 though Parker J found that Gamby was aware of various issues but did nothing.

[62]   Ibid at 464.

[63]   G. Kirkpatrick, 'The Corporate Governance Lessons from the Financial Crisis', *Financial Market Trends*, 2009 at http://www.oecd.org/dataoecd/32/1/42229620.pdf (accessed 14 January 2011).

into the crisis, its risk management systems were inadequate[64] and the FSA's report bears this out.[65]

Yet it is open to directors to argue (and the courts to find) that there are material differences between the situation of the Barings directors and those of bank directors more recently, which would defeat a straight-forward comparison with *Re Barings*.

To explain, in *Re Barings* Parker J found that not only the risks Leeson posed but also the steps needed to address them were obvious, and the mistakes the directors made in failing to act, were 'elementary and fundamental'.[66] Baker himself recognized that the manner in which Leeson was permitted to operate was 'fundamentally wrong in principle' and that the systems to control him were inadequate.[67] Moreover even if the problems had not been self evident to the directors, both risks and remedies had been highlighted by an internal audit report in October 1994 that recommended that Leeson's trading and settlement roles should be segregated, his activities subject to independent monitoring and that risk limits should be observed.[68] In contrast, prior to the financial crisis, the risks facing banks appear to have been far less obvious: not only did boards fail to identify these, so did regulators, policy makers and many financial experts.[69] Furthermore the steps that bank boards needed to take to address these risks are unlikely to have been quite as straightforward to identify and implement as the measures required in *Barings*. On the other hand, over-reliance on short and medium term wholesale funding and excessive leverage were, arguably, elementary mistakes and these were significant causes of the difficulties banks faced.[70] Again Northern

---

[64]   The House of Commons Treasury Committee, *Banking Crisis: Dealing with the Failure of the UK Banks,* Seventh Report of Session 2008–09 (HC 416) (21 April 2009) at para 33.

[65]   FSA, *The Failure of the Royal Bank of Scotland* (December 2011) at 236–238 for example.

[66]   *Secretary of State for Trade and Industry v Baker (No 5)* [1999] 1 BCLC 433 at 451.

[67]   Ibid at 539.

[68]   Ibid 551 and 572.

[69]   As the FSA repeatedly pointed out in its report into the collapse of RBS. It is a moot question as to how relevant the FSA's failings in this regard were, or should have been, to any decision not to pursue bank directors: see FSA, *The Failure of the Royal Bank of Scotland* (December 2011) at 29, 113–114.

[70]   W. Sahlman, 'Management and the Financial Crisis (We have met the enemy and he is us ...)' Harvard Business School Working Article No. 10–033 at http://www.hbs.edu/research/pdf/10–033.pdf (accessed 15 January 2011) at 26. See also FSA, *Final Notice: Bank of Scotland plc* (9 March 2012)

Rock's failure to obtain sufficient insurance against liquidity risk was arguably an obvious and unnecessary mistake.[71]

Another significant aspect of *Re Barings* was that the directors disregarded clear red flags raised by, in particular, the internal audit report and a significant accounting discrepancy.[72] It might be argued that, prior to the financial crisis, no one was waving a red flag and no one predicted what was coming. However this is not quite correct. While the full extent of the crisis was not predicted, alerts were being sounded about banks' business models, and there were other indicators of problems. In April 2007, the Bank of England had warned that the wholesale funding of banks was a potential risk if markets became less liquid, and the FSA had issued similar warnings.[73] Although the board of Northern Rock was aware of this, Northern Rock continued to rely on the wholesale markets. In addition, the sharp fall in Northern Rock's share price in the summer of 2007 should have raised red flags.[74] Meanwhile the FSA raised concerns as far back as 2004 about the risks that key parts of HBOS' business posed, yet the board continued to expand its business base even in 2007 when it was apparent that there were problems in the property market.[75] On the basis of *Re Barings*, it may be easier to establish a breach of the duty of care and skill where directors have disregarded such warning signs.

However, the board of Northern Rock asserted that, far from ignoring warnings, it reviewed the matter and considered that the institution was safeguarded because it operated in different wholesale markets. The board did not anticipate a shutdown of all the markets. Furthermore, it took advice from the FSA, the UK Listing Authority and its own legal

---

[71]   The House of Commons Treasury Committee, *The Run on the Rock* (HC 56–1) (January 2008) at 13–14.

[72]   This was the SLK receivable: an accounting discrepancy of £50 million for which Leeson could provide no satisfactory explanation: *Secretary of State for Trade and Industry v Baker (No 5)* [1999] 1 BCLC 433 at 561.

[73]   The House of Commons Treasury Committee, *The Run on the Rock* (HC 56–1) (January 2008) at 14–15.

[74]   Ibid at 23.

[75]   FSA, *Final Notice: Bank of Scotland* plc (9 March, 2012); A. Arora, 'The Corporate Governance Failings in Financial Institutions and Directors' Legal Liability' (2011) 32 *Company Lawyer* 3 at 10; The House of Commons Treasury Committee, *Banking Crisis: Dealing with the Failure of the UK Banks*, Seventh Report of Session 2008–09 (HC 416) (21 April 2009) at paras 41–43. See also FSA, *The Failure of the Royal Bank of Scotland* (December 2011) at 136.

advisers on the bank's position.[76] Again HBOS directors asserted that they had recognized the risks and had taken steps to mitigate them.[77] In contrast, in *Re Barings* the directors were criticized for completely abdicating their managerial responsibility.[78] In some instances this was so negligent as to be irrational, such as the failure to challenge Leeson over an accounting discrepancy of £50 million pounds and the inconsistent explanations he had given for this,[79] and Gamby's failure to report a funding discrepancy of US $170 million, which the judge said beggared belief.[80] Where directors demonstrate a 'total abrogation of responsibility'[81] by failing to monitor at all then the courts have been willing to find them at fault. After all, in such cases it would be difficult to conclude that they had fulfilled their duty to be reasonably diligent. It is less clear what the courts' response would be where directors do monitor but ineffectively. Moreover there is a difference between failing to monitor one high-risk individual, as in *Re Barings*, and failing to monitor for the risks inherent in a business model. The latter issue is far more complex, and the steps required to address it are far less obvious, than those facing the Barings directors.

In summary, directors will be in breach of their duty to monitor where they completely abdicate their responsibilities to monitor the company's business, where they ignore red flags and obvious risks, and where the response needed to avert those risks is also obvious. Where, however, the risks and the steps needed to avert them are not so obvious, and where

---

[76]   R. Tomasic, 'Corporate Rescue, Governance and Risk Taking in Northern Rock: Part 2' (2008) 29 *Company Lawyer* 330 at 332 and 333.

[77]   The House of Commons Treasury Committee, *Banking Crisis: Dealing with the Failure of the UK Banks,* Seventh Report of Session 2008–09 (HC 416) (21 April 2009) at para 44. In addition since completion of this chapter the FSA has sanctioned both HBOS and one of its directors, finding that adequate systems were not in place to control and monitor for risk: FSA, *Final Notice: Bank of Scotland plc* (9th March 2012); FSA, *Final Notice: Peter Cummings* (12 September 2012). It has not been possible to fully analyse these decisions.

[78]   Parker J repeatedly refers to the abdication of management responsibilities by the directors and a failure to exercise judgment: see for example *Secretary of State for Trade and Industry v Baker (No 5)* [1999] 1 BCLC 433 at 522–524, 574–575, 595–598; on appeal, *Re Secretary of State for Trade and Industry v Baker (No 6)* [2001] BCC 272 at 283 at 292.

[79]   *Secretary of State for Trade and Industry v Baker (No 5)* [1999] 1 BCLC 433 at 465 and 568, describing this as 'well-nigh incomprehensible'.

[80]   Ibid at 593.

[81]   *Re Westmid Packing Services Ltd* [1998] 2 BCLC 646 at 653.

the directors have taken some steps to monitor, it may be more difficult to establish fault. The case law does not clearly support finding directors negligent when they fail to respond appropriately to complex situations.

(b)   Failure to Keep Informed

Directors have a continuing duty to keep themselves informed. If they fail to do so they will be unable to monitor effectively.[82] Given that a contributing cause of the problems faced by banks may have been the lack of industry experience of independent non-executive directors, or their failure to devote sufficient time to the business, those directors may have breached their duty to keep themselves informed about their institutions' activities and risk exposure. It has also been suggested that even the executive directors did not understand what was going on.[83]

Once again there appear to be similarities between the alleged failings of bank boards and those of the Barings senior management. In *Re Barings* it was found that Baker had 'wholly failed to inform himself' of how Leeson's trading was so profitable and his understanding of it was 'sketchy'.[84] Meanwhile Tuckey's knowledge of Leeson's switching business was 'very limited', 'very general' and superficial and he had no real idea of how it could be so profitable.[85] Given the size of the apparent profits generated by Leeson (in 1994 these amounted to £45 million and the total revenue for the whole banking group was £85 million[86]) this was 'woefully inadequate'.[87] Tuckey had also failed to understand the real level of profitability of Leeson's group before he and his fellow directors agreed the bonuses the group was entitled to.[88] Parallels can be drawn with banks where executives were also rewarded with compensation and

---

[82]   *Secretary of State for Trade and Industry v Baker (No 5)* [1999] 1 BCLC 433 at 500.

[83]   FSA, *The Failure of the Royal Bank of Scotland* (December 2011) at 143–144, 220.

[84]   *Secretary of State for Trade and Industry v Baker (No 5)* [1999] 1 BCLC 433 at 537 and 539.

[85]   Ibid at 508 and see also 506–507.

[86]   *Secretary of State for Trade and Industry v Baker (No 6)* [2001] BCC 273 at 277.

[87]   *Secretary of State for Trade and Industry v Baker (No 5)* [1999] 1 BCLC 433 at 508.

[88]   Ibid at 508–509.

bonuses that failed to take account of the risks they had exposed their institutions to and so over-valued their contributions.[89]

Other cases, however, show a far greater reluctance to hold even executive directors to account for failing to understand what was going on in their company. In *Re Continental Assurance Company of London plc (in liquidation) (No 4) (Re Continental)*[90] action was taken by the liquidators of an insurance company against the managing director and five non-executive directors (the action against the finance director was settled before trial) for wrongful trading under s.214 Insolvency Act 1986 and for misfeasance under s.212 Insolvency Act 2006.[91] The gist of the s.214 case was that the directors should have realized that the company had adopted inappropriate accounting policies and that they had failed to realise that the company was insolvent.[92] In other words, they had failed to ensure that they were properly informed about the company's true financial position.

The court exonerated all the directors, holding that they were not required to possess specialist accounting expertise. Rather, they were required to exercise the skill of intelligent laymen with knowledge of basic accounting principles relevant to their business, which in that case was an insurance company, and should be able to understand the company's accounts with guidance.[93] Park J accepted that a higher level of knowledge could be expected of the finance director than of the non-executives and that the former might have breached his duty of care in failing to spot problems even when the latter had not.[94] However, while Park J accepted that the managing director had a general responsibility to oversee the company's activities, including its accounting operations,[95] this did not require specialist knowledge of accountancy.[96]

---

[89]   House of Commons Treasury Committee, *Banking Crisis: Reforming Corporate Governance and Pay in the City* Ninth Report of Session 2008–09 (12 May 2009) (London, Stationery Office, 2009) at paras 19–20.

[90]   [2007] 2 BCLC 287. The approach in this case can be contrasted with that in the Australian case of *ASIC v Healey* [2011] FCA 717 in which the Federal Court of Australia held the non-executive directors liable for failing to spot mistakes in the accounts.

[91]   [2007] 2 BCLC 287 at 333–334.

[92]   Ibid at 364.

[93]   Ibid at 401–403.

[94]   Ibid at 411 and 444.

[95]   Ibid at 443.

[96]   Ibid at 440. Compare the Australian case of *Daniels v Anderson* (1995) 16 ACSR 607 in which both the non-executive directors and the chief executive were sued but only the latter was liable. The former were entitled to rely on the

Again in *Re Produce Marketing Consortium Ltd* Knox J stated that the executive directors had to apprise themselves of such information as can be ascertained with reasonable diligence and an appropriate level of *general* knowledge skill and experience.[97] However, he pointed out that this was a minimum standard and that in determining what a director should be expected to know it was necessary to have regard to the functions the director carried out, the particular type of company in question and its business. He commented that the

> 'general knowledge, skill and experience postulated will be much less extensive in a small company in a modest way of business, with simple accounting procedures and equipment, than it will be in a large company with sophisticated procedures.'[98]

It is suggested that it would not be unreasonable to expect a sophisticated understanding of the financial services business, together with the ability to recognize when their institutions were exposed to very high risks, from the executive directors of banks, particularly the finance and managing directors. However in the light of *Re Continental* this is open to doubt, at least as far as managing directors are concerned.

As for non-executive directors, as *Re Continental* demonstrates, they will not be required to have as much information and understanding about the company's business as executives. Consequently, even if executives were at fault for failing to understand business models and the implications of complex securitization (for example), non-executives might not be. Langley J in *Equitable Life v Bowley* seemed to entertain the possibility of more onerous requirements being expected of non-executives, namely that they should have understood the financial implications of a particular policy, realized that it was legally problematic, and that a particular commercial decision was wrong.[99] However, he also warned that it could not be assumed in the context of the case before him, which was a strike out application, that he considered the allegations against the non-executives to be right.[100]

---

information they had been provided with by management, the latter was not: at 668–677. In *ASIC v Healey* [2011] FCA 717 the non-executive directors were liable as well as the CEO.

[97]   [1989] 5 BCC 569 at 595.

[98]   Ibid at 594–595.

[99]   *Equitable Life Assurance Society v Bowley* [2003] EWHC 2263 (Comm); [2003] BCC 829 at 842–845.

[100]   Ibid at 846.

Re Continental demonstrates that a failure to understand exactly what is going on cannot necessarily be equated with a failure to keep oneself informed. Given that it has been asserted that for bank directors to have understood the risks their institutions were exposed to would have required them to become 'true financial expert[s], knowledgeable about insurance, derivatives, valuation and accounting',[101] it seems unlikely that non-executive directors of banks would have breached their duty of care in not understanding such information. It may even be difficult to establish a case against executive directors.

(c) Undue Reliance on Others and Inappropriate Delegation

It has been argued that even if bank directors had had the requisite financial expertise to enable them to understand their company's business, 'they could not possibly have spent enough time to figure out what was going on'.[102] This is particularly likely to have been the case with non-executive directors. As a result, many must have been heavily reliant on executive directors and senior management to explain the accounts and business models to them and to provide them with the information they required to discharge their monitoring duties satisfactorily.

There is some uncertainty over the extent to which non-executive directors are permitted to rely on management for these purposes. Early cases were undemanding.[103] Thus in *Re City Equitable Fire Insurance Co Ltd* it was held that directors could trust those to whom they delegated in the absence of grounds for suspicion.[104] However, in *Equitable Life Assurance Society v Bowley* Langley J stated that this did not represent modern law, but then added the qualification 'at least if … it means unquestioning reliance upon others to do their job.' Rather what was required of non-executives was 'independence of judgment and supervision of the executive management.'[105] Meanwhile in *Re Sherborne*

---

[101] W. Sahlman, 'Management and the Financial Crisis (We have met the enemy and he is us …)' Harvard Business School Working Article No. 10–033 at http://www.hbs.edu/research/pdf/10–033.pdf (accessed 15 January 2011) at 15.
[102] Ibid.
[103] See for example *Land Credit v Lord Fermoy* (1870) LR 5 Ch App 763; *Re Denham & Co* (1884) 25 Ch D 752.
[104] [1925] Ch 407 at 429.
[105] *Equitable Life Assurance Society v Bowley* [2003] EWHC 2263 (Comm); [2003] BCC 829 at [41].

Associates Ltd it was confirmed that non-executives could rely on highly experienced executives.[106]

The question therefore is whether, in the light of the case law, non-executive directors of banks placed undue reliance on the executives. This is a fact-sensitive inquiry and so it is difficult to predict how courts would determine this issue.[107] In *Re Continental* non-executive directors who were unable to understand the company's financial information by themselves did not breach their duties when they relied on erroneous guidance by the auditors and the finance director, nor were they required to ensure that the company had adopted appropriate accounting policies and had applied these in an appropriate way. This would have required them to have specialist accounting knowledge and to overrule executive directors in their fields of expertise, and this was not necessary.[108] Rather they had to probe, test and discuss the information provided by the experts as intelligent laymen, which they had done.[109]

Consequently, non-executive directors of banks and other financial institutions were not necessarily negligent if they relied on erroneous or incomplete information provided by executives. They were entitled to accept what they were told, as long as they weighed and considered that information, asking questions about it and testing it. If however they failed to challenge executives, as has been alleged, they may have been in breach of their duty of care.[110]

Executive directors meanwhile are entitled to delegate tasks to others, although they must supervise those to whom they delegate.[111] In a company of any significant size, it is also inevitable that they will rely on others to bring material information to their attention. However they cannot be passive in relation to delegated tasks and react only when problems are brought to their attention: they must also pro-actively monitor. In *Re Barings*, it was unacceptable that Tuckey, who chaired a committee responsible for monitoring risk within the Group, delegated

---

[106]   [1995] BCC 40 at 55. In this case it was acceptable to rely on a highly experienced chairman.

[107]   *Equitable Life Assurance Society v Bowley* [2003] EWHC 2263 (Comm); [2003] BCC 829 at 837.

[108]   [2007] 2 BCLC 287 at 443.

[109]   Ibid at 402–403 and 411. See also *Re Sherborne Associates Ltd* [1995] BCC 40 at 54.

[110]   FSA, *The Failure of the Royal Bank of Scotland* (December 2011) at 225–226, 409.

[111]   *Secretary of State for Trade and Industry v Baker (No 5)* [1999] 1 BCLC 433 at 489.

this task to a sub-committee and was prepared to intervene only if some extraordinary situation was brought to his notice. He assumed, but did not check, that others would deal with problems.[112] It is clear therefore that while others within banks and financial institutions may have had the task of monitoring and managing risks, boards carried the ultimate responsibility for ensuring that there was effective risk management and for mitigating excessive risk. This remained so before, and at the time of, the financial crisis.[113] The fact that no-one else warned about the risks, either within or outside the banks, will not excuse the directors if they ought to have realized that these risks were excessive.

Executive directors would be expected to spot flaws in information that would not be apparent to non-executives, at least where the subject matter fell within an area in which they had specialist responsibility or where they had acquired particular skills.[114] However, *Norman v Theodore Goddard*[115] indicates that it may be difficult to prove that executive directors have breached their duty if they rely upon others in matters lying outside their field of expertise. In this case a director responsible for maintaining a property portfolio, who relied on another for advice on financial matters, paid away large sums of the company's money on the basis of a lunchtime conversation. He had not breached his duty because he had not allowed himself to be a mere nominee of the fraudster.[116] While this decision seems to be generous to the director, it was a small company, and Knox J's comments in *Re Produce Marketing Consortium Ltd* regarding the low level of expertise required of directors in such companies need to be borne in mind.[117] The courts may be more prepared to hold executive directors of large dispersed share-ownership companies liable if they demonstrate the same degree of reliance on others when disposing of large amounts of the company's assets.

Norman v Theodore Goddard[118] also draws attention to the role of professional advice and, in particular, legal advice, a matter that has

---

[112]   Ibid at 503–504 and at 519.
[113]   See FRC, Combined Code on Corporate Governance (2006) at 3; House of Commons Treasury Committee, *Banking Crisis: Reforming Corporate Governance and Pay in the City* Ninth Report of Session 2008–09 (12 May 2009) (London, Stationery Office, 2009) at paras 154–158.
[114]   *Secretary of State for Trade and Industry v Bairstow (No 2)* [2004] EWHC 1730 (Ch); [2005] 1 BCLC 136.
[115]   [1992] BCC 14.
[116]   Ibid at 18–22.
[117]   [1989] 5 BCC 569 at 594–595.
[118]   [1992] BCC 14.

surfaced at various points during the crisis. For example, the board of Northern Rock took legal advice on its flawed business strategy,[119] whilst the RBS board sought advice from Linklaters in May 2007 on whether it had given the takeover of ABN AMRO proper consideration.[120] In September 2007 the RBS board again received legal advice on whether RBS could withdraw from the bid in the face of deteriorating market conditions.[121] Assuming that this advice supported the boards' actions, this raises the question of to what extent directors are entitled to rely on it to escape findings of negligence. For example, if Linklaters had told the RBS board that the directors had given sufficient consideration to the takeover to comply with their legal obligations (including the duty of care), could this prevent a finding that the directors were negligent even though the due diligence carried out by RBS was 'inadequate'?[122] In *Re Bradcrown Ltd* it was stated that reasonable reliance on wrong advice might lead to a finding that there was no breach of duty.[123] In that case, however, a breach of duty was established because the director had simply relied on the advice unquestioningly and 'abdicated all responsibility'.[124] This leaves open whether reliance on legal advice would ever be unreasonable where directors did not completely abdicate their responsibilities and did ask questions of the advisers. The position is far from clear. In those cases which suggested that seeking legal advice could be an exonerating or mitigating factor, directors were in fact usually disqualified.[125] Moreover such an approach must be treated with caution since it is the responsibility of directors, not lawyers, to assess not only whether a decision is commercially sound or overly reckless but also whether the directors have received sufficient information to make such an assessment. In the case of ABN AMRO, as the FSA pointed out, the board of RBS had not. If directors were permitted to hide behind legal advice in this way, this would allow them to shirk responsibility for decisions that lie within their field of expertise. In addition, as Hannigan

---

[119] R. Tomasic, 'Corporate Rescue, Governance and Risk Taking in Northern Rock: Part 2' (2008) 29 *Company Lawyer* 330, 332 and 333.

[120] FSA, *The Failure of the Royal Bank of Scotland* (December 2011) at 227.

[121] Ibid at 164 and 415.

[122] Ibid at 160.

[123] [2002] BCC 428 at 439.

[124] Ibid.

[125] See for example *Re Aldermanbury Trust plc* [1993] BCC 598; *Re Bradcrown Ltd* [2002] BCC 428. See also *Re McNulty's Interchange Ltd* (1988) 4 BCC 533. In *Official Receiver v Jones* [2004] EWHC 2096 (Ch) the director was excused but there were other exonerating factors.

points out, it could lead to directors spending company money on professional advisers simply to reduce their personal exposure to litigation.[126]

So far, as with the failure to monitor decisions, cases in which directors have been found to have unduly relied on others or to have failed to supervise delegated tasks, all involved total avoidance of responsibility, where the directors failed to apply their minds to the issues and were completely passive.[127] In contrast, when directors have asked questions they have escaped liability.[128] Whether directors would be found negligent because the questions they asked were not searching enough or because, having asked questions, they unreasonably relied on the information, is unresolved. In other words it is far from clear when the courts will find directors liable for acting negligently, rather than not acting at all, a point that will be explored further below.

(d)   Negligent Decisions

So far the discussion has focussed on when the courts may impose liability upon directors for errors of omission. However bank directors not only failed to act, on occasion they actively took decisions (which turned out disastrously). Thus the Northern Rock board claimed that far from disregarding warnings provided by the Bank of England and FSA it took them into account by selling certain operations and diversifying the markets in which the bank sought retail funding so that if one market shut down Northern Rock could still have recourse to other markets.[129] Bradford and Bingley directors defended their business model as the

---

[126]   B. Hannigan, *Company Law* 2nd edn (Oxford: Oxford University Press, 2009) at 240.

[127]   *Re City Equitable Fire Insurance Co Limited* [1925] Ch 407 at 473–474: the directors simply relied on the auditors' certificate and the assurances of the chairman; *Dorchester Finance Co Ltd v Stebbing* [1989] BCLC 498; *Bishopsgate Investment Management Ltd (in liquidation) v Maxwell (No 2)* [1993] BCLC 1282; *Re Westmid Packing Services Ltd* [1998] 2 BCLC 646; *Re Bradcrown Ltd* [2002] BCC 428; *Lexi Holdings Plc (in administration) v Luqman* [2009] EWCA Civ 117; [2009] BCC 716.

[128]   *Norman v Theodore Goddard* [1992] BCC 14, 18–22.

[129]   The House of Commons Treasury Committee, *The Run on the Rock* (HC 56–1) (January 2008) at 5.

product of a strategic analysis that higher risk mortgages were acceptable because they paid a higher interest rate.[130] As for the board of RBS, it:

> 'made judgments about the balance of risk and return, which under different circumstances might have served stakeholders' interests but which in retrospect were poor. But these were not ... made without consideration of relevant information. They were therefore doing what executives and boards in other sectors of the economy do: sometimes getting judgments right and sometimes wrong.'[131]

This section therefore considers when directors might be held liable for breach of their duty of care when they take decisions with poor outcomes.

It is well-established that directors are not to be held liable simply because their decisions turned out badly, nor for mere errors of judgment. As Park J stated in *Re Continental Assurance Company of London plc*:

> 'The duty is not to ensure that the company gets everything right. The duty is to exercise the reasonable care and skill up to the standard which the law expects of a director of the sort of company concerned, and also up to the standard capable of being achieved by the particular director concerned'.[132]

So it is not enough that bank directors took risky decisions that had catastrophic consequences. As is often pointed out, directors are required to take risks, and society on the whole is better served by promoting entrepreneurial activity. Imposing liability for risky decisions that go wrong could lead to directors being overly cautious, with detrimental consequences for the economy.[133]

Moreover, as Worthington has argued, the courts are more reluctant to hold directors to account where the claim is that they acted negligently, rather than that they failed to act at all because the former requires the

---

[130] The House of Commons Treasury Committee, *Banking Crisis: Dealing with the Failure of the UK Banks,* Seventh Report of Session 2008–09 (HC 416) (21 April 2009) at para 27 and also para 23.

[131] A. Turner, 'Rules to Keep Bankers Honest' *The Financial Times,* 7 December 2010.

[132] [2007] 2 BCLC 287 at [399].

[133] C. Riley, 'The Company Director's Duty of Care and Skill: the Case for an Onerous but Subjective Standard' (1999) 62 *Modern Law Review* 697 at 709, although Riley suggests that such arguments should be treated with caution.

courts to evaluate the merits of different business policies.[134] Second guessing business judgment is something that the courts try to avoid.[135]

Courts are also extremely wary of the dangers of judging behaviour with hindsight, distanced from the fast-moving commercially pressurized situation that directors find themselves in.[136] In this respect it is significant that although much of what the banks did seems reckless now, at the time there were few who recognized the risks.

The case law supports the view that it will be very difficult to hold directors to account where they have exercised judgment and made a decision. Thus in *Re Continental* directors who had not 'shut their eyes to the financial situation of their company' when they decided that the company should continue to trade were not negligent when that decision turned out to be mistaken.[137] The directors had a 'wholly responsible and conscientious attitude'[138] and 'did do their best to behave responsibly and properly'.[139] Moreover in response to the claimant's argument that although the directors did their best, they got it wrong and were at fault for doing so, Park J commented 'This is an austere attitude'.[140]

This comment is interesting because it was made in the context of a claim under the Insolvency Act 1986 s.214 and so in the course of applying an objective standard in assessing whether the directors' conduct was reasonable. Austere or not, s.214 and s.174 require that even directors who are doing their best should be held to account where that best falls below the minimum objective standard. However Park J's approach seems closer to that advocated by Riley who argues that while directors should be held to a rigorous subjective standard, they should not be found liable where they have genuinely done their best.[141]

Occasionally, though, the courts have been prepared to hold directors to account for their actions, as opposed to failures to act. Thus in *Simtel*

---

[134]   S. Worthington, 'The Duty to Monitor: A Modern View of the Director's Duty of Care' in F. Patfield (ed.), *Perspectives on Company Law: 2* (London, Kluwer Law International, 1997) at 189, 191–192.

[135]   *Howard Smith Ltd v Ampol Petroleum Ltd* [1974] AC 821 at 832.

[136]   *Re Sherborne Associates Ltd* [1995] BCC 40 at 54; *Re Brian D Pierson (Contractors) Ltd* [1999] BCC 26 at 50; *Re Continental Assurance Company of London plc (in Liquidation) (No 4)* [2007] 2 BCLC 287 at 360.

[137]   [2007] 2 BCLC 287 at [30] per Park J and at [106].

[138]   Ibid at [107].

[139]   Ibid at [109].

[140]   Ibid.

[141]   C. Riley, 'The Company Director's Duty of Care and Skill: the Case for an Onerous but Subjective Standard' (1999) 62 *Modern Law Review* 697.

Communications Ltd v Rebak[142] a director breached his duty of care and skill by causing the company to enter into a contract to purchase a large quantity of goods without arranging for the goods to be on-sold. The judge found that this 'was the height of folly' which went beyond a mere error of judgment and constituted an unacceptable level of risk taking.[143] The director was gambling with the company's money 'without having any real regard to the high degree of risk involved in the transaction'[144] and he had attempted to conceal what was going on.[145] However the judge found that not only had the director breached his duty of care but also his fiduciary duties to act in good faith in the interests of the company for a proper purpose, and to avoid conflicts of interest. No intelligent and honest man could have reasonably believed the transactions were for the benefit of the company.[146]

Similarly in *Bishopsgate Investment Management Ltd (in liquidation) v Maxwell (No 1)*, a director, who unwittingly signed away the company's assets because his brother had asked him to, was in breach of fiduciary duty to act for a proper purpose, as well as negligent. There were no grounds 'upon which it could honestly have been thought that the transactions were for the benefit of the company'.[147]

In both these cases the directors' behaviour was so unreasonable that it breached their fiduciary duties as well as their duty of care. These are not therefore strong authorities for proceeding against bank directors who have not been accused of breaching fiduciary duties. The FSA, for example, explicitly stated that it had found no evidence of misconduct in RBS.[148]

There are, though, some decisions which appear to have gone further. In *Swan v Sandhu* Evans-Lombe J found directors liable for negligent

---

[142]   [2006] EWHC 572; [2006] 2 BCLC 571. The case is relevant because although the judge accepted that *Re City Equitable Fire Insurance Co Ltd* accurately set out the standard of care required, he also accepted that an employed director would be held to a more stringent objective standard of care as an employee: at 577–578. This standard is very similar to the objective standard of care expected of directors under the later common law and now under s.174: P.L. Davies, *Gower and Davies' Principles of Company Law*, 8th edn (Sweet and Maxwell, London, 2008) at 487.

[143]   [2006] EWHC 572; [2006] 2 BCLC 571 at [39].

[144]   Ibid at [39].

[145]   Ibid.

[146]   Ibid at 582 and 596.

[147]   [1993] BCLC 1282 at 1285.

[148]   FSA, *The Failure of the Royal Bank of Scotland* (December 2011) at 354–355.

misfeasance when they advanced loans to a third party without taking security.[149] In *Brian D Pierson (Contractors) Ltd* directors were negligent for agreeing to postpone repayment of the loans to a fixed date ten years in the future without making provision for repayment at an earlier date and in failing to demand payment for goodwill on the sale of a company's business.[150] In *Re Loquitur Ltd* Etherton J was able to determine that a challenged transaction made no commercial sense and was simply a tax avoidance scheme.[151]

In these cases the courts seem to be assessing the directors' commercial judgment and finding it wanting. Thus in *Brian D Pierson (Contractors) Ltd* the need to charge for goodwill 'was perfectly obvious, or *should have been to any businessman*' (emphasis added) and that there 'was a deal to be done'.[152] Again in *Re Loquitur Ltd* the judge assessed the projections in the company's accounts and the assumptions made by the directors in relation to the income the company could obtain on a property and found that these were unreasonable and 'wholly unrealistic'.[153] In none of these cases would the mistakes necessarily have been obvious to a layman: their identification required a certain amount of business expertise.

Nevertheless these decisions involved small companies with unsophisticated directors, not large dispersed share ownership institutions operating in fast-moving markets, and the types of decisions involved were a far cry from the complex judgments that bank directors had to make. Courts may be much more reluctant to assess business judgment in more complex scenarios although, as *Re Loquitur Ltd* demonstrates, they could be assisted by expert evidence.[154]

A further consideration is that the mistakes that attracted liability were often the result of directors failing to take into account material information or shutting their eyes to the obvious.[155] Arguably the courts assigned liability in these cases not just because the decisions were incorrect but because the process the directors used to reach their

---

149   [2005] EWHC 2743(Ch); [2006] BPIR 1035 at [45]–[46].
150   [1999] BCC 26 at 43.
151   [2003] EWCA 999 (Ch); [2003] 2 BCLC 442 at 469.
152   [1999] BCC 26 at 47 and 43 respectively per Hazel Williamson QC.
153   [2003] EWCA 999 (Ch); [2003] 2 BCLC 442 at 484 and [222].
154   Ibid at 485. It should be noted that the evidence was not provided by independent experts, but by the company's managing agents who were acting for the company at the time of the breach of duty.
155   *Re Brian D Pierson (Contractors) Ltd* [1999] BCC 26 at 54; *Re Loquitur Ltd* [2003] EWCA 999 (Ch); [2003] 2 BCLC 442 at 484.

decision was defective. The courts may have been more willing to impose liability because doing so did not involve them in second-guessing the directors' substantive commercial judgment. Rather, it only required them to review the procedure followed in making that judgment.[156] In contrast the courts have refused to find directors negligent when directors have taken account of all the relevant information that they could reasonably be expected to know.[157] With this in mind, insofar as bank directors did take into account commercial considerations before making bad decisions,[158] it seems unlikely that an action in respect of those decisions would be successful.

One exception may be the acquisition of ABN AMRO by RBS, a deal that was 'fatal to [RBS's] survival as a privately owned company',[159] which was described as a gamble by the FSA.[160] The FSA found that the due diligence carried out by RBS on ABN AMRO comprised two lever arch files and a CD-Rom.[161] It concluded that the due diligence was 'insufficient in its scope and depth and inappropriate in relation to the

---

[156]   S. Worthington, 'The Duty to Monitor: A Modern View of the Director's Duty of Care' in F. Patfield (ed.), *Perspectives on Company Law: 2* (London, Kluwer Law International, 1997) at 191–192, 197.

[157]   *Re Welfab Engineers Ltd* [1990] BCC 600; *Re Continental Assurance Company of London plc (in Liquidation) (No 4)* [2007] 2 BCLC 287.

[158]   See, for example, the account of the board's reasoning at Northern Rock: The House of Commons Treasury Committee, *The Run on the Rock* (HC 56–1) (January 2008) at 14–17; The House of Commons Treasury Committee, *Banking Crisis: Dealing with the Failure of the UK Banks,* Seventh Report of Session 2008–09 (HC 416) (21 April 2009) at paras 43–44.

[159]   The House of Commons Treasury Committee, *Banking Crisis: Dealing with the Failure of the UK Banks,* Seventh Report of Session 2008–09 (HC 416) (21 April 2009) at para 35. See also the decision by HBOS to pursue aggressive growth when it was already heavily exposed to a market downturn and when it was obvious that market conditions were worsening: FSA *Final Notice: Bank of Scotland plc* (9th March 2012). The FSA found that HBOS and one of its directors failed to exercise reasonable care. This lack of care was not solely the decision to aggressively expand but to do so without proper controls in place: FSA, *Final Notice: Peter Cummings* (12 September 2012) at para 5.51. It is notable that the FSA did not pursue any other directors, suggesting that it thought it could not establish that others failed to exercise due care.

[160]   FSA, *The Failure of the Royal Bank of Scotland* (December 2011) at 179.

[161]   The House of Commons Treasury Committee, *Banking Crisis: Dealing with the Failure of the UK Banks,* Seventh Report of Session 2008–09 (HC 416) (21 April 2009) at para 35.

nature and scale of the acquisition and the risks involved'.[162] Arguably, reaching this conclusion did not involve second-guessing complex business judgments. Moreover, by proceeding with limited due diligence, it could be claimed that the RBS board failed to properly inform itself. If so, its decision was the product of a defective process. For example, the board's conclusion that due diligence had thrown up nothing which undermined the commercial rationale for the bid[163] looks unreasonable given the limited due diligence carried out.[164] It ignored the obvious, namely that if one does not or cannot look for problems, one will not find them.[165] Meanwhile, the non-executive directors may not have had sufficient opportunity to review the due diligence findings and some did not attend a crucial board meeting on the takeover in person and so did not see a slide presentation relating to the bid.[166]

Despite these shortcomings, the FSA failed to pursue the RBS directors on the basis that the limited due diligence carried out by RBS was normal for that time.[167] This raises two issues.

First, whether the board's conduct only looks poor with the benefit of hindsight, in which case the courts are unlikely to find the directors liable. Although no RBS director appears to have raised any concerns at the time about the limited due diligence, this conclusion seems untenable.[168]

The second issue is whether, even if such conduct was obviously unreasonable, the directors would be excused because they acted in accordance with market norms. This depends on whether the standard of care is norm-reflecting or norm-setting. The fact that the standard is objective suggests the latter, but the courts may nevertheless be very reluctant to find directors liable where their conduct conforms to market norms, even where those norms are unreasonable. Setting a standard of care which is higher than that adopted by the market at the relevant time may be viewed as too onerous, and as creating the risk that people may be deterred from taking up directorial positions or from engaging in risky

---

[162] FSA, *The Failure of the Royal Bank of Scotland* (December 2011) at 408.
[163] Ibid at 178.
[164] Ibid at 413.
[165] Thus the due diligence carried out did not provide adequate information on the quality of ABN AMRO's key risk management policies, the quality of its assets in its structured credit portfolios nor a valuation of those positions: ibid at 412.
[166] Ibid at 419.
[167] Ibid at 33.
[168] Ibid at 179.

behaviour that drives entrepreneurial behaviour and the economy.[169] However, the question is unresolved.

To conclude, directors are most likely to be liable for actions and decisions where these are so irrational that they cannot possibly serve the interests of the company. This cannot be said about the RBS decision to take over ABN AMRO. While one of the impetuses behind the deal may have been the CEO's desire for empire-building,[170] its stated purpose was to advance RBS's interests.[171] Although some courts have been more willing to question bad business decisions, it may be that this will be confined to when the directors' process of reasoning can be faulted. Even then, if, as seems likely, the process of decision-making at RBS was defective, it remains unclear whether the courts would impose liability for acting irrationally when the market as whole was engaged in irrational behaviour.

IV. CAUSATION

Assuming that a breach of duty can be established, no action against bank directors could succeed unless it was shown that the breach caused the loss complained of. This is likely to be very difficult in the context of the financial crisis.

The first stage in establishing causation is for a claimant to show, on balance of probabilities, that but for the directors' breach of duty the loss would not have occurred. It is clear that some institutions did better than others during the financial crisis, which suggests that the decisions taken by these institutions, and the business models they adopted, did make a difference to the losses they suffered once the crisis broke.[172] However the causal link will be complex. Moreover, it may be difficult to trace relevant differences in banks' business models to any breaches of their directors' duty of care.

Establishing causation in relation to omissions is particularly difficult. It would be necessary to demonstrate what bank directors should have

---

[169]   C. Riley, 'The Company Director's Duty of Care and Skill: the Case for an Onerous but Subjective Standard' (1999) 62 *Modern Law Review* 697 at 709.

[170]   FSA, *The Failure of the Royal Bank of Scotland* (December 2011) at 166.

[171]   Ibid at 145 and 162.

[172]   See also D. Walker, *A Review of Corporate Governance in UK Banks and Other Financial Industry Entities: Final Recommendations* (26 November 2009) at para 2.1; FSA, *The Failure of the Royal Bank of Scotland* (December 2011) at 52–53.

done had they fulfilled their duties and that if they had done this it would have prevented the damage.[173] Directors will not escape liability by showing that they would never have taken the steps necessary to avert catastrophe if such a failure was itself a breach of duty to the company.[174] Nevertheless, in cases of omission the claimant is required to construct a 'hypothetical edifice'[175] and may therefore have difficulties in establishing a convincing 'worked-out causation analysis'.[176] Moreover when it is known in retrospect that certain steps would have averted the disaster, it is tempting to argue that these steps were so obviously necessary that the defendants should have taken them at the time. This, however, does not necessarily follow and the courts would be wary of applying hindsight to the causation analysis.[177] For these reasons causation may often prove an insurmountable hurdle and it is unsurprising that few cases have overcome these difficulties.[178]

Furthermore, while satisfying the 'but for' test is necessary, it is not sufficient.[179] In cases of economic loss, both in contract and in tort (at least in situations analogous to contract), the courts have drawn a distinction between a breach of duty that causes the loss and a breach of

---

[173] *Cohen v Selby* [2002] BCC 82 at 89; *Lexi Holdings Plc (in administration) v Luqman* [2008] 2 BCLC 725 at 735.

[174] *Lexi Holdings Plc (in administration) v Luqman* [2009] EWCA Civ 117; [2009] BCC 716 at 726. For example although the FSA thought that even with better due diligence RBS would have gone ahead with the takeover of ABN AMRO, this in itself was due to a weak understanding of the risks of CDOs and in the face of deteriorating market conditions in the spring of 2007. Consequently pressing ahead even with better due diligence may have been a breach of the directors' duty of care: FSA, *The Failure of the Royal Bank of Scotland* (December 2011) at 145–146.

[175] *Lexi Holdings Plc (in administration) v Luqman* [2008] EWHC 1639 (Ch); [2008] 2 BCLC 725 at [28] per Briggs J.

[176] Ibid at [150].

[177] *Lexi Holdings Plc (in administration) v Luqman* [2008] EWHC 1639 (Ch); [2008] 2 BCLC 725 at 762. See also FSA, *The Failure of the Royal Bank of Scotland* (December 2011) arguing that many of the RBS board's decisions appear poor only with the benefit of hindsight at 26, 355.

[178] However in *Lexi Holdings Plc (in administration) v Luqman* while the claim failed at first instance on the basis of causation, it succeeded in the Court of Appeal.

[179] *Re Continental Assurance Company of London plc (in liquidation) (No 4)* [2007] 2 BCLC 287 at 445.

duty that provides the opportunity for the loss to be incurred.[180] Thus, in *Re Brian D Pierson (Contractors) Ltd*, (a s.214 action), the judge held that while the company would have avoided incurring losses had the directors not engaged in wrongful trading, the decision to continue trading had not been the cause of all the losses. To find otherwise would be applying only the 'but for' test, which was impermissible. Rather, the cause was bad weather conditions. The directors' breach of duty had provided the opportunity for the company to suffer those losses but it had not caused the losses in the sense that the directors ought to be held liable.[181] Again, in *Re Continental*, relying on this distinction, Park J held that, even if the directors had been in breach of duty, the company's losses had been caused by adverse trading and the actions of the liquidator.[182]

If Northern Rock had had a more robust business model which relied less on short and medium term wholesale funding, or if RBS had not expanded so aggressively then neither bank would have been so exposed when the crisis hit and it is likely that each institution would have fared better.[183] It is, however, a moot question as to whether the courts would view the prior conduct of the boards as a cause of the loss or as merely providing the opportunity for it to be incurred.

Furthermore directors would not be held liable for all the losses they caused. As Lord Hoffmann stated in *South Australian Asset Management Corporation v York Montague Ltd*[184] (SAAMCO), 'Normally the law limits liability to those consequences which are attributable to that which made the act wrongful'.[185]

As to this, Gray has commented:

> 'Quite how the law and its processes of accountability views the loss of liquidity which stalled Northern Rock and caused the run on it will be a key practical and not just philosophical question. Exactly where any court ... will

---

[180]   *Galoo Ltd v Bright Grahame Murray* [1994] 1 WLR 1360 (involving a claim for trading losses against auditors who failed to detect the true financial state of the company audited).

[181]   [1999] BCC 26 at 56.

[182]   [2007] 2 BCLC 287 at 445–446. See also *Re Brian D Pierson (Contractors) Ltd* [1999] BCC 26 at 56 applying a similar test in the context of s.214.

[183]   The House of Commons Treasury Committee, *Banking Crisis: Dealing with the Failure of the UK Banks,* Seventh Report of Session 2008–09 (HC 416) (21 April 2009) at para 32.

[184]   [1997] AC 191.

[185]   Ibid at 213, cited in *Re Continental Assurance Company of London plc (in liquidation) (No 4)* [2007] 2 BCLC 287 at [380] in the context of the s.214 claim.

draw the line between 'unexpected yet still foreseeable' risk on the one hand, and complete blindsiding uncertainty on the other could end up being a key determinant of responsibility.'[186]

Similar questions can be asked in relation to the losses suffered by the other banks and in particular whether the courts will find that the losses that came out of the financial crisis were foreseeable. In contract the courts have limited recovery to losses arising naturally, according to the normal course of things, from the breach of contract and which is in the reasonable contemplation of the parties and for which they have assumed responsibility.[187] Many consider that the total shutdown of the financial markets in 2007 was entirely unforeseeable,[188] or, at best, foreseeable but unexpected.[189] In tort however the general rule is that a claimant can recover for losses that are reasonably foreseeable even in the most unusual case unless the risk is so small that a reasonable man would in the whole circumstances feel justified in neglecting it.[190] Defendants are liable for losses that are more extensive than anticipated so long as the kinds of loss are foreseeable. Arguably, therefore, the fact that the financial losses incurred by banks were far higher than reasonably anticipated would not excuse directors if the loss was of a foreseeable type. However in *Camerata Property Inc v Credit Suisse Securities (Europe) Limited*[191] in a claim brought in both negligence and contract, Flaux J stated obiter that the loss caused to an investor who had purchased a Lehman Brothers structured product was not caused by his financial adviser's negligent advice to purchase the product, but by the collapse of Lehman Brothers, and this was unforeseeable.[192] In contrast however, in *Rubenstein v HSBC Bank Plc*, in a claim brought in tort, contract and for breach of statutory duty, the Court of Appeal found that

---

[186] J. Gray, 'Lessons from BCCI Saga for the Current Accountability Debate Surrounding Northern Rock?' (2008) 23 *Journal of International Banking Law and Regulation* 37 at 43.

[187] *Hadley v Baxendale* (1854) 9 Ex 341; *Transfield Shipping Inc v Mercator Shipping Inc (The Achilleas)* [2008] UKHL 48; [2009] 1 AC 61.

[188] R. Adams,'Governance and the Financial Crisis' ECGI Finance Working Paper No 248/2009 at http://papers.ssrn.com/sol3/papers.cfm?abstract_id= 1398583 (accessed 23 April 2011) at 14.

[189] J. Gray, 'Lessons from BCCI Saga for the Current Accountability Debate Surrounding Northern Rock?' (2008) 23 *Journal of International Banking Law and Regulation* 37 at 43.

[190] *Koufos v C Czarnikow Ltd* [1969] 1 AC 350 at 385–386.

[191] [2012] EWHC 7 (Comm)..

[192] Ibid at [101–102].

the loss a consumer suffered after being advised to purchase an investment product, and which was caused by the markets falling after Lehman
Brothers' collapse, was foreseeable. The consumer had been negligently
advised to purchase a product which was vulnerable to market move-
ments having indicated that he did not wish to be exposed to risk.[193] The
Court of Appeal did not dispute that the collapse of Lehman's was
unforeseeable but found that the risk of loss due to market movement
was entirely foreseeable, albeit its scale was unforeseeable.[194] Moreover
the foreseeable market volatility caused the claimant's loss and was the
very thing that the bank's breach of duty exposed him to.[195] In the light
of this, the question of whether bank directors would be liable for losses
caused by breach of their duty of care could turn on whether those losses
are found to have been caused by foreseeable market volatility or
unforeseeable events. It would also depend on what constituted an
unforeseeable event: it does not follow that an event causing a loss which
outsiders, such as financial advisers, could not reasonably foresee-such as
a bank getting into serious difficulty-is also one that insiders such as
directors should not have foreseen.

A recent approach to limiting liability has been to ask whether the
damage fell within the scope of the duty owed by the defendant to the
claimant.[196] In cases involving economic loss this has been used to avoid
imposing liability even where the foreseeability test has been satisfied.[197]
Moreover in *SAAMCO* Lord Hoffmann stated that the scope of the duty
of care and skill in tort was the same as that in contract,[198] and thus the
recoverable losses in both would be similar. He stated that the scope of
the defendants' duty in tort would 'depend upon the purpose of the rule
imposing the duty' while in contract it would be defined by the relevant

---

[193]   [2012] EWCA Civ 1184 at [15]–[16]
[194]   Ibid at [117].
[195]   Ibid at [124].
[196]   *SAAMCO* [1997] AC 191 at 212. It should though be noted that in
Haugesund Kommune v Depfa ACS Bank [2011] EWCA Civ 33; [2012] Bus LR
230 at [51] the Court of Appeal stated that the SAAMCO principle did not go to
either causation or foreseeability but to the scope of the duty of care. However
the relationship between the scope of duty rule and what was formerly known as
legal causation is murky: see M. Jones, 'Scope of the Duty of Care and
Causation' (2007) 23 *Professional Negligence* 49.
[197]   *SAAMCO* [1997] AC 191 at 214; *Nykredit Mortgage Bank plc v Edward
Erdman Group Ltd (No 2)* [1997] 1 WLR 1627 at 1631; *Haugesund Kommune v
Depfa ACS Bank* [2011] EWCA Civ 33; [2012] Bus LR 230 at 86.
[198]   [1997] AC 191 at 211.

contractual term.[199] So the relevant question would be whether the directors were under a duty to protect their companies from the kind of loss suffered.

The courts have been slow to impose responsibility for losses caused by volatile markets,[200] trading losses[201] and a counterparty's lack of credit-worthiness,[202] but many of these cases have involved claims against professional advisers, whose liability is limited by the terms of their retainer.[203] Directors' liability is not so constrained: they are required to supervise and monitor across the whole sphere of the company's activities, albeit at a high level, and so could be liable for a broader range of loss than advisers. Nevertheless in *Re Continental* Park J held that even if the directors had breached a duty to ensure that the company used appropriate accounting principles in preparing its accounts, the purpose of such a duty was not to protect the company from losses caused by adverse trading conditions.[204] Could directors ever be liable for losses caused by adverse trading conditions such as those presented by the financial crisis? The answer to this could turn on the precise question posed. For example, asking whether the purpose of the directors' duty to ensure that they understood the company's business and to monitor management was so that they could guard their institutions against the consequences of the financial crisis could lead to one answer. Asking whether its purpose was to ensure that their institutions did not suffer losses as a result of taking reckless risks might lead to another.

However, given that the courts have been wary of imposing dispropor-tionate liability on defendants in either contract or tort for even foresee-able economic loss,[205] it may be unlikely that the courts would be prepared to hold directors responsible for the scale of the losses incurred

---

[199]   Ibid at 212.
[200]   *Transfield Shipping Inc v Mercator Shipping Inc (The Achilleas)* [2008] UKHL 48; [2009] 1 AC 61: admittedly this case did not concern the contractual duty to take reasonable care but the majority adopted the SAAMCO scope of duty reasoning in reaching their conclusion.
[201]   *SAAMCO* [1997] AC 191.
[202]   *Haugesund Kommune v Depfa ACS Bank* [2011] EWCA Civ 33; [2012] Bus LR 230.
[203]   See for example, *Haugesund Kommune v Depfa ACS Bank* ibid at [73–77].
[204]   [2007] 2 BCLC 287 at 446.
[205]   *Haugesund Kommune v Depfa ACS Bank* [2011] EWCA Civ 33; [2012] Bus LR 230 at [86]. However see *Lexi Holdings Plc (in administration) v Luqman* [2009] EWCA Civ 117; [2009] BCC 716 in which the non-executive directors were held liable for over £41 million and £37 million arising out of

by their institutions in the wake of the financial crisis. Courts may be more willing to entertain claims that can be traced to a particular transaction but, even so, since the losses would be greater than could have been anticipated, full recovery may be unlikely.

V. CONCLUSION

Although bank directors have been the target of significant public anger and criticism, an action against them for breach of their duty of care, skill and diligence faces significant obstacles.

First, while courts have been willing to hold directors to account where they have abdicated their managerial responsibilities, courts have been far less prepared to impose liability where directors have exercised judgment but made bad decisions. Yet much of the information that has emerged from the crisis suggests that many of the problems suffered by the banks were a result of bad decision-making rather than no decision-making.

Second, while much criticism has been directed at non-executive directors, claims against executive directors (especially, it is suggested, finance and managing directors) have a greater chance of success. Their roles require them to have a sounder understanding of their institutions' business models and exposure to significant risks than other directors. Nevertheless, proving causation against even executive directors could be a major obstacle, particularly given the unforeseeability of the financial crisis and the scale of losses that materialized.

Opinion is likely to be divided on the question of whether this position is desirable. On the one hand it has been argued that 'liability rules need to be tempered against the need to ensure that the attention of directors is not significantly diverted from the pursuit of maximizing shareholder wealth' and that too stringent a standard could do just this by making directors overly defensive.[206] It could also increase agency costs by

---

their brother's fraud. The discussion in the case did not focus on legal causation, foreseeability or scope of the duty as a limit on recoverable loss.

[206] Directors' Duties and Corporate Governance: Corporate Law Reform Program, Proposals for Reform: Paper No 3 cited in the Law Commission, *Company Directors: Regulating Conflicts of Interest and Formulating a Statement of Duties* (Law Com, Report No 261, Cm 4436) (Scot Law Commission No 173) (London, Stationery Office, 1999) at para 15.38.

causing directors to seek more compensation.[207] Insurance may not be available to cover liability risks and if it were available, there could be an increase in litigation, as claimants pursued deep pocket defendants. This could deter directors, particularly non-executive directors who have limited access to inside information, from taking positions on boards and could dampen 'incentives for innovation'.[208]

On the other hand, it can be said in response that: the financial crisis demonstrates that in the absence of accountability innovation became unrestrained, leading to the creation of products such as CDO squareds and other complex derivatives that served no socially useful purpose and were in fact toxic;[209] risk-taking behaviour has been under, not over, deterred; and the focus on shareholder wealth maximisation has, on more than just this occasion, led to the destruction of shareholder wealth.[210] Again, a low level of enforcement of the director's duty of care, skill and diligence may be of less concern if companies were primarily private arrangements between shareholders and directors, since the former can take other steps to deal with poor directors, such as removing them under the Companies Act 2006 s.168.[211] It is not the place to assess this

---

[207] Ibid. Agency costs is the economic concept that refers to the costs that arise when one person (the principal) engages another (the agent) to act on their behalf and include the costs of incentives, monitoring costs and bonding costs: M.C. Jensen and W. Meckling, 'Theory of the Firm: Managerial Behavior, Agency Costs and Ownership Structure' (1976) 3 *Journal of Financial Economics* 305.

[208] Ibid paras 3.87–3.88. For a detailed analytical discussion of the arguments for and against a strict standard of care for directors, and of the Law Commission's approach, see C. Riley, 'The Law Commission's Questionable Approach to the Duty of Care and Skill' (1999) 20 *Company Lawyer* 196 and C. Riley, 'The Company Director's Duty of Care and Skill: the Case for an Onerous but Subjective Standard' (1999) 62 *Modern Law Review* 697.

[209] The House of Commons Treasury Committee, *Banking Crisis: Dealing with the Failure of the UK Banks,* Seventh Report of Session 2008–09 (HC 416) (21 April 2009) at para 74.

[210] A. Beltratti and R. Stulz, 'Why Did Some Banks Perform Better during the Credit Crisis? A Cross-Country Study of the Impact of Governance?' ECGI Working Paper Series in Finance No. 254/2009 at: http://papers.ssrn.com/sol3/papers.cfm?abstract_id=1433502 (accessed 14 January 2011). This study found that banks with more shareholder friendly boards fared worse during the crisis.

[211] For a discussion of the options open to shareholders see V. Finch, 'Company Directors: Who Cares about Skill and Care?' (1992) 55 *Modern Law Review* 179 at 179–189; A. Keay, 'Company Directors Behaving Poorly: Disciplinary Options for Shareholders' (2007) *Journal of Business Law* 656.

argument as far as shareholders go[212] but this view of the company is arguably indefensible when the negligent conduct of boards has repercussions not only for shareholders but also the wider community, as the financial crisis has demonstrated very clearly.

Some argue that banks are special cases and that a different, stricter, standard of care should be applied to bank directors because bank disasters have a much greater impact than other corporate collapses and can undermine the fabric of the financial system and the real economy. Furthermore, insofar as imposing a stricter standard would deter risk-taking, this would be desirable in banks, as these should take less risks than ordinary commercial companies.[213]

Arguably, suing directors for breach of their duty of care and skill is not the best way to hold them to account because, inter alia, it exposes them to disproportionate financial liability. Other accountability mechanisms may be preferable, such as disqualification or the wrongful trading provisions. However disqualification has been criticized precisely because it does not require directors to repay monies to their companies even when they received high levels of compensation in the course of presiding over corporate collapses.[214] Moreover, given that disqualified directors can return to successful careers after their period of disqualification[215] it is not clear that disqualification constitutes an adequate deterrent for unduly risky conduct. Meanwhile the efficacy of the wrongful trading provisions has also been questioned.[216]

---

[212]   As to which see Finch ibid and see also critique of shareholders' role in R. Tomasic and F. Akinbami, 'Shareholder Activism and Litigation Against UK Banks: The Limits of Company Law and the Desperate Last Resort to Human Rights Claims?' at Chapter 5 of this book.

[213]   See J. H. Farrar, 'The Global Financial Crisis and the Governance of Financial Institutions' (2010) *Australian Journal of Corporate Law* 22 reviewing the debate on whether bank directors should be held to a stricter standard of care.

[214]   For a critique of disqualification as a response to the banking crisis see D. Arsalidou, 'The Banking Crisis: Rethinking and Refining the Accountability of Bank Directors' (2010) 4 *Journal of Business Law* 284 at 294–296.

[215]   In relation to the Barings directors, for example, Tuckey became a consultant to blue chip firms: 'Few Escaped from Glittering Class of 1995' *The Observer*, 20 February 2005. A Tony Gamby, described as director of Baring Brothers up until 1995, went on to be a director of Standard Bank and is now a director of a company providing services to the banking industry, LinkedIn listing, (accessed 11 April 2011).

[216]   A. Keay, 'The Duty of Directors to Take Account of Creditor's Interests: Has It Any Role to Play?' (2002) *Journal of Business Law* 393–394; A. Keay,

More effective enforcement of the duty of care and skill could address these issues but only if more actions are brought and only if the courts showed greater readiness to hold directors liable. But leaving enforcement to companies and shareholders may lead to sub-optimal levels of disciplining, for reasons explored in detail here and elsewhere in this book. The case law on the director's duty of care shows that claims are not easily won and so those acting on a company's behalf are unlikely to litigate except in the most clear-cut cases. As a result the financial crisis is unlikely to give rise to a wave of litigation based on the director's duty of care.

'Wrongful Trading and the Liability of Company Directors' (2005) 25 *Legal Studies* 431, 439–442.

2 The duty to promote the success of the company: is it fit for purpose in a post-financial crisis world?

Andrew Keay

I. INTRODUCTION

It has been said that the underlying reason for the financial crisis of 2007–2009 and the problems connected to it, was the mispricing of risk,[1] and/or the employment of foolish and irresponsible lending practices all the way down the finance chain.[2] Some have focused on the failure to manage risk as the reason for the crisis.[3] Others have identified a broader reason, namely the short-termist pressure placed on directors as a result of the demands of shareholders for unsustainable ever-increasing earnings growth that was possible only by way of the shortcut of over-leverage and reduced investment, and the dangerous route of excessive risk. Such commentators have emphasised the fact that the stability and financial strength needed to endure economic cycles were sacrificed for

---

[1] T. Kirchmaier, 'Inject Governance, and Not Just Cash: Some Thoughts on the Governance of Banks' 27 October 2008 and at http://ssrn.com/abstract= 130320 (accessed 31 May 2010); G. Kirkpatrick, 'The Corporate Governance Lessons from the Financial Crisis' (2009) 96 *Financial Market Trends* 1 at 4; M. Peters, 'Corporate Governance of Australian Banking: A Lesson in Law Reform or Good Fortune?' at http://ssrn.com/abstract=1567726 (accessed 23 June 2010).

[2] C. Jordan and A. Jain, 'Diversity and Resilience: Lessons from the Financial Crisis,' Research article, Centre for Corporate Law and Securities Regulation, University of Melbourne, 8 September 2009 at 5.

[3] W. Sahlman, 'Management and the Financial Crisis (We have met the enemy and he is us...)' Harvard Business School, Working Article No. 10–033 at http://www.hbs.edu/research/pdf/10–033.pdf (accessed 15 July 2010); G. Kirkpatrick, 'The Corporate Governance Lessons from the Financial Crisis' (2009) 96 *Financial Market Trends* 1 at 17–23; P. Rose, 'Regulating Risk by "Strengthening Corporate Governance"' at http://ssrn.com/abstract=1630122 (accessed 15 July 2010).

immediate satisfaction.[4] Some commentators have identified the complexity of the finance products employed as a key reason for the crisis.[5] But many commentators have opined that failures in corporate governance in financial institutions caused the crisis,[6] a view also taken by the UK's Financial Services Authority (FSA),[7] even though it has been shown that the governance of these companies is no worse than

---

[4] M. Lipton, T. Mirvis and J. Lorsch, 'The Proposed 'Shareholder Bill of Rights Act of 2009' Harvard Law School Forum on Corporate Governance & Financial Regulation (12 May, 2009) at http://blogs.law.harvard.edu/corpgov/2009/05/12/the-proposed-%e2%80%9cshareholder-bill-of-rights-act-of-2009%e2%80%9d (accessed 1 June 2010). Some support for this comes from the views of company officials interviewed in a small study of FTSE 350 companies in the UK: see P. Taylor, 'Enlightened Shareholder Value and the Companies Act 2006' (unpublished PhD thesis, May 2010), Birkbeck College, University of London at 179. The issue of immediate satisfaction is probably tied up with the fact that it had been said many years before the current crisis that the markets placed pressure on directors to meet their views of what results companies should be achieving: see C. Williams, 'A Tale of Two Trajectories' (2006) 75 *Fordham Law Review* 1629 at 1654–1655; N. Sharpe, 'Rethinking the Board Function in the Wake of the 2008 Financial Crisis' (2010) 5 *Journal of Business and Technology Law* 99 at 110–111. Also see J. Grinyer, A. Russell and D. Collision, 'Evidence of Managerial Short-termism in the UK' (1998) 9 *British Journal of Management* 13 at 14, 15; J. Graham, C. Harvey and S. Rajgopal, 'The Economic Implications of Corporate Financial Reporting' Duke University Research Article, 11 January 2005 at http://ssrn.com/abstract=491627 (accessed 21 June 2010).
[5] L. Buchheit, 'Did We Make Things Too Complicated?' (2008) 27 (3) *International Financial Law Review* 24.
[6] T. Kirchmaier, 'Inject Governance, and Not Just Cash: Some Thoughts on the Governance of Banks' (27 October 2008) at http://ssrn.com/abstract=130320 (accessed 31 May 2010); G. Kirkpatrick, 'The Corporate Governance Lessons from the Financial Crisis' (2009) 96 *Financial Market Trends* 1; M. Peters, 'Corporate Governance of Australian Banking: A Lesson in Law Reform or Good Fortune?' at http://ssrn.com/abstract=1567726 (accessed 23 June 2010); R. Adams, 'Governance and the Financial Crisis' at http://ssrn.com/abstract=1398583 (accessed 23 June 2010) at 15; W. Sahlman, 'Management and the Financial Crisis (We have met the enemy and he is us ...)' Harvard Business School Working Article No. 10–033 at http://www.hbs.edu/research/pdf/10–033.pdf (accessed 15 July 2010); P. Mulbert, 'Corporate Governance of Banks after the Financial Crisis – Theory, Evidence, Reform' (April 2010) at http://ssrn.com/abstract=1448118 (accessed 23 June 2010) at 8–9. Mulbert expresses some doubts as to whether poor corporate governance was a major cause: ibid at 27–28. Brian Cheffins expresses a similar doubt: B. Cheffins, 'Did Corporate Governance "Fail" During the 2008 Stock Market Meltdown? The Case of the S & P 500' at http://ssrn.com/abstract=1396126 (accessed 24 June 2010).
[7] 'Effective Corporate Governance' (January 2010) at para 1.1.

companies conducting businesses in other fields.[8] Some might well argue
that failures in risk management are themselves failures in corporate
governance.[9] It is perhaps notable that UBS, the Swiss-based financial
services company, linked the two when it provided a frank assessment of
its risk management and governance failures to its shareholders.[10]

The OECD Steering Group on Corporate Governance has argued that
weak governance across the spectrum of companies was a major cause of
the financial crisis.[11] The UK's Treasury Select Committee supports the
view that corporate governance problems were a cause of the financial
crisis, stating that it had spotted 'important ... corporate governance
failures in the banking sector.'[12] The Turner Review[13] stated that
improvements in the effectiveness of firm governance are essential.[14] The
Walker Review, undertaken to consider corporate governance in UK
financial institutions, said that:

'The need is now to bring corporate governance issues closer to centre stage
... These entities [financial institutions] need to be better governed.'[15]

---

[8]   R. Adams, 'Governance and the Financial Crisis' at http://ssrn.com/
abstract=1398583 (accessed 23 June 2010) at 15. Also, see B. Cheffins, 'Did
Corporate Governance "Fail" During the 2008 Stock Market Meltdown? The
Case of the S & P 500' at http://ssrn.com/abstract=1396126 (accessed 24 June
2010) where the learned commentator accepted that corporate governance
mistakes were made more widely.
[9]   P. Rose, 'Regulating Risk by "Strengthening Corporate Governance"' at
http://ssrn.com/abstract=1630122 (accessed 15 July 2010).
[10]   UBS AG, *Shareholder Report on UBS's Write Downs* (April 18 2008) and
referred to in Rose, ibid.
[11]   See G. Kirkpatrick, 'The Corporate Governance Lessons from the Financial Crisis' (2009) 96 *Financial Market Trends* 1.
[12]   House of Commons Treasury Committee, *Banking Crisis: Reforming
Corporate Governance and Pay in the City* Ninth Report of Session 2008–09 (12
May 2009) (London, Stationery Office, 2009) and quoted in M. Arden, 'Regulating the Conduct of Directors' (2010) 10 *Journal of Corporate Law Studies* 1
at 1.
[13]   FSA, 'A regulatory response to the global banking crisis' March 2009.
[14]   Ibid at para 2.8.
[15]   D. Walker, *A Review of Corporate Governance in UK Banks and Other
Financial Industry Entities: Final Recommendations* (26 November 2009) at 9
(Executive summary). One of the problems that exist is that little is known about
the characteristics of boards of banks. See D. Ferreira T. Kirchmaier,T and D.
Metzger, 'Boards of Banks' at http://ssrn.com/abstract=1620551 (accessed 23
June 2010).

It is trite to say that the role played by directors of companies is essential to any consideration of corporate governance.[16] Obviously, they are critical to any corporate governance system that exists. As part of this system, directors are made accountable for how they have conducted the affairs of their company, and this is achieved through a number of mechanisms. That is, they are, or may be, called to account in various forms for what they have done or not done. Importantly in this regard certain duties are imposed on how directors act in managing their companies' affairs. If they fail to fulfil these duties the directors may be subject to legal proceedings and they may, ultimately, be held liable by the courts.

The position as far as duties of directors in the UK are concerned is that the law has seen a recent upheaval, at least on the face of things. After so many years when directors' duties were provided for by common law rules and equitable principles, the UK has now decided to follow other common law jurisdictions,[17] and it has codified the duties in the Companies Act 2006, principally in Chapter 2 of Part 10 of that statute. These duties, which became operational on either 1 October 2007,[18] or 1 October 2008,[19] now act as guides for many of the management activities of directors and determine whether directors have acted properly.

The statutory duties became operational at a time when the financial life of not only the UK, but much of the rest of the world, was in turmoil. Most of the actions of directors that related to this financial crisis, and even contributed to it, were regulated by the previous law on duties, and so whether directors are liable for what they did, or did not do, will depend on those previous duties. It is highly likely that any actions that are instituted will be on the basis of an alleged breach of the duty of care and skill, now codified in s.174. What this chapter seeks to do, in light of the events of the financial crisis which began in 2007 and is still unravelling and having a significant effect on the UK and many parts of the world, is to look forward and assess whether one of the duties imposed by the Companies Act 2006 is fit for purpose. Is the duty likely

---

[16]   See J. Carver, 'A Case for Global Governance Theory' (2010) 18 *Corporate Governance: An International Review* 149 at 149, 150.

[17]   For example, Australia, New Zealand, Ghana and Singapore.

[18]   Sections 170–176 and 178. See Companies Act 2006 (Commencement No. 3, Consequential Amendments, Transitional Provisions and Savings) Order 2007 (SI 2007/2194).

[19]   Sections 175–177. See Companies Act 2006 (Commencement No 5, Transitional Provisions and Savings) Order 2007 (SI 2007/3495).

to fulfil its purpose, as determined by the legislature, and will it prove to be effective in providing better corporate governance and regulating how directors act for the future?

The duty upon which the chapter focuses is that contained in s.172 of the Companies Act 2006 (the Act). Arguably, this 'core duty'[20] has been the most controversial and challenging duty that has been introduced in the Act,[21] and the one that has given lawyers, companies and their directors the most concern.[22] The provision led to more debate in the UK Parliament than any other provision contained in the whole Act, and, interestingly, the section has attracted quite a reasonable amount of interest and comment in the US.[23] The section may be said to impose a duty on directors to require them to be more inclusive in their decision-making, namely taking into account the relationships which the company has with its stakeholders in seeking to benefit the members. Unlike other duties such as that in s.175 which involves a revamping of the no conflict and no profit rules, it has no obvious precursor. However, it has clear links to the duty to act bona fide in the best interests of the company, which was the predominant and core fiduciary duty owed by directors before the codification of the duties, and it is probably fair to see s.172 as a successor to this duty. The only cases that have addressed the provision, albeit briefly, have stated that s.172 merely sets out the pre-existing law on the subject, that is, decisions made in relation to the duty to act bona fide in the best interests of the company.[24] Having said that, some have

---

[20] P.L. Davies, *Gower and Davies' Principles of Company Law*, 8th edn (Sweet and Maxwell, London, 2008) at 506.

[21] See, for example, the debates in the House of Commons in Standing Committee D on 11 July 2006 (at col. 543) at http://www.publications. parliament.uk/pa/cm200506/cmstand/d/st060711/am/60711s01.htm (accessed 31 May 2010).

[22] Institute of Chartered Secretaries and Administrators (ICSA), *Guidance on Directors' General Duties* (January 2008) at para 3.2.3.

[23] For example see C. Williams and J. Conley, 'An Emerging Third Way? The Erosion of the Anglo-American Shareholder Value Construct' (2005) 38 *Cornell International Law Journal* 493 at http://articles.ssrn.com/sol3/ articles.cfm?abstract_id=632347 (accessed 29 October 2009) at 500; V. Ho, '"Enlightened Shareholder Value": Corporate Governance Beyond the Shareholder-Stakeholder Divide' abstract at http://ssrn.com /abstract=1476116 (accessed 10 December 2009); D. Millon, 'Enlightened Shareholder Value, Social Responsibility, and the Redefinition of Corporate Purpose Without Law' at http://articles.ssrn.com/abstract=1625750 (accessed 28 July 2010).

[24] For instance, see *Re West Coast Capital (LIOS) Ltd* [2008] CSOH 72; 2008 Scot (D) 16/5 (Outer House, Court of Sessions, Lord Glennie) at [21];

argued that as the duty provided for in s.172 is obviously different from the duty to act in the best interests of the company it requires fresh consideration.[25] While the section does require fresh consideration, it is submitted that important aspects of the section will be interpreted and applied in conformity with previous case law.

The duty is probably the most wide-ranging duty of the general duties in the Act, and the most difficult to interpret at this stage. Thus, and because it is not as closely aligned to any previous duty when compared with other duties in Chapter 2 of Part 10 of the Act, parts of this article, while informed by existing case law and academic opinion, involve some speculation.

This chapter examines the duty in s.172 and assesses whether the duty is fit for purpose and whether, assuming that directors' duties are designed to facilitate, at least partly, improved corporate governance, the duty is likely to ensure that better corporate governance is delivered. The chapter does not focus only on financial institutions, the companies whose corporate governance has been called into question most often since the crisis. The chapter seeks to consider large public companies in general, while accepting that much of it applies to the governance of financial institutions, because boards of financial institutions owe the same duties to their companies and shareholders[26] as non-financial institutions.[27] It is probably fair to say that not as much is known about the governance of boards of financial institutions compared with non-financial institutions as the empirical research undertaken has tended to be directed to the latter kind of companies.[28] The fact is that non-financial companies have suffered in the aftermath of the financial crisis, and their corporate governance may have contributed to the state in which they find themselves. One important thing to emphasise is that

---

Cobden Investments Ltd v RWM Langport Ltd [2008] EWHC 2810 (Ch). The judgments did not go on to discuss the section at all.

[25] See for example, Maclay Murray Spens *Guide to the Companies Act 2006* at http://www.mms.co.uk/ (accessed 6 January 2006) at 6. Cf Cameron McKenna 'Companies Act 2006: Deferred Reform' *Law-Now* (29 November 2006) at http://www.law-now.com/ law-now/default (accessed 22 March 2007) at 6; Ashurst *The Companies Act 2006: Directors Duties* (November 2006), at http://www.ashurst.com/publication-item.aspx?id_Content=2784 (accessed 22 March 2007).

[26] Christopher Bruner is of the view that a new corporate governance paradigm might have to be developed for banks: 'Corporate Governance Reform in a Time of Crisis' at http://ssrn.com/abstract=1617890 (accessed 23 June 2010).

[27] Ibid.

[28] Ibid.

although s.172 was conceived and enacted some time before the financial crisis developed, at least publicly, it was not put in force until the financial problems causing the crisis had started to unravel. The provision had a long gestation period and was conceived during an economically halcyon period, certainly for the UK (latter part of the 1990s and first two years of this century). So it is important to recognize that the provision cannot in anyway be regarded as a response to the financial crisis.

The chapter does not seek to examine[29] the views of some that the provision is moving the UK towards a more 'stakeholder conscious corporate society,'[30] that 'UK corporations are now moving towards a more stakeholder centred model of governance,'[31] or that it is providing for an emerging third way, somewhere between shareholder primacy theory and stakeholder theory.[32] That really is another issue, consideration of which is undoubtedly laudable, but not totally relevant to the thrust of this chapter.[33]

The chapter develops as follows. First, it sets out the section and places it in context. Second, the chapter provides some background to the evolution of s.172. Following this the chapter addresses the section's purpose. Fourth, the main part of the chapter provides an assessment of the duty and whether it is likely to be effective in the terms set out above. Fifth, some general reflections are given in relation to the section and its likely application. Finally, the chapter provides some conclusions.

---

[29]   For an article that does, see A. Keay, 'Moving Towards Stakeholderism? Enlightened Shareholder Value, Constituency Statutes and More: Much Ado About Little?' at http://ssrn.com/abstract=1530990 (accessed 17 July 2010).

[30]   S. Kiarie, 'At Crossroads: Shareholder Value, Stakeholder Value and Enlightened Shareholder Value: Which Road Should the United Kingdom Take?' (2006) 17 *International Company and Commercial Law Review* 329 at 329.

[31]   A. Mickels, 'Beyond Corporate Social Responsibility: Reconciling the Ideals of a For-Benefit Corporation with Director Fiduciary Duties in the US and Europe' (2009) 32 *Hastings International and Comparative Law Review* 271 at 293.

[32]   See C. Williams and J. Conley, 'An Emerging Third Way? The Erosion of the Anglo-American Shareholder Value Construct' (2005) 38 *Cornell International Law Journal* 493 at 500 at http://articles.ssrn.com/sol3/articles. cfm?abstract_id=632347 (accessed 29 October 2009); S. Kiarie, 'At Crossroads: Shareholder Value, Stakeholder Value and Enlightened Shareholder Value: Which Road Should the United Kingdom Take?' (2006) 17 *International Company and Commercial Law Review* 329 at 339.

[33]   See, A. Keay, "Moving Towards to Stakeholderism? Enlightened Shareholder Value, Constituency Statutes and More: Much Ado About Little?" (2011) 22 *European Business Law Review* 1.

II. SECTION 172(1)

It is worthwhile setting out s.172(1) in full. It provides that:

A director of a company must act in a way that he considers, in good faith, would be most likely to promote the success of the company for the benefit of its members as a whole, and in doing so have regard (amongst other matters) to

(a) the likely consequences of any decision in the long term;
(b) the interests of the company's employees;
(c) the need to foster the company's business relationships with suppliers, customers and others;
(d) the impact of the company's operations on the community and the environment;
(e) the desirability of the company maintaining a reputation for high standards of business conduct, and
(f) the need to act fairly between the members of the company.

While s.172 is regarded as imposing a new duty on directors, there are indications in previous case law that the directors have had a similar duty in the past. In the classic case of *Aberdeen Railway Co v Blaikie Brothers,*[34] Lord Cranworth said that:

'A corporate body can only act by agents, and it is of course the duty of those agents so *to act as best to promote the interests of the corporation* whose affairs they are conducting.'[35] (emphasis added)

More recently, in *Scottish Co-operative Wholesale Society Ltd v Meyer,*[36] Lord Denning said that the duty of directors 'was *to do their best to promote its business* and to act with complete good faith towards it'[37] (emphasis added).

So, it would appear, as one might expect, that directors have always been under a duty to promote the company's business. This would surely require actions that would be consistent with fulfilling the duty to act in good faith for the benefit of the company.

The Government stated that Chapter 2 of Part 10 of the Act can be viewed in one of two ways, either as simply codifying the existing equitable and common law obligations of company directors, or as

---

[34]   (1854) 1 Macq 461.
[35]   Ibid at 471 per Lord Cranworth LC.
[36]   [1959] AC 324.
[37]   Ibid at 367.

marking a radical change in articulating the connection between what is good for a company and what is good for society at large, and the minister overseeing the enactment of the companies legislation said that s.172 of the Act falls into the latter category.[38] This is considered later.

It is possible to say that this duty is the fundamental duty of directors, and that other duties mentioned elsewhere in the Act are applications of this duty.[39] Certainly this is the case with s.175 which deals with ensuring that directors are not in conflict situations and do not exploit company opportunities for their own benefit.

Although s.172(1) has attracted by far the greatest attention, s.172 contains two other sub-sections, which provide exceptions to the duty laid down in s.172(1).

First, s.172(2) provides that where there is a company that includes purposes other than the benefit of the members, it operates as if the reference to promoting the success of the company for the benefit of its members were to achieving the purposes set by the company. According to the Explanatory Notes to the Act this provision deals with altruistic, or partly altruistic, companies. Examples that are given are charitable companies and community interest companies, but the notes accept that it is possible for any company to have objectives that are unselfish and are paramount over the members' own interests.

The second exception is contained in s.172(3).[40] It provides that the duty to promote the success of the company for the benefit of the members is subject to any enactment or rule of law requiring directors to consider the interests of the company's creditors. What the sub-section does is to recognize, inter alia, the common law development of a duty of directors to take into account the interests of the creditors of the company

---

[38] *Duties of Company Directors* (DTI, June 2007), Introduction and Statement of Margaret Hodge MP. Clearly the Government was caught between business not wanting to see any change to the law, and many of the constituents of the Labour Party who wished to see the nature of companies changed. The Government sought to steer a course that took it down the middle. For an interesting discussion on this topic and others, see P. Bovey, 'A Damn Close Run Thing – The Companies Act 2006' (2008) 29 *Statute Law Review* 11.

[39] See *Shepherds Investments Ltd v Walters* [2006] EWHC 836 at [106]; *Item Software (UK) Ltd v Fassihi* [2004] EWCA Civ 1244; [2004] BCC 994 at [41] in relation to the previous law.

[40] For a discussion of the subsection, see A. Keay, *The Enlightened Shareholder Value Principle and Corporate Governance* (London, Routledge, 2012) at 218–230.

in certain circumstances.[41] The provision does not state when creditors' interests are to be considered in the course of the directors' decision-making. This is left to the common law.[42] The circumstances which will require directors to have to take into account creditor interests involve situations where the company is insolvent and even where the company is in some form of financial difficulty, short of insolvency. Consequently until the company has become solvent again or moved out of the financial mire in which it finds itself, the s.172(1) duty is suspended.[43]

Section 172(1) requires directors to have regard to the interests of various stakeholders, such as employees, yet many argue that this is what directors have done for many years, even when operating under a shareholder value approach to governance.[44] This approach was acknowledged in the Hampel Report when it was said that to ensure that there is

---

[41] The development of this area of the law may well reduce the incidence of risk-taking when companies are in financial straits.

[42] For some of the case law see: Winkworth v Edward Baron Development Co Ltd [1986] 1 WLR 1512; [1987] 1 All ER 114; Liquidator of West Mercia Safetywear v Dodd [1988] 4 BCC 30; Facia Footwear Ltd (in administration) v Hinchliffe [1998] 1 BCLC 218; Re Pantone 485 Ltd [2002] 1 BCLC 266; Gwyer v London Wharf (Limehouse) Ltd [2002] EWHC 2748; [2003] 2 BCLC 153; Re MDA Investment Management Ltd [2003] EWHC 227 (Ch), [2004] BPIR 75; Re Cityspan Ltd [2007] EWHC 751 (Ch), [2007] 2 BCLC 522; Ultraframe (UK) Ltd v Fielding [2005] EWHC 1638 (Ch); Re Bakewell Management Ltd [2008] EWHC 3633 (Ch). The case law in other Commonwealth jurisdictions has been very influential. For example see, Walker v Wimborne (1976) 137 CLR 1, 3 ACLR 529; Kinsela v Russell Kinsela Pty Ltd (1986) 4 ACLC 215, 10 ACLR 395; Jeffree v NCSC (1989) 7 ACLC 556, 15 ACLR 217; Spies v The Queen [2000] HCA 43, [2000] 201 CLR 603; Nicholson v Permakraft (NZ) Ltd (1985) 3 ACLC 453; Hilton International Ltd (in liquidation) v Hilton [1989] NZLR 442. For academic consideration, see for example, D. Prentice, 'Creditor's Interests and Director's Duties' (1990) 10 Oxford Journal of Legal Studies 265; V. Finch, 'Directors' Duties: Insolvency and the Unsecured Creditor' in A. Clarke (ed), Current Issues in Insolvency Law (London, Stevens, 1991); A. Keay, Company Directors' Responsibilities to Creditors (Abingdon, Routledge-Cavendish, 2007) at 151–286; A. Keay, Directors' Duties (Jordan, Bristol, 2009), Ch 13.

[43] For suggestions as to how this would work, see A. Keay, 'Formulating a Framework for Directors' Duties to Creditors: An Entity Maximisation Approach' (2005) 64 Cambridge Law Journal 614.

[44] Michael Jensen has argued that it is part of his enlightened stakeholder value theory: 'Value Maximisation, Stakeholder Theory, and the Corporate Objective Function' (2001) 7 European Financial Management 297.

long-term shareholder wealth, directors have to develop and sustain relationships with stakeholders.[45]

Section 172(1) was the first of two mechanisms that was to introduce the concept of enlightened shareholder value ('ESV'), as conceived by the Company Law Review Steering Group ('CLRSG'). The CLRSG was established in 1998 to review UK company law. Section 172(1) imposes a duty on directors to be more inclusive in their decision-making, namely taking into account the relationships the company has with stakeholders while seeking to benefit the members. The second mechanism was the requirement for listed companies to provide an operating and financial review that would compel such companies 'to disclose a range of 'qualitative' and 'forward-looking' information of a kind that is not normally found in traditional financial statements.'[46] The operating and financial review never actually saw light of day, but was replaced by the requirement to produce a business review.[47] The duty in s.172 cannot be considered, given the aims of the article, without some examination of the business review and that is done later in the chapter.[48]

III.   LEGISLATIVE DEVELOPMENT[49]

It is not intended in this article to rehearse the background to the enactment of s.172 and what issues were considered first by the CLRSG,[50] and then the Government in their decisions to draft and to enact respectively the section as it is. I have done that elsewhere in some detail.[51] But a few words are appropriate to set the scene. Section 172

---

[45] *Final Report of the Committee on Corporate Governance* (Hampel Report) (1998) at para 1.18.

[46] A. Johnston, 'After the OFR: Can UK Shareholder Value Still Be Enlightened?' (2006) 7 *European Business Organisation Review* 817 at 818.

[47] See s.417 of the Companies Act 2006.

[48] See also C. Villiers, 'Narrative Reporting and Enlightened Shareholder Value Under the Companies Act 2006' in chapter 3 of this book.

[49] The following is distilled from A. Keay, *Directors' Duties* (Bristol, Jordans, 2009) at 106–110.

[50] For a detailed discussion, see A. Keay, *The Enlightened Shareholder Value Principle and Corporate Governance* (London, Routledge, 2012) Chapter 3.

[51] A. Keay, 'Enlightened Shareholder Value, the Reform of the Duties of Company Directors and the Corporate Objective' [2006] *Lloyds Maritime and Commercial Law Quarterly* 335; A. Keay, 'Tackling the Issue of the Corporate Objective: An Analysis of the United Kingdom's 'Enlightened Shareholder Value Approach' (2007) 29 *Sydney Law Review* 577.

developed during the course of the CLRSG's consideration of duties of directors. The CLRSG believed that UK company law embraced the shareholder value approach (also known as 'shareholder primacy' or 'shareholder wealth maximization'), namely the directors are to manage the company so as to enhance ultimately the interests of the shareholders.[52] This is opposed to the stakeholder or pluralist approach which holds, to put it simply, that the directors must run the company so as to benefit all stakeholders of the company.[53] The CLRSG stated that directors were obliged to 'achieve the success of the company for the benefit of the shareholders by taking proper account of all the relevant considerations for that purpose' and this involved taking

> 'a proper balanced view of the short and long term; the need to sustain effective ongoing relationships with employees, customers, suppliers and others' as well as to 'consider the impact of its operations on the community and the environment.'[54]

When the Government published its first White Paper in July 2002 on what was going to be the new companies legislation,[55] it expressly endorsed the CLRSG's approach.[56] The draft Companies Bill that was

---

[52] For discussion of this approach, on which much has been written, see (for example): D. G. Smith, 'The Shareholder Primacy Norm' (1998) 23 *Journal of Corporate Law* 277; L. Stout, 'Bad and Not-So-Bad Arguments for Shareholder Primacy' (2002) 75 *South California Law Review* 1189; J. Fisch, 'Measuring Efficiency in Corporate Law: The Role of Shareholder Primacy' 31 *Journal of Corporations Law* 637 (2006); A. Keay, 'Shareholder Primacy in Corporate Law. Can it Survive? Should it Survive? (2010) 7 *European Company and Financial Law Review* 369. It is to be noted that one commentator argues somewhat persuasively that the UK has a more shareholder-centric approach than the US: C. Bruner, 'Power and Purpose in the 'Anglo-American' Corporation' (2010) 50 *Virginia Journal of International Law* 579.

[53] For discussion of this approach, see for example: R. E. Freeman, *Strategic Management: a Stakeholder Approach* (Boston, Pitman/Ballinger, 1984); R. Karmel, 'Implications of the Stakeholder Model' (1993) 61 *George Washington Law Review* 1156; J. Clarke, 'The Stakeholder Corporation: A Business Philosophy for the Information Age' (1998) 31 *Long Range Planning* 182; A. Campbell, 'Stakeholders, the Case in Favour'(1997) 30 *Long Range Planning* 446; A. Keay, 'Stakeholder Theory in Corporate Law: Has it Got What it Takes?' (2010) 9 *Richmond Journal of Global Law and Business* 249.

[54] Company Law Review, *Modern Company Law for a Competitive Economy: Developing the Framework* (London, DTI, 2000) at para 2.19.

[55] Department of Trade and Industry, *Modernising Company Law*, Cm 5553 (London, Stationery Office, 2002).

[56] Ibid at para 3.6.

part of the White Paper included an embryonic s.172. In its second White Paper, in March 2005, the Government confirmed that it was going to pursue the CLRSG's recommendations in relation to directors' duties.[57] The second White Paper provided that there are two elements to the way in which directors are to run the company.[58] First, they are to do that which they consider, in good faith, is most likely to promote the success of the company for the benefit of the members as a whole. Second, in carrying out the first element, the directors are to take into account, where relevant, and as far as is reasonably practicable, several factors (in order to reflect wider consideration of responsible business behaviour) that are listed, but not intended to be exhaustive. These factors are now contained in s.172(1)(a)–(f) as set out above

IV. THE PURPOSE OF THE DUTY

Directors' duties have been provided by common law and equity since the beginning of the major developments of company law in the mid-nineteenth century. It has been said that to get a picture of the duties of directors one had to digest 'a confusing and compendious mass of case law and the occasional statutory measure.'[59] The purpose of codification was, according to the joint Report of the Law Commission and the Scottish Law Commission,[60] to restate the law on directors' duties in order to clarify it and make it more accessible, with the aim of bringing about a change in directors' behaviour by educating directors and providing them with greater certainty regarding what the law required of them.[61] Subsequently, in the debates on the Company Law Reform Bill 2005, later to be re-named the Companies Bill 2006, the Government,

---

[57]   Department of Trade and Industry, *Company Law Reform* Cm 6456 (London, Stationery Office, 2005).

[58]   Ibid Explanatory Notes at para B17.

[59]   L. Roach 'The Legal Model of the Company and the Company Law Review' (2005) *26 Company Lawyer* 98.

[60]   Law Commission, *Company Directors: Regulating Conflicts of Interest and Formulating a Statement of Duties*, (Law Com, Report No 261, Cm 4436) (Scot Law Commission No 173) (London, Stationery Office, 1999).

[61]   Ibid at paras 4.40–4.41. The Law Commission and the Institute of Directors have expressed concerns in the past that directors have a generally low level of understanding of their duties: Company Law Review, *Modern Company Law for a Competitive Economy: Developing the Framework* (London, DTI, 2000) at para 3.37; Law Commission, *Company Directors: Regulating Conflicts of Interest and Formulating a Statement of Duties* (Law Com, Report No 261,

through the statements of Lord Goldsmith in the House of Lords, indicated that clarifying and making accessible the duties was the main reason for codification.[62] Earlier the CLRSG, in its Final Report to the then Department of Trade and Industry gave three reasons for codification,[63] two of which reflected the points mentioned above. The Final Report said that codification would provide greater clarity on what is expected of directors and make the law more accessible. It was said that this would help to improve standards of corporate governance. A second reason was that a codified statement of duties would enable 'defects in the present law to be corrected in important areas where it no longer corresponds to accepted norms of modern business practice.'[64] Third, the CLRSG said that it would address the scope of duties, namely in whose interests are the company's affairs to be run?[65]

The purpose behind s.172, within the framework just discussed, was primarily to emphasize the fact that directors should not run a company for short-term gains alone,[66] but to take into account long-term consequences.[67] The policy intention is to encourage decision-making based

---

Cm 4436) (Scot Law Commission No 173) (London, Stationery Office, 1999) at paras 4.25–4.26 and Appendix B.

[62] Lords Grand Committee, HL 6 February 2006, Col 254. For a consideration of the purpose behind codification see A. Keay, *Directors' Duties* (Jordans, Bristol, 2009) at 56–58.

[63] Company Law Review, *Modern Company Law for a Competitive Economy: Final Report* (London, DTI, 2001) vol 1 at para 3.7.

[64] Ibid.

[65] Ibid.

[66] Short-termism has been defined as 'seeking short-term gain to the exclusion of long-term achievement': D. Mullins, 'Foreword' in M. Jacobs, *Short-term America* (Harvard Business School Press, Boston, MA, 1991) and quoted in J. Grinyer, A. Russell and D. Collision, 'Evidence of Managerial Short-termism in the UK' (1998) 9 *British Journal of Management* 13 at 13 and as 'forgoing economically worthwhile investments with longer-term benefits in order to increase reported earnings for the current period': Grinyer, Russell and Collision ibid at 15. There is some debate as to whether UK markets at the time of the CLRSG's reports were short-termist: see P. Marsh, *Short-termism on Trial* (Institutional Fund Managers Association, London, 1990); D. Miles, *Testing for Short-termism in the UK Stock Market* (Economics Division, Bank of England, London, 1992).

[67] This accorded with the UK's Combined Code (now the UK Code of Corporate Governance), sanctioned by the Financial Reporting Council, which provided in its preamble that: 'Good governance should facilitate efficient, effective and entrepreneurial management that can deliver shareholder value over the longer term.': Financial Reporting Council, *Combined Code on Corporate Governance* (June 2008) at para 1.

upon a longer-term perspective and not just immediate returns. Also, the section, together with the business review (required by s.417 of the Act), was to make the process of management more enlightened and it did this to ensure that directors would consider a much wider range of interests, with the hope that there would be more responsible decision-making. The business review was introduced to try to ensure that the directors not only were more inclusive in their actions, but that they justified what they did.

Besides the purposes set out above, and which might be regarded as ground-breaking, the section was included to take over the role previously played by the duty to act bona fide in the best interests of the company. That is, to act as the central fiduciary duty, at the very heart of which is the requirement of loyalty, as loyalty is concerned, inter alia, with the exercising of power in a good faith effort to foster the interests of the company.[68]

V. FITNESS FOR PURPOSE

(a) Introduction

The article now turns to a study of s.172 to assess how it is likely to be applied by the courts and with the ultimate objective of assessing whether the section is fit for purpose. Is it likely to achieve what the Government intended it to achieve? Does the provision requiring loyalty to the company assist in enhancing corporate governance and help to overcome the problems that existed during the period leading up to the financial malaise?

What has to be noted at the outset is that the provision includes either novel or elusive concepts, such as 'success of the company' and 'good faith.' This means that to a degree, the application of the section is uncertain.

Hitherto, and despite the fact that the section has been in force for a little over three years, there is little case law to illustrate how s.172 might be viewed by the courts. The only decisions, outside of the derivative action cases,[69] that have covered the section are the Scottish case of *Re*

---

[68]   E. Pan, 'Rethinking the Board's Duty to Monitor: A Critical Assessment of the Delaware Doctrine' at http://ssrn.com/abstract=1593332 (accessed 17 July 2010). Also see P.L. Davies, *Gower and Davies' Principles of Company Law*, 8th edn (Sweet and Maxwell, London, 2008) at 506.

[69]   There have been several other cases that have mentioned s.172 in dealing with an application by shareholders for permission (in England and Wales) or leave (in Scotland and Northern Ireland) under s.263(2)(a) (applying to England and Wales and Northern Ireland) or s.268(1)(a) (applying to Scotland) to

West Coast Capital (LIOS) Ltd[70] and the English case of *Cobden Investments Ltd v RWM Langport Ltd.*[71] In the former case Lord Glennie merely said that the provision seemed to do little more than set out the pre-existing law on the subject. In the latter case Warren J seemed to agree, saying

'The perhaps old-fashioned phrase acting "*bona fide* in the interests of the company" is reflected in the statutory words acting "in good faith in a way most likely to promote the success of the company for the benefit of its members as a whole". They come to the same thing with the modern formulation giving a more readily understood definition of the scope of the duty.'[72]

If s.172 merely reflects the previous duty then it is not fit for purpose as the Government had expectations that the section would achieve more than the previous duty did. As with the previous duty, the duty is based on loyalty and it aims to have directors consider the interests of the company and to act in good faith, but the Government wanted more. Furthermore the view that s.172 merely restates the previous duty does not sit well with the fact that the Government said at one point that the new provision 'marks a radical departure in articulating the connection between what is good for a company and what is good for society at large.'[73]

---

continue a derivative action. However this has been simply because where a court is satisfied that a person acting in accordance with s.172 would not seek to continue the claim, the court must refuse permission or leave. For example see *Mission Capital Plc v Sinclair* [2008] EWHC 1339 (Ch), [2008] BCC 866; *Franbar Holdings Ltd v Patel* [2008] EWHC 1534 (Ch), [2008] BCC 885; *Wishart* [2009] CSIH 65, 2009 SLT 812; *Iesini v Westrip Holdings Ltd* [2009] EWHC 2526 (Ch), [2010] BCC 420; *Stimpson v Southern Landlords Association* [2009] EWHC 2072 (Ch), [2010] BCC 420; *Kiani v Cooper* [2010] EWHC 577 (Ch), [2010] BCC 463; *Stainer v Lee* [2010] EWHC 1539 (Ch), [2011] BCC 134. None of these cases have cast any light on s.172 and its scope, and one would not really expect them to do so.

[70]   [2008] CSOH 72; 2008 Scot (D) 16/5 (Outer House, Court of Sessions, Lord Glennie) at [21].

[71]   [2008] EWHC 2810 (Ch). The decision in *Re Phoenix Contracts (Leicester) Ltd* [2010] EWHC 2375 (Ch) did address s.172(1) very briefly as well, but the focus was on s.994 of the Act.

[72]   [2008] EWHC 2810 (Ch) at [52].

[73]   *Duties of Company Directors* (DTI, June 2007) Introduction and Statement of the Margaret Hodge MP.

(b) Application

The first thing to note is that s.170(1) states that directors owe their duties to the company. If that is the case, how does that line up with the s.172(1) requirement that directors have to promote the success of the company for the benefit of the members as a whole? It must surely mean that the directors' overall duty is to the company and that duty encompasses all of the individual duties contained in ss.171–177. If there was a possible conflict between the company's interests and those of the members the former should prevail. This assumes that the interests of the company and those of the shareholders are not necessarily common, and of course some take the view that the company's interests are those of the shareholders. But provided that an action is not against the interests of the company, s.170(1) means that one duty that the directors have to the company is to act in such a way that will foster the interests of the members as a whole. Section 172 does not give the shareholders, individually or a group of them, short of a derivative action, the right to enforce the duty as it is owed to the company. This has always been the case. The company has always had to take any action for a breach of duties of directors as the company is the one to whom the duties were owed,[74] except where the courts were willing to apply one or more of a number of so-called exceptions to the rule in *Foss v Harbottle*.[75]

1. Good faith[76]

The first thing to note is that, consistent with its predecessor duty, s.172 requires directors to act in good faith. This concept is central to the provision. A director is to act in such a way that *he considers*, in good faith, will promote the success of the company. Under the predecessor duty directors were obliged to act 'bona fide in what they consider – not what a court may consider – is in the interests of the company ... '.[77] The focus was very much on what the directors themselves considered. The courts would neither impose their own views as to whether the decisions made by the director were in the best interests of the company,[78] nor

---

[74] See *Foss v Harbottle* (1843) 2 Hare 46; 67 ER 189.

[75] Arguably there was only one true exception to the rule, namely the fraud on the minority ground.

[76] For further discussion, see A. Keay, *The Enlightened Shareholder Value Principle and Corporate Governance* (London, Routledge, 2012) at 93–107.

[77] *Re Smith & Fawcett Ltd* [1942] Ch 304 at 306 per Lord Greene MR.

[78] Ibid at 306; *Regentcrest plc v Cohen* [2002] 2 BCLC 80; *Extrasure Travel Insurance Ltd v Scattergood* [2003] 1 BCLC 598.

would they hold a director liable simply because his actions happened, in the event, to cause injury to the company.'[79] Further, no reasonableness test was applied. Whether a director had breached his or her duty came down to an examination of the director's state of mind and provided that directors believed in good faith that they were acting in the best interests of the company they were not in breach. In *Regentcrest plc v Cohen*[80] Jonathan Parker J, when dealing with the duty to act bona fide in the best interests of the company, said that if the directors give unequivocal evidence that they had honestly believed that they had acted in the best interests of the company,[81] and if that evidence were accepted, then there had been no breach.[82] The new duty would seem to attract the same approach. This is evident in the statement of the Government Minister responsible for the legislation, Margaret Hodge MP, when she said, in relation to s.172, that:

'We believe it is essential for the weight given to any factor to be a matter for the director's good faith judgment. Importantly, the decision is not subject to the reasonableness test.'[83]

Nevertheless, courts will not accept without question a director's statement that he or she acted in good faith. Where it is patent that the act complained of led to significant detriment to the company, a director will have, according to Jonathan Parker J in *Regentcrest plc v Cohen*, a more difficult task to convince the court that he or she honestly believed the action to be in the best interests of the company.[84] The judge hearing a case might not believe the evidence of the directors as to his or her state of mind. This is, arguably, consistent with what Harman J said in *Re a Company*[85]: 'It is, in my judgment, vital to remember that actions of boards of directors cannot simply be justified by invoking the incantation that there has been 'a decision taken bona fide in the interests of the company.'[86]

So an assertion by a director is not impregnable and judges are not prevented from declining to accept it. In *Extrasure Travel Insurance Ltd*

<hr>

[79] *Extrasure Travel Insurance Ltd v Scattergood* [2003] 1 BCLC 598 at [90].
[80] [2002] 2 BCLC 80.
[81] Ibid at [124].
[82] Ibid at [125].
[83] Hansard, HC Comm D, 11 July 2006, Cols 591–593.
[84] [2002] 2 BCLC 80 at [90]. Also, see Arden LJ in *Item Software (UK) Ltd v Fassihi* [2004] EWCA Civ 1244; [2005] 2 BCLC 91 at [52].
[85] [1988] BCLC 570.
[86] Ibid at 577.

v Scattergood[87] Jonathan Crow (sitting as a deputy High Court judge) plainly did not believe the directors when they said that they believed that they were acting in the best interests of the company. The learned deputy judge said: 'I am satisfied that the defendants did not think, on 17 August 1999, that the transfer of £200,000 was in the best interests of Extrasure.'[88] He was of view that the directors' evidence was not plausible, given the surrounding evidence, and he found against them.[89] But it is likely to be difficult to demonstrate, except in cases of really bad behaviour, that the directors have breached their duty of good faith.[90] It is onerous, in many cases, to impugn the actions of someone who is able to state clearly that he or she believed that what was done was in the company's best interests. Directors will normally assert that their motives were pure. Courts are reluctant to reject evidence given by directors concerning their motives. Davies has opined, adroitly, that it is difficult to say that a director has failed to act in good faith 'except in egregious cases or where the directors, obligingly, have left a clear record of their thought processes leading up to the challenged decision.'[91]

Nevertheless, there is *one* situation where reasonableness might be an issue. This is where directors had actually failed to consider whether an action taken would be in the interests of the company. In *Charterbridge Corp Ltd v Lloyds Bank Ltd*[92] Pennycuick J said that in such a situation the court has to ask whether an intelligent and honest man in the position of a director of the company involved, could, in the whole of the circumstances, have reasonably believed that the transaction was for the benefit of the company.[93]

In *Cobden Investments Ltd v RWM Langport Ltd*[94] Warren J was of the view that the duty in s.172 is subjective, just as its precursor was.[95] This seems to be right as the section states that: 'A director of a company must act *in a way that he considers, in good faith,* would be most likely to

---

[87]   [2003] 1 BCLC 598.

[88]   Ibid at [105].

[89]   Ibid at [106].

[90]   *Re Smith & Fawcett Ltd* [1942] Ch 304.

[91]   P.L. Davies, *Gower and Davies' Principles of Company Law*, 8th edn (Sweet and Maxwell, London, 2008) at 510.

[92]   [1970] Ch 62; [1969] 3 All ER 1185.

[93]   *Charterbridge Corp Ltd v Lloyds Bank Ltd* [1970] Ch 62 at 74; [1969] 3 All ER 1185 at 1194. Also, see *Shuttleworth v Cox Bros (Maidenhead) Ltd* [1927] 2 KB 9 at 23.

[94]   [2008] EWHC 2810 (Ch).

[95]   Ibid at [53]. Proudman J in *Re Phoenix Contracts (Leicester) Ltd* [2010] EWHC 2375 (Ch) at [104] agreed.

promote the success of the company…'(emphasis added). Such a view is confirmed by the Explanatory Notes to the Act. They provide that the decision as to what will promote the success of the company, and what constitutes such success, is one for the director's good faith judgment, and this ensures that business decisions on, for example, strategy and tactics are for the directors, and not subject to decision by the courts, always provided directors acted in good faith.[96] Furthermore, a problem for a claimant in an action against the directors is that he or she has the burden of proving an absence of good faith on the part of the directors.[97]

In conclusion, the position under the old duty was that provided the courts believed directors when they gave evidence that any action taken was in good faith the directors would not be liable for breach. However a judge might, given all the evidence in the case, opine that the directors are not to be believed concerning their state of mind, and hold them liable. If a director did act in good faith, but unreasonably (in the view of the judge), then it would seem that he or she would not be in breach of the duty to act in the best interests of the company, provided he or she had considered that what they were doing was in the best interests of the company. There is nothing to suggest that the new provision will be interpreted any differently. Where a director has acted in good faith, but not reasonably, any claimant would have to seek to make out a case for breach of another duty, perhaps under s.174.

2. Success

The directors must act to promote the success of the company.[98] Success is quite a slippery term and this might well be as vague as 'best interests'[99] under the previous duty. In its response to the second White Paper and the draft Bill in 2005 the Law Society said, in relation to the clause that was the precursor to s.172, that the term 'success' would create practical problems of some significance.[100] The Confederation of British Industry in its submission was concerned about how success was

---

[96] Explanatory Notes to the Companies Act 2006, at para 327. Also see Department of Trade and Industry, *Guidance to Key Clauses in the Company Law Reform Bill 2005* (London, Stationery Office, 2005) at clause 64.

[97] *Re Phoenix Contracts (Leicester) Ltd* [2010] EWHC 2375 (Ch) at [94].

[98] For more discussion of this element, see A. Keay, *Directors' Duties* (Jordan, Bristol, 2009) at 118–120.

[99] See J. Edelman, 'When Do Fiduciary Duties Arise?' (2010) 126 *Law Quarterly Review* 302 at 322.

[100] Law Society's Company Law Committee, June 2005 at 6.

to be measured.[101] It might be said that it means the achievement of the business objectives that the company has laid down for itself, and these could include financial, strategic or others. The Government's intention is that the decision as to what will promote the success of the company, and what constitutes such success, is one for the director's good faith judgment.[102] The directors' interpretation of any business objectives could be important. It might be argued that what is done to fulfil that interpretation can only be impugned where the directors did not have a good faith belief in the strategy they had for promoting the company's success.

Lord Goldsmith, in an address to the Parliament in February 2006, considered what success would entail. He said that:

'... for a commercial company, success will normally mean long-term increase in value, but the company's constitution and decisions made under it may also lay down the appropriate success model for the company. ... it is essentially for the members of a company to define the objectives they wish to achieve. The normal way for that to be done – the traditional way – is that the members do it at the time the company is established. In the old style, it would have been set down in the company's memorandum. That is changing ... but the principle does not change that those who establish the company will start off by setting out what they hope to achieve. For most people who invest in companies, there is never any doubt about it – money. That is what they want. They want a long-term increase in the company. It is not a snap poll to be taken at any point in time'.[103]

3. Benefit members as a whole

The previous duty to s.172 involved directors having to act in the best interests of the company. 'The interests of the company' has probably been one of the most problematical expressions in company law, and it has often been misunderstood.[104] Many have said that it means the interests of the shareholders as a whole,[105] namely the shareholders as a general body, although there are cases in which judges have played down the pre-eminence of shareholders' interests. It has been argued that there is not a clear strain of authority running through UK and Commonwealth case law that holds that only shareholder interests are to be the concern

---

[101]   CBI, Submission to the DTI, June 2005 at 25.
[102]   Explanatory Notes to the Companies Act 2006 at para 327.
[103]   Hansard, Lords Grand Comm, HL 6 February 2006, Col 256.
[104]   For example, see the comments of Nourse LJ in *Brady v Brady* (1987) 3 BCC 535 at 552.
[105]   Company Law Review, *Modernising Company Law: The Strategic Framework*, (London, DTI, 1999) at para 5.1.5.

of the directors.[106] A number of cases do suggest that the focus should be on shareholders, while others either merely state that the directors are to act in the interests of the company, or indicate that the interests of the company involves something more than the interests of shareholders.[107]

Parliament has been congratulated for removing the reference to 'interests of the company' and replacing it in s.172(1) with the expression 'members as a whole.'[108] This latter expression has been used on several occasions in company law and, consequently, one would assume that the judicial comments on the meaning of the expression would be pressed into service here. The courts have tended to hold that it means the present and future shareholders, certainly in relation to companies for profit.[109] In relation to this expression Lord Goldsmith said in Parliament that:

'the duty is to promote the success for the benefit of the members as a whole – that is, for the members as a collective body – not only to benefit the majority shareholders, or any particular shareholder or section of share-holders, still less the interests of directors who might happen to be share-holders themselves'.[110]

As far as the meaning of the benefit involved, the courts have tended to hold that it means the financial well-being of the shareholders.[111]

It would appear that the phrase 'members as a whole' embraces future shareholders. The CLRSG envisaged this when it said that directors should not ignore events that may occur after the present members have ceased being members.[112] All of this seems to indicate that the phrase is likely to be applied by many courts in the same way as 'interests of the

---

[106] A. Keay, 'Enlightened Shareholder Value, the Reform of the Duties of Company Directors and the Corporate Objective' [2006] *Lloyds Maritime and Commercial Law Quarterly* 335 at 345. Also see S. Deakin, 'Squaring the Circle? Shareholder Value and Corporate Social Responsibility in the UK' (2002) 70 *George Washington Law Review* 976 at 977.

[107] See for instance, *Fulham Football Club Ltd v Cabra Estates plc* [1992] BCC 863 at 876.

[108] P.L. Davies, 'Enlightened Shareholder Value and the New Responsibilities of Directors,' W.E. Hearn Lecture, delivered at the Law School, University of Melbourne, 4 October 2005, at 4–5.

[109] For instance, see *Gaiman v National Association for Mental Health* [1971] Ch 317 at 330; *Brady v Brady* (1987) 3 BCC 535 at 552.

[110] Hansard, Lords Grand Comm, HL 6 February 2006, Col 256.

[111] See *Gaiman v National Association for Mental Health* [1971] Ch 317 at 330; *Brady v Brady* (1987) 3 BCC 535 at 552.

[112] Company Law Review *Modern Company Law For a Competitive Economy: Developing the Framework* (London, DTI, 2000) at para 3.54.

company' was under the old duty. If that is correct, it makes the assessment of the directors' decisions difficult, for some actions can be more beneficial for the present shareholders than future ones and vice versa, depending on how much of a long-term view is taken.

4. The prescribed factors

One of the novel aspects of s.172(1) is that it provides that the directors are, in the course of discharging their duty to promote the success of the company, to have regard to[113] a list of factors. It must be noted that this does not introduce a new duty, owed to the constituencies referred to in s.172(1)(a)-(f). The director's duty is to the company, as required by s.170(1). Margaret Hodge MP made this plain when she said that: 'a director will not be required to consider any of the factors [in s.172(1)] beyond the point at which to do so would conflict with the overarching duty to promote the success of the company.'[114]

On one view the listing of these factors does not introduce anything new. Arguably there was nothing in the existing case law that forbade directors from taking into account the long-term consequences of what they were proposing to do and even the interests of other parties besides shareholders, as long as the directors acted in good faith in the best interests of the company as a whole. In fact, many have said that directors would be acting prudently if they considered the interests of the company's stakeholders in their decision-making. Naturally, the interests of shareholders are not likely to be enhanced if, for example, the company's workers are on strike or even discontented, or the company's customers are dissatisfied with the company's products or way of doing business.

Nevertheless there are at least three potential problems with the requirement to have regard to the factors. First, how do directors have regard to the interests set out in s.172(1) where one or more of the factors are in conflict with promoting the overall success of the company? To make sense s.172(1) must mean that directors are to have regard to the factors and if they find that any or all are inconsistent with promoting the success of the company, they must surely dismiss them from their decision-making. This is consistent with what Margaret Hodge MP said above. Second, what if there is a conflict between one or more of the factors on the one hand, and interests of the members, on the other? Examples given by the CLRSG include the closing down of a plant or the

---

[113] For a discussion of the meaning of 'having regard to,' see A. Keay, *Directors' Duties* (Jordan, Bristol, 2009), at 138–143.

[114] Hansard, HC Comm D, 11 July 2006, Cols 591–593.

termination of a long-term supply contract when the continuation of either will impact adversely on shareholder returns.[115]

Third, what if there is conflict between the various interests mentioned in s.172(1)(a)-(f) which does not have an impact on the promotion of the success of the company?[116] That is, favouring any one of the interests will promote the success of the company, so which one should be chosen? If there is a conflict, do the directors have to balance competing factors where they conflict? If so, how are they to do that? For instance, should a company purchase new technology that might benefit the environment, but which might also mean accompanying job losses?[117] Also, what weight is to be given to each factor?[118] While not taking the view that directors need to balance interests, Proudman J in *Re Phoenix Contracts (Leicester) Ltd*[119] did not criticize a director for doing so.[120] The concern of some is that directors could use a balancing exercise as an opportunity to foster their own self-interest.[121] With directors having greater discretion in deciding what interests to take into account, it might be thought that shareholders will have more difficulty in monitoring the performance of directors, and directors might resist claims of breach of duty on the basis that what they did was based on a consideration of the interests of one or more constituencies that are mentioned in s.172(1). Some might doubt whether company managers are in a position to carry out a fair and efficient balancing of the interests on the basis that they might well be looking to take into account their own interests, often at odds with those of some constituencies.[122] This might be particularly

---

[115]   Ibid.

[116]   The same concern that was expressed in regard to the US constituency statutes. It has been said that these statutes place burdens on directors to consider a wide range of interests that might well conflict without 'establishing sufficient standards by which directors may evaluate them': J. D. Springer, 'Corporate Constituency Statutes: Hollow Hopes and False Fears' (1999) *Annual Survey of American Law* 85 at 107.

[117]   Example given in CMS Cameron McKenna, 'Companies Act 2006: An Overview' (September 2007).

[118]   For further discussion of this point see, A. Keay, *Directors' Duties* (Jordans, Bristol, 2009) at 124.

[119]   [2010] EWHC 2375 (Ch).

[120]   Ibid at [103].

[121]   M. Roe, 'The Shareholder Wealth Maximization Norm and Industrial Organization' (2001) 149 *University of Pennsylvania Law Review* 2063 at 2065.

[122]   J. Parkinson, 'Models of the Company and the Employment Relationship' (2003) 41 *British Journal of Industrial Relations* 481 at 498. In an article by the Special Representative of the Secretary-General (SRSG) on the Issue of Human

pertinent when one considers s.172(1)(f) and the need to ensure that the directors act fairly between the members of the company.[123]

The Explanatory Notes to the Act state that 'it will not be sufficient to pay lip service to the factors [set out in s.172(1)(a)-(f)], and, in many cases the directors will need to take action to comply with this aspect of the duty.'[124]

But it can be asserted, as we have seen, that when directors have acted in good faith the court is not to question, for the most part, the directors' actions. It is hard to see where there is a statement from the directors that they acted in good faith and considered the factors in s.172(1), how a court will be able to ascertain whether the directors just paid lip service to the factors, and even more what a court would do if it came to the conclusion that mere lip service was paid to the factors. Would a court be willing to make a business judgment and say that X should have been done rather than Y because the directors did not really have regard for one or more of the factors in s.172(1)(a)-(f)? It is unlikely, given the fact that courts are often reluctant to decide on commercial decisions made by directors.

Although not overtly stated, it is likely that the duty to foster the success of the company for the benefit of the members and the duty to take into account other interests can be seen in a hierarchal way, with the former being regarded more highly than the latter. The CLRSG advocated a hierarchy of obligations when it proposed a similar approach,[125] and this involved the promotion of the benefit of the members' interests above those of the broader interests set out in s.172(1)(a)-(f). This causes one to wonder whether the provision provides any, or any significant, enlightenment concerning the aim of the Government. The situation is as before; directors will consider stakeholder interests as far as they promote the success of the company, but only where it will benefit of shareholders.

Rights and Transnational Corporations and other Business Enterprises titled 'Corporate Law Project: Overarching Trends and Observations' (July 2010) at http://www.reports-and-materials.org/Ruggie-corporate-law-project-Jul-2010.pdf (accessed 28 July 2010) it was indicated that little guidance is provided around the world to assist directors in balancing.

[123]   On which see the decision pre-codification in *Re BSB Holdings Ltd (No2)* [1996] 1 BCLC 155.

[124]   At para 328.

[125]   Company Law Review, *Modern Company Law for a Competitive Economy: Completing the Structure* (London, DTI, 2000) at para 3.19.

(c) The Section 417 Business Review[126]

At one stage, before the Act was enacted, s.172 was only one half of the concept of enlightened shareholder value ('ESV') that the Government wanted to bring into force. The other half was the requirement for companies to prepare and publish an operating and financial review (OFR)[127] with the directors' report. The clause covering the need for the OFR provided that companies were to publish material information on the activities of the company and this was to include details concerning future plans, opportunities and risks. The Government envisaged the OFR providing a major benefit to a 'wider cross-section of a company's stakeholders.'[128] The material that directors had to consider was relevant to the interests of stakeholders other than shareholders, such as the company's policies in relation to: employment; environmental issues relevant to the company's business; and the company's policies on social and community issues relevant to the company's business.[129] But in the end the Government shelved the OFR.[130] The then Chancellor of the Exchequer, Gordon Brown, said that if companies were required to produce the OFR it would add to their administrative burdens. The need for the OFR was replaced with the requirement that all but small companies have to include a business review ('the Review') with the

---

[126] For a detailed discussion, see A. Keay, The Enlightened Shareholder Value Principle and Corporate Governance (London, Routledge, 2012) at 145–184.

[127] Department of Trade and Industry, *Modernising Company Law*, Cm 5553-I (London, Stationery Office, 2002) at para 4.28. The need for such a review was included in clauses of a draft Companies Bill attached to a White Paper in July 2002.

[128] Ibid at para 4.32. For a detailed discussion of the OFR and its withdrawal by the Government, see A. Johnston, 'After the OFR: Can UK Shareholder Value Still Be Enlightened?' (2006) 7 *European Business Organisation Review* 817.

[129] Clause 75(2) the Draft Clauses on the Operating and Financial Review, Department of Trade and Industry, Modernising Company Law, Cm 5553 (London, Stationery Office, 2002) Annex D.

[130] The Government instead enacted the Companies Act (Operating and Financial Review (Repeal) Regulations 2005 (SI 2005/3442). See 'Chancellor Gives ONS Independence,' BBC News, November 28 2006 at http://news.bbc.co.uk/1/hi/business/4477516.stm; see also C. Williams and J. Conley, 'Triumph or Tragedy? The Curious Path of Corporate Disclosure Reform in the UK' (2007) 31 *William and Mary Environmental Law and Policy Review* 317 at 327–361 and referred to in G. L. Clark and E. R. W. Knight, 'Implications of the UK Companies Act 2006 for Institutional Investors and the Market for Corporate Social Responsibility' (2009) 11 *University of Pennsylvania Journal of Business Law* 259 at 275.

directors' report.[131] While this was a blow to many who had lobbied for the OFR, it must be acknowledged that the provisions providing for the Review require similar things to those required in the OFR.[132] But Johnson asserted that the Review will: 'be considerably less prescriptive and will offer even less guidance than the OFR about what should be disclosed.'[133]

Notwithstanding Johnson's concern, the information required under s.417 is, prima facie, quite extensive. Besides being required to include a fair review of the company's business and a description of the principal risks and uncertainties faced by the company,[134] quoted companies have to include, to the extent necessary to understand the development, performance and position of the company's business, information about environmental matters, the employees, social and community issues and the people with whom the company has contractual arrangements.[135] The Review ties in with s.172 in that the Review's objective was, as indicated in s.417(2), 'to inform members of the company and help them assess how the directors have performed their duty under section 172.' To this end, the Review is where directors should indicate how they have considered the factors set out in s.172(1)(a)-(f).

Nevertheless, there is nothing to prevent directors making quite neutral statements which give little detail about their thinking and discussions at board level. Davies seems to agree when he says that there is a risk that the Review: 'will be productive of self-serving and vacuous narrative rather than analytical material which is of genuine use.'[136] One outcome from a small empirical study conducted by Peter Taylor, involving interviews of senior officials of FTSE 350 companies and representatives of some institutional investors, undertaken since s.172 came into operation, was that companies were prepared to disclose in the Review how

[131]   Andrew Johnson saw this as 'a regressive step': 'After the OFR: Can UK Shareholder Value Still Be Enlightened?' (2006) 7 *European Business Organisation Review* 817 at 842.
[132]   Although one view put forward by respondents in an empirical study undertaken by Peter Taylor was that the preparation of the business review was, in comparison to the OFR, easier: P. Taylor, 'Enlightened Shareholder Value and the Companies Act 2006' (unpublished PhD thesis, May 2010), Birkbeck College, University of London at 182.
[133]   A. Johnson, 'After the OFR: Can UK Shareholder Value Still Be Enlightened?' (2006) 7 *European Business Organisation Review* 817 at 841.
[134]   Companies Act 2006 s.417(3).
[135]   Companies Act 2006 s.417(5).
[136]   P.L. Davies, *Gower and Davies' Principles of Company Law*, 8th edn (Sweet and Maxwell, London, 2008) at 740.

risk was managed as a formal process, but not the actual risks to the company's business and which risks might be critical to the viability of the business.[137] One institutional investor responding to the study[138] was sceptical about the impact of the Review in relation to risk, and said that in most companies the risk disclosures are many pages of boilerplate risk factors, as the focus is on defensive disclosures to ensure that the board is not sued. Villiers's research, discussed in the next chapter, and the studies she refers to, also bear this finding out. It is highly debatable whether the Review is able to verify whether directors have discharged their duty under s.172.

As indicated above, the Review is designed to inform members. While some members who might be said to have a social conscience or who are focused on long-term issues, may be concerned about environmental matters, the employees and so on, most members are likely to be concerned about the bottom line. Is the company making profits, and what do the shareholders get out of it? The Review could be used in evidence in any claim against the directors for breach, but the claim must reach a court, and as we shall see later, that is a problematic.

One interesting matter that is worth dwelling on, in light of the fact that at the outset of this chapter it was noted that according to many one cause of the financial crisis was that companies embraced excessive risk, is the issue of corporate risk.[139] Will the requirement in s.417(3)(b) that companies must include in the Review a description of the principal risks and uncertainties that the company is facing be likely to make boards more risk averse to the point of not repeating some of the mistakes of the past decade (and perhaps longer) or enable shareholders to take action to thwart the board taking on unacceptable risk? The rather imprecise answer is 'maybe.' A positive response to either of the questions raised above depends on financial institutions rightly identifying the risks inherent in the deals in which they are, or about to be, engaged, so that they can disclose the risks in the Review. There are indications that boards of at least some financial institutions did not appreciate the full

---

[137]   P. Taylor, 'Enlightened Shareholder Value and the Companies Act 2006' (unpublished PhD thesis, May 2010), Birkbeck College, University of London at 196.

[138]   Ibid.

[139]   M. Lipton, T. Mirvis and J. Lorsch, 'The Proposed 'Shareholder Bill of Rights Act of 2009' Harvard Law School Forum on Corporate Governance & Financial Regulation (May 12, 2009) at: http://blogs.law.harvard.edu/corpgov/2009/05/12/the-proposed-%e2%80%9cshareholder-bill-of-rights-act-of-2009%e2%80%9d (accessed 1 June 2010).

extent of the risks that their companies were taking before the financial crisis, partly because they did not understand many of the transactions being entered into[140] and the possible ramifications of default, so they might not be able to disclose risk factors accurately in the future. Furthermore, it is likely that many companies will be most reluctant to disclose their major risks, as that might provide their competitors with ammunition and/or place themselves in a weak bargaining position when dealing with others.

(d) Long Termism

Clearly at the heart of the concerns of both the CLRSG in its deliberations as far as directors' duties were concerned, and the Government when it introduced s.172, was to encourage companies to be managed for the long term. Whilst some who have advocated the employment of shareholder value in company management felt that businesses should be run for the long term,[141] not all have favoured such a view,[142] and for the most part shareholder value has been linked to short-termism, with Enron, the disgraced American energy company, and the effects of its business approach, being synonymous with short termism. According to several finance academics, the shareholder value approach produces a short-term focus and short-term earnings performance overshadows all else.[143] While logically shareholder value should not necessarily lead

---

[140]   D. Arsalidou, 'The Banking Crisis: Rethinking and Redefining the Accountability of Bank Directors' [2010] *Journal of Business Law* 284 at 292.

[141]   For example see M. Jensen, 'Value Maximisation, Stakeholder Theory and the Corporate Objective Function' (2001) 14 *Journal of Applied Corporate Finance* 8; H. Hansmann and R. Kraakman, 'The End of History for Corporate Law' (2001) 89 *Georgetown Law Journal* 439 at 439; G. Dent, 'Corporate Governance: Still Broke, No Fix in Sight' (2006) 31 *Journal of Corporations Law* 39 at 57.

[142]   M. Lipton, T. Mirvis and J. Lorsch, 'The Proposed 'Shareholder Bill of Rights Act of 2009' Harvard Law School Forum on Corporate Governance and Financial Regulation (May 12, 2009) at: http://blogs.law.harvard.edu/corpgov/2009/05/12/the-proposed-%e2%80%9cshareholder-bill-of-rights-act-of-2009%e2%80%9d (accessed 1 June 2010) refers to the fact that short-termism is still rife. Also, see Aspen Institute, 'Overcoming Short-Termism' Business and Society Program (9 September 2009) at http://www.aspeninstitute.org/sites/default/files/content/docs/pubs/overcome_short_state0909_0.pdf) (accessed 28 July 2010).

[143]   S. Wallman 'The Proper Interpretation of Corporate Constituency Statues and Formulation of Director Duties' (1991) 21 *Stetson Law Review* 163 at 176–177; M. Lipton and S. Rosenblum 'A New System of Corporate Governance: The Quinquenial Election of Directors' (1991) 58 *University of Chicago*

toshort-termism, with a concomitant fixation on the quarterly earnings of companies and their share value,[144] in practice it often has. This was certainly the view of the CLRSG, for it said that:

> 'the state of directors' duties at common law are often regarded as leading to directors having an undue focus on the short term and the narrow interests of members at the expense of what is in a broader and a longer term sense the best interests of the enterprise ... '[145]

Perhaps a good example of neglecting the long term is where a company engages in drastic cost-cutting that might achieve short-term results by improving the bottom line for a short while, and providing shareholders with good dividends and an enhanced share value, but in the long-run this might adversely affect the company's business.[146]

A potential problem is that differentiating between what is the short-term and what is the long-term is not easy. As William Allen, the former Chancellor of the Delaware Court of Chancery, said extra-judicially: '[t]he law 'papered over' the conflict in our conception of the corporation by invoking a murky distinction between long-term profit maximization and short-term profit maximization.'[147] Short-termism has been defined as: 'foregoing economically worthwhile investments with longer-term benefits in order to increase reported earnings for the current period.'[148] This could mean scrimping on research and development, failing to renew plant and equipment or making employees redundant (even though the company might need to hire more in the medium term, this provides a short term boost to profits at least). It has been said that to apply a short-term approach strictly in this context would mean that the directors would be paying out to shareholders every amount earned as profit and

---

Law Review 187 at 205–215; M. E. van der Weide 'Against Fiduciary Duties to Corporate Stakeholders' (1996) 21 *Delaware Journal of Corporate Law* 27 at 61.

[144] See D. Millon 'Why is Corporate Management Obsessed with Quarterly Earnings and What Should be Done About it?' (2002) 70 *George Washington Law Review* 890 especially at 902.

[145] Company Law Review *Modern Company Law for a Competitive Economy*: The Strategic Framework (London, DTI, 1999) at para 5.1.17.

[146] E. Orts 'The Complexity and Legitimacy of Corporate Law' (1993) 50 *Washington and Lee Law Review* 1565 at 1592.

[147] W. Allen, 'Our Schizophrenic Conception of the Business Corporation' (1992) 14 *Cardozo Law Review* 261 at 273.

[148] J. Grinyer, A. Russell and D. Collision, 'Evidence of Managerial Short-termism in the UK' (1998) 9 *British Journal of Management* 13 at 15.

with no consideration for investing funds and expansion of the company's market.[149] If maximizing for long-term value, it might be thought that directors would aim to balance the seeking of opportunities to make profits now with opportunities to make profits in the future.[150]

While s.172 provides an entreaty, in s.172(1)(a), for directors to manage whilst having regard for the long-term effects of an action, it is questionable whether this will in fact happen. First, it is going to be difficult to enforce the long-term requirement, especially where directors resolutely maintain that they have acted in good faith. Second, managing for the long term is often antithetical to the interests of the company's managers. Managers could favour the short term because they only have a temporary interest in the company, primarily limited to their time in the job. Managers get no or little benefit from planning for the long term as it is likely to be their successors who will receive the plaudits, and benefit from economic advantages that come to the company under that approach.[151] In fact, planning for the long term could make the performance of today's managers look decidedly average, as the share price might not increase and higher dividends would not be paid as quickly as if short-term plans were implemented. Also managers' remuneration has often been aligned with short-term shareholder interests (in order, it is said, to reduce agency costs[152]). Third, and linked to the point just made, the short-term approach seems to have been favoured in the past in the UK and the US and, arguably, still holds sway due to a number of factors, including shareholder pressure. How long are shareholders going to keep their powder dry before they look at pressuring the board to oust a CEO (or other manager(s)) who does not seem 'to be doing the

---

[149] J. Heydon, 'Directors' Duties and the Company's Interests' in P. Finn (ed), *Equity and Commercial Relationships* (Sydney, Law Book Co, 1987) at 135.

[150] See S. Lydenberg, *Corporations and the Public Interest: Guiding the Invisible Hand* (San Francisco, Berrett-Koehler, 2005) and quoted in A. White, 'What is Long-Term Wealth?' Business for Social Responsibility article (September 2007) at http://www.bsr.org/reports/bsr_awhite_long-term-wealth.pdf (accessed 30 March 2010) at 4.

[151] F. Allen and D. Gale, *Comparing Financial Systems* (Cambridge, MA, MIT Press, 2000) at 382.

[152] Agency costs is the economic concept that refers to the costs that arise when one person (the principal) engages another (the agent) to act on their behalf and include the costs of incentives, monitoring costs and bonding costs: M.C. Jensen and W. Meckling, 'Theory of the Firm: Managerial Behavior, Agency Costs and Ownership Structure' (1976) 3 *Journal of Financial Economics* 305.

business'? How long will they accept the directors' reports that things are being done for the long term and there will be benefits 'down the track?'

While there is often emphasis placed on managers reacting to the pressure of shareholders, it is not just the shareholders who have to be kept on-side. It has been said quite recently by highly respected commentators in this field, Lipton, Mirvis and Lorsch that:

> 'Short-termism is a disease that infects American business and distorts management and boardroom judgment. But it does not originate in the boardroom. [It] is bred in the trading rooms of the hedge funds and professional institutional investment managers who control more than 75 per cent of the shares of most major companies.'[153]

Due to the threat of hostile takeovers, some directors may tend to act in the short-term interests of their shareholders – to keep the shareholders satisfied so they would reject any takeover offer and, therefore, to keep the directors (it is hoped) in control of the management of the company.

Fourth, how are the actions of directors to be measured in order to ascertain if they have been acting in the long term? As suggested above, the concept of the 'long term' is not precise. How far in the future are the directors of the company required to provide for in their decision-making? Defining what is the short term is difficult enough, but it has been argued that the long term is even harder to define.[154] For some businesses which are established for one or two specific reasons, next year is the long term and yet for more traditional businesses the long term will be much further into the future.

The common law permitted directors to consider short-term and long-term issues in making decisions. Now s.172 also appears to do so. It enables directors not necessarily to aim for a high increase in the market value of the company's shares. In the Company Law Reform Bill that was part of the Government's 2005 White Paper,[155] clause B3 stated, inter alia, that directors have to have regard to: '(a) The likely consequences of any decision in both the long and the short term.' The omission of any reference to the short term in s.172(1) has led Mayson,

---

[153] M. Lipton, T. Mirvis and J. Lorsch, 'The Proposed Shareholder Bill of Rights Act of 2009' Harvard Law School Forum on Corporate Governance and Financial Regulation (May 12, 2009) at: http://blogs.law.harvard.edu/corpgov/2009/05/12/the-proposed-%e2%80%9cshareholder-bill-of-rights-act-of-2009%e2%80%9d (accessed 1 June 2010).

[154] E. Elhauge, 'Sacrificing Corporate Profits in the Public Interest' (2005) 80 *New York University Law Review* 733 at 756.

[155] Cm 6456, 2005, DTI.

French and Ryan to conclude that the long term is more important.[156] I am unsure whether one can necessarily draw that conclusion as undoubtedly the general thrust of the provision, with the benefit of members being the end result, would still permit consideration of the short term. The CLRSG had said that directors were obliged to 'achieve the success of the company for the benefit of the shareholders by taking proper account of all the relevant considerations for that purpose' and this involved taking 'a proper balanced view of the short and long term.'[157] Perhaps the omission of any reference to the short term in s.172 is designed merely to emphasize the relevance of the long term when it has been eschewed by many in the past. The reference to the long term does not mean, it is submitted, that the directors are not able to focus on the short term if they believe that it will promote the success of the company for the benefit of the members. And for reasons already given, they may do so.

Clearly, there appears to be a difference between the position that existed under the previous law compared with that under the new law, especially seeing that the Government said that the new provision 'marks a radical departure in articulating the connection between what is good for a company and what is good for society at large.'[158] But as suggested above, before the inclusion of s.172(1)(a) directors of many companies did look at the long term in certain situations and did not only focus on the short-term effects of their decisions. For example, if a company were to expand and open a new factory, it would be clear that the short-term costs of facilitating this process[159] would be huge, but it might well produce handsome benefits in the long term.

Finally, what might constitute a failure to have regard to the long term? This depends on a lot of factors, such as the size of the company, the company's business and the nature of the relevant marketplace. The

---

[156] *Company Law* 24th edn, (Oxford, Oxford University Press, 2007) at 457.

[157] Company Law Review *Modern Company Law for a Competitive Economy: Developing the Framework* (London, DTI, 2000) at para 2.19. It has been said that directors should be at liberty to use their commercial judgment in order to balance short- and long-term considerations: Australian Parliamentary Joint Committee on Corporations and Financial Services 'Corporate Responsibility: Managing Risk and Creating Value,' (21 June 2006) at: www.aph.gov.au/Senate/committee/corporations_ctte/corporate_responsibility/report/report.pdf (accessed 17 July 2008) at para 3.82.

[158] *Duties of Company Directors* (DTI, June 2007) Introduction and Statement of Margaret Hodge MP, and available at http://www.dti.gov.uk/files/file40139.pdf

[159] Including building the factory, creating more jobs and so on.

Institute of Chartered Secretaries and Administrators' Guidance on Directors' General Duties gives the example of a failure to consider the long term where a pharmaceutical company cuts the research and development budget.[160] Another possible strategy that could be regarded as long term is taking action that will increase corporate reputation, not perhaps in the short term, but it will lead to long-term benefits.

Importantly for the context of this chapter, it has been asserted by several reputable commentators that banks have been operating under short-term strategies for years.[161] UBS reported to shareholders in 2008 that it had a culture that was focused on short-term profits and had 'insufficient incentives to protect the UBS franchise long-term.'[162] Certainly there seems to be some evidence that the finance institutions in the period that preceded the crisis of 2007–2009 failed to take into account the long term for they embraced risks which proved lucrative in the short term, but have turned out to be catastrophic for future shareholders (and many others). Some will undoubtedly argue that convenient hindsight is being used to come to that conclusion, but it is suggested that there were indications at various stages in the time running up to the advent of the downturn, and before everything fell apart, that the risks adopted by these institutions were potentially too high and, arguably, too short term.

Will s.172 change the approach of boards? Much of what we say amounts to speculation, although the empirical study undertaken by Taylor indicates that the pressure on short-termism in favour of more long-term thinking had not been reduced since the enactment of s.172.[163] The more recently published study of Olaojo Aiyegbayo and Charlotte Villiers provides support for this view.[164]

---

[160]   (February 2008) at para 3.2.1. Research and development is usually an investment made in order to generate future cash and profit flows: J. Grinyer, A. Russell and D. Collison 'Evidence of Managerial Short-termism in the UK' (1998) 9 *British Journal of Management* 13 at 14.

[161]   L. Bebchuk and H. Spamann, 'Regulating Bankers' Pay' (2010) 98 *Georgetown Law Journal* 247; S. Bhagat and R. Romano, 'Reforming Executive Compensation: Focusing and Committing to the Long-Term' (2009) 26 *Yale Journal on Regulation* 359.

[162]   UBS AG, *Shareholder Report on UBS's Write Downs* at 42 and referred to in P. Rose, 'Regulating Risk by "Strengthening Corporate Governance"' at http://ssrn.com/abstract=1630122 (accessed 15 July 2010).

[163]   P. Taylor, 'Enlightened Shareholder Value and the Companies Act 2006' (unpublished PhD thesis, May 2010), Birkbeck College, University of London at 162.

[164]   'The Enhanced Business Review: Has It Made Corporate Governance More Effective?' [2011] *Journal of Business Law* 699.

(e)   Enforcement

As with the law that existed before the Act, the only persons who can enforce a breach of duty by a director, is the board (which is, usually, given the power to manage the company's affairs by the articles of association) and the shareholders, if the board does not take action.[165] This is despite the fact that s.172(1) might be seen as couched in stakeholder-oriented language. As with the repealed s.309 of the Companies Act 1985, which provided that directors *must* take into account the interests of employees as well as shareholders, s.172 gives no power to stakeholders expressly or implicitly to take proceedings against miscreant directors.

Even the shareholders' power might be somewhat circumscribed in the context of s.172. Shareholders have the right to take derivative proceedings against directors if they believe the directors are in breach, but they have to obtain the court's permission ('leave' in Scotland and Northern Ireland) to continue such proceedings.[166] Taking the reported decisions where shareholders have sought permission/leave to continue derivative actions against directors decided thus far under the new regime in the Act, we can see that shareholders have generally found things difficult.[167] It is likely that there will be few occasions, especially in public companies, when derivative actions will be initiated. Importantly, any prospective litigant would have to take into account the fact that there is likely to be a cost element in any derivative claim. As one commentator has said: 'Deep-pocketed hedge funds could be encouraged to take action to apply pressure on company boards to implement the sorts of strategy required to produce the high returns their investors demand,'[168] but they are unlikely to do so because directors have not had regard for the interests of other stakeholders.

There are only a few situations where one could envisage an action being brought by a member other than in the cases mentioned above. First,[169] where a member makes an investment in the company for the long term, and it is felt that the action of the directors does not have

---

[165]   By way of derivative action.

[166]   See Companies Act 2006 ss.260ff.

[167]   For an analysis of the relevant case law, see A. Keay and J. Loughrey, 'An Assessment of the Present State of Statutory Derivative Proceedings', Chapter 5 of this book.

[168]   P. Beale 'Directors Beware' (2007) 157 *New Law Journal* 1033.

[169]   The following is taken from A. Keay, *Directors' Duties* (Jordans, Bristol, 2009) at 146–147.

regard for the long term. Second, a member is also an employee of the company and is concerned that the directors did not, in what they have done, have regard to the interests of the employees. Third, a member is concerned that the directors have not had regard for the need to promote business relationships with suppliers, customers or others and this is likely to damage the company in the future. Fourth, there are members of the company living in the community in which the company operates, and they believe that the community will be adversely affected by the actions of the directors, and that will, as a consequence, affect the lives of those members. An example might be where a company, which operates several factories, decides to close one that is in the community where a member resides or has other business interests. Fifth, so-called shareholder activists, who have concerns wider than their own interests, take proceedings because of a heightened sense of community interest or concern for the environment, and they believe that directors failed to consider community interests and/or the environment in the decisions which they have made.

In his empirical study, Taylor, found that all of the institutional investors interviewed were pessimistic about the successful use of derivative proceedings in this context. They indicated that they would not employ proceedings either at all or rarely.[170] This is consistent with the fact that the respondents in the study who were officials in companies did not see derivative proceedings as providing any threat to, or constraint on, directors in what they did or did not do.[171]

As far as financial institutions are concerned Bruner is of the view that there is nothing to suggest that providing opportunities for shareholders to take legal action against directors will help the governance of such companies.[172]

Absent shareholders' actions or a decision by the board to initiate proceedings against a miscreant director, there will be no proceedings unless either: control of the company falls into the hands of different persons; or the company enters administration or liquidation. In any case it may be difficult to establish that the directors should not have done what they did, perhaps several years in the past.

---

[170]   P. Taylor, 'Enlightened Shareholder Value and the Companies Act 2006' (unpublished PhD thesis, May 2010), Birkbeck College, University of London at 188.
[171]   Ibid at 190.
[172]   C. Bruner, 'Corporate Governance Reform in a Time of Crisis' at http://ssrn.com/abstract=1617890 (accessed 23 June 2010).

VI. REFLECTIONS

It would seem that practitioners' views on the duty's effect in practice
vary from the duty being a 'damp squib' which does not introduce any
new liabilities or responsibilities for directors,[173] to assertions that the
duty to promote the success of the company will lead to 'radical
change'[174] and a real prospect of increased litigation against directors.[175]
Loughrey, Keay and Cerioni found in a study of law firms' responses to
s.172 in 2007 that most were agnostic about whether the section would
alter the outcome of directors' decisions in the ordinary course of
business.[176] Although it is still early days, the view that nothing much
will change seems to be in the ascendancy, together with the fact that we
see little movement as far as actions under s.172 are concerned. While
the section has only been in operation for five years, one would expect by
now that we would have seen some cases that have addressed it in some
detail, certainly if there was any groundswell of opinion that the section
made things significantly different. The fact that we have not seen any
significant case law on the provision[177] could be because of one or more
of a number of reasons. First, lawyers are uncertain of the meaning of the

---

[173]   Bruce Hanton of Ashursts, quoted in 'Companies Act to Regulate
Directors' Behaviour' *Financial Director*, 26 November 2006 at http://
www.financialdirector.co.uk/financial-director/analysis/2169965/companies-act
(accessed 26 March 2007).

[174]   J. Gauntlett and R. Dattani (Norton Rose), *Directors Duties Codified*
(November 2006) at http://www.nortonrose.com/html_pubs/view.asp?id=11331
(accessed 22 March 2007).

[175]   G. Milner Moore and R. Lewis (Herbert Smith), *In the Line of Fire –
Directors Duties under the Companies Act 2006* at http://www.herbertsmith.com/
NR/rdonlyres/94EEE30C-72B6–4B74–8F81–4EB93F332FF6/2976/
Inthelineoffirearticle.pdf (accessed, 22 March 2007) at 4.

[176]   J. Loughrey, A. Keay and L. Cerioni 'Legal Practitioners, Enlightened
Shareholder Value and the Shaping of Corporate Governance' (2008) 8 *Journal
of Corporate Law Studies* 79 at 90 and referring to Cameron McKenna,
'Companies Act 2006: Deferred Reform' *Law-Now*, 29 November 2006 at
http://www.law-now.com/law-now/default (accessed 22 March 2007) at 4–5;
Freshfields Bruckhaus Deringer, *Companies Act 2006: Directors Duties* (November
2006)   at   http://www.freshfields.com/publications/pdfs/2006/17062.pdf
(accessed 22 March 2007) at 4.

[177]   Cases that have mentioned it have not engaged in any exposition or
explanation of the provision. For example see *Re West Coast Capital (LIOS) Ltd*
[2008] CSOH 72; 2008 Scot (D) 16/5 (Outer House, Court of Sessions, Lord
Glennie); *Cobden Investments Ltd v RWM Langport Ltd* [2008] EWHC 2810
(Ch).

provision and its effect and have been counselling caution in their advice to would-be litigants (namely shareholders and office-holders like administrators and liquidators) who wish to take action against directors for breach. Second, actions are still in the pipeline. Third, directors are simply not breaching the section, or at least not patently. Directors might be taking extremely conservative action in line with legal advice, and this would be consistent with the fact that some firms have been concerned about the changes that would be caused by the introduction of s.172.[178] Fourth, litigants are relying on other breaches as the basis for actions against directors.

As actions under s.172 cannot be successful unless directors are shown to have failed to exercise good faith and as enforcement of any breach might be difficult, it might be thought that the section lacks effective teeth and directors will not have to be overly concerned with non-shareholder interests, and so the problems of the past where directors have focused on short-termism may not be rectified. We know that some banks, for example, paid out significant dividends after making huge profits in the years leading up to the financial crisis. For example, the Royal Bank of Scotland plc paid out a final dividend of 17 per cent in 2005, 22 per cent in 2006 and 23 per cent in 2007.[179] Lloyds TSB Bank plc had a similar record.[180] Arguably, the banks and other financial institutions did not take into account the interests of future shareholders and the long term (and other stakeholders). There are indications that insufficient consideration was given to the possible default of borrowers in the sub-prime mortgage market and the problems associated with other risks. It would seem that in fact at least some involved in company management did not understand the deals in which a lot of company funds were tied up.[181]

---

[178] See the discussion in J. Loughrey, A. Keay and L. Cerioni, 'Legal Practitioners, Enlightened Shareholder Value and the Shaping of Corporate Governance' (2008) 8 *Journal of Corporate Law Studies* 79.

[179] See at http://www.investors.rbs.com/our_performance/dividend.cfm (accessed 7 June 2010). Also see the position of the Bank of New York Mellon which slashed its dividend payable in 2009 by 63 per cent (Ben Steverman, 'The Ever-Shrinking Bank Dividend' *Bloomberg Businessweek*, 21 April, 2009 at http://www.businessweek.com/investing/insights/blog/archives/2009/04/the_ever-shrink.html (accessed 7 June 2010).

[180] 23.5 per cent in 2005 and 2006, 24.7 per cent in 2007: http://www.investorrelations.lloydstsb.com/ir/uk_dividend_history_page.asp (accessed 7 June 2010).

[181] L. Buchheit, 'Did we make things too complicated?' (2008) 27 (3) *International Financial Law Review* 24.

It is debatable whether s.172 changes things much, or at all. Birds is probably right when he states that the effect of the section is largely educational and that decisions taken in good faith are not likely to be more easily challenged than under the previous law.[182] The CLRSG was confident that the statutory code would have 'a major influence in changing behaviours and the climate of decision-making' by deterring short termism.[183] This was not because the new formulation of directors' duties changed the law, for the CLRSG thought that it simply reflected existing law and best practice. However it had noted considerable evidence that the law was widely misunderstood as a result of the manner in which it was expressed and interpreted.[184] Perhaps the CLRSG was hoping that a new provision would bring a change of approach by directors, lawyers and judges.

Arguably one benefit of the ESV model is that it enables directors to take into account non-shareholder interests when making decisions, without being in breach of their duties, always providing that their decisions do in fact ultimately promote the success of the company for the benefit of its members as a whole. Of course if the actions of the directors do achieve this objective it is unlikely that shareholders would be complaining about the fact that directors have considered the interests of other stakeholders. Absent where activist shareholders are moved to object to the fact that directors have not considered certain factors set out in s.172(1), there are only two scenarios where shareholders might take umbrage at what the directors have done. First where the company would have been more successful had the directors not taken into account non-shareholder interests or if they had taken into account other non-shareholder interests. Second, where shareholders with a vision for the long term would impugn the actions of the directors on the basis that the directors have not had regard to long-term considerations. It is probably true to say that the enactment of s.172 will make little difference to the state of affairs in corporate life in the UK as the list of interests that are found in s.172(1) were almost certainly considered by the directors of many listed companies and large private companies that were subject to

---

[182]   A. Alcock, J. Birds and S. Gale, *Companies Act 2006: The New Law*, (Jordans, Bristol, 2007) at 146.

[183]   Company Law Review *Modern Company Law for a Competitive Economy: Developing the Framework* (London, DTI, 2000) at para 3.58.

[184]   See Company Law Review *Modern Company Law for a Competitive Economy: The Strategic Framework* (London, DTI, 1999) at para 5.1.20 (for instance).

public scrutiny before the enactment of the provision.[185] One would expect that any company secretary worth his or her salt would now ensure that the minutes of board meetings record that the board, in making its decisions, considered the matters mentioned in the section.

In 2005, in the second White Paper dealing with the proposed companies legislation, it was said that:

> 'The basic goal for directors should be the success of the company for the benefit of its members as a whole; but that, to reach this goal, directors would need to take a properly balanced view of the implications of decisions over time and foster effective relationships with employees, customers and suppliers, and in the community more widely. The Government strongly agrees that this approach, which [is] called 'enlightened shareholder value', is most likely to drive long-term company performance and maximise overall competitiveness and wealth and welfare for all.'[186]

But, as mentioned above, it can be said that many companies practised the contents of s.172 before its enactment, mainly because it made sense and the shareholder value theory often depends on using the company's stakeholders as the means to the end that is the maximization of the shareholders' wealth. Many adherents to the shareholder value theory always accepted the fact that it was wise to consider the interests of stakeholders where it would foster shareholder wealth. Section 172 appears to require the same, given the fact that the bottom line is: how do the shareholders fare as a result of what directors have done?[187] The fact that stakeholder interests are actually enumerated in the section might, conceivably, persuade boards to take into account such interests in a more patent way than before s.172 emerged, and if this were the case it would be, to a degree, confirmation of the Birds' view that the impact is going to be, essentially, educational.

Can we conclude that s.172, together with s.417, is going to prevent the worst kind of short-termism so that there is some sustainability created by companies that are endeavouring to practise shareholder

---

[185] A. Alcock, 'An Accidental Change of Directors' Duties?' (2009) 30 *Company Lawyer* 362 at 368.

[186] Department of Trade and Industry, *Company Law Reform* Cm 6456 (London, Stationery Office, 2005) at para 3.3.

[187] Section 172 may be seen simply as codifying the shareholder primacy principle. In the bastion of shareholder value in the US, Delaware, there is judicial opinion that directors are entitled to have regard for the interests of constituencies other than shareholders provided that some benefit will accrue to shareholders. See *Revlon Inc v MacAndrews & Forbes Holdings Inc* 506 A. 2d 173 at 176 (Del, 1986).

value? In line with many answers to questions on the subject the answer is 'maybe.' Undoubtedly it will depend on a lot of factors, including the attitude of shareholders and how far boards are willing to embrace the philosophy behind ESV. Taylor concludes from his study that the Review:

> 'fails in its objective to provide investors with the information necessary for a full understanding of the businesses in which they invest. That being the case, it must also fail to provide the means by which shareholders can verify that directors are performing their duties in accordance with s.172(1).'[188]

Many have called for more accountability, or a greater depth of accountability, where directors are concerned, and perhaps the main point to note is that there does not seem to be any framework in place to ensure that directors are held accountable for their decision-making process. As it is, there are likely to be few occasions where a director is going to have to justify what he or she did. Of course, very often, and especially with what might be regarded as the daily affairs of the company, those constituencies which are mentioned in s.172(1) will not know what the directors have done (no mention of it being contained in the Review), and when they do become aware of it, it will be too late to do anything that is effective.

Members might be able to secure permission to continue derivative proceedings against directors where there is thought to be a breach of s.172(1), but except where directors have failed to benefit the members from the action that they have taken, such proceedings are likely to be few and far between. Those who are numbered among other constituencies in the sub-section will not be entitled to initiate any legal proceedings against directors, so where directors fail to have regard for the interests set out in the sub-section, it is unlikely that they will be called to account, except, perhaps, where activist shareholders are minded to take action.

One prominent problem with the application of s.172 is that non-executive directors will often lack the expertise and information that will enable them to say whether some action will promote the success of the company. This is a long-standing problem. It is one that is linked with the need for directors to ensure that they fulfil their duty of care to the company, and it is probably better left to a consideration of that duty. But suffice it to say, there are indications that some of the problems at board

---

[188]   P. Taylor, 'Enlightened Shareholder Value and the Companies Act 2006' (unpublished PhD thesis, May 2010), Birkbeck College, University of London.

level experienced by some of the financial institutions were that there was a lack of expertise and understanding of the finance industry. Roman Tomasic, in his interesting study of Northern Rock plc,[189] said that:

> 'the qualifications of the former chairman of Northern Rock, Dr Matt Ridley, did not escape comment in the media when it was noted in the *Financial Times* that he was a zoologist and a successful science writer. He had joined the board of Northern Rock in 1994 and then served as non-executive chairman from 2004 until 2007; he resigned after being criticised in Parliament for harming the reputation of British banking and for lacking financial experience.' (footnotes omitted)

This state of affairs is not abnormal. An empirical study by Ferreira, Kirchmaier and Metzger of 12,010 directors working for 740 large banks in 41 countries found that few outside (non-executive) directors had previous banking experience.[190]

Would the financial malaise that hit British banks and other financial institutions in 2007 and onwards have occurred if s.172 and s.417 had applied beforehand? Would boards have focused more on the long term? As I have said earlier, the actions that precipitated the crisis pre-dated the enactment of s.172, so the provision would not have applied. It is not possible to answer the questions which I have just posed with any degree of certainty. It is quite possible that the exact risks that the banks had adopted would not have been specified in sufficient detail for anyone perusing the Review to have appreciated the extent and seriousness of the risks. In the Taylor study[191] several respondents indicated significant apprehension about disclosing in the Review their companies' major risks and what was intended to be done to address them. Even if they had done so before the advent of the financial crisis, would shareholders have been in a position to have done anything? Due to the impotence of most shareholders,[192] it is doubtful. Institutional investors might have been able to do so, perhaps through discussions with the boards, but whether institutional investors have made, or are making, any difference as far as

---

[189]   R. Tomasic 'Corporate Rescue, Governance and Risk taking in Northern Rock: Part 2' (2008) 29 *Company Lawyer* 330 at 334.

[190]   D. Ferreira, T. Kirchmaier and D. Metzger, 'Boards of Banks' at http://ssrn.com/abstract=1620551 (accessed 29 July 2010).

[191]   P. Taylor, 'Enlightened Shareholder Value and the Companies Act 2006' (unpublished PhD thesis, May 2010), Birkbeck College, University of London at 175.

[192]   See A. Keay, 'Company Directors Behaving Poorly: Disciplinary Options for Shareholders' [2007] *Journal of Business Law* 656.

corporate governance goes is a moot point, for the evidence appears to be conflicting.[193]

One might think that given the fact that the CLRSG stated that the primary reason for rejecting the pluralist position in company law (namely requiring directors to take into account a multitude of stakeholder interests), was that it would grant an unpoliced discretion to directors,[194] the CLRSG would not sanction the granting of a wide discretion to directors. So it is rather ironic that the CLRSG drafted, and the Government agreed to, a virtually unpoliced discretion to directors under s.172. Directors are granted a completely unfettered discretion as to what actions they take provided that they are acting in a way that *they* consider would most likely promote the success of the company for the benefit of the members. While the CLRSG rejected the pluralist position, inter alia, on the basis that it would involve directors having to consider the interests of all constituencies, and it would give no formal remedy for abuse by the directors,[195] this is what we have with s.172. Arguably, the section might have the same failings that the CLRSG identified with the pluralist theory that is, how to choose between a number of competing and inconsistent constituent interests? We could end up with what has been said to be wrong with stakeholder theory, namely directors are left in a position of *not being accountable* for the stewardship of their company's resources.[196] Perhaps the real problem is that unlike in the past where the law has sought to require directors to meet acceptable standards of behaviour, such as not acting in self-interest, it is now

---

[193]   For instance see B. Black, 'Shareholder Passivity Reexamined (1990) 89 *Michigan Law Review* 520; J. Dean, *Directing Public Companies*, (London, Cavendish, 2001) at 49; S. Bainbridge, 'Director Primacy: The Means and Ends of Corporate Governance' (2003) 97 *Northwestern University Law Review* 547 at 555 and 571; C. Williams and J. Conley, 'An Emerging Third Way? The Erosion of the Anglo-American Shareholder Value Construct' (2004) at http:// articles.ssrn.com/sol3/articles.cfm?abstract_id=632347 (accessed 17 July 2010); P. Hosking, 'Fund Managers 'soft on company directors' *The Times*, 28 April 2005; M. Goergen, L. Renneboog and C. Zhang, 'Do UK Institutional Shareholders Monitor Their Investee Firms?' (2008) 8 *Journal of Corporate Law Studies* 39.
[194]   Company Law Review, *Modern Company Law for a Competitive Economy: Developing the Framework* (London, DTI, 2000) at para 3.24.
[195]   Company Law Review *Modern Company Law for a Competitive Economy: Strategic Framework* (London, DTI, 1999) at paras 5.1.21 and 5.1.30.
[196]   M. Jensen 'Value Maximisation, Stakeholder Theory and the Corporate Objective Function' (2001) 7(3) *European Financial Management* 297 at 305.

seeking to compel directors to act in a particular manner,[197] and this is far harder to regulate.

It was indicated earlier that directors are usually regarded as being accountable to the shareholders. It appears that s.172 dilutes the accountability to shareholders because of the fact that s.172 does not circumscribe the directors' discretion in determining what will promote the success of the company in any significant way, and the prosecuting of derivative actions might not be seen as a satisfactory control device. While accountability to shareholders is diluted, this state of affairs occurs without any commensurate creation of accountability to stakeholders as the latter have no locus standi if directors do not have regard for any factors in s.172(1).

What s.172 appears to permit is directors following a long-term strategy, provided that they have good reasons for saying that it will promote the success of the company. It would seem to prevent directors being forced by shareholders to pay dividends if they can establish that what they are doing falls within s.172, for example, following a long-term plan, providing facilities for workers and so forth. It would enable directors to pay out more modest dividends, compared with those paid out in recent years, on the basis that they need to build for the long term. However, whether directors could weather pressure from shareholders and the markets if they took this approach is another issue.

In the House of Lords during the debate on the Company Law Reform Bill 2005, Lord Goldsmith, who led for the Government, said[198] that the ESV principle is proper as it:

> 'resolves any confusion in the mind of directors as to what the interests of the company are, and prevents any inclination to identify those interests with their own. It also prevents confusion between the interests of those who depend on the company and those of the members.'

However, certainly at the moment it would appear that s.172 does not resolve confusion in the minds of directors or anyone else. This is recognized to some degree by what an Australian Joint Parliamentary Committee on Corporations and Financial Services report stated in 2006, when addressing the precursor of s.172 (clause 156 in the Company Law Reform Bill) in the context of considering whether to recommend changes to Australian law. It stated that:

---

[197] S. Worthington 'Reforming Directors' Duties' (2001) 64 *Modern Law Review* 439 at 448.

[198] Hansard, Lords Grand Comm, HL 6 February 2006, Col 255.

'The committee does not support the British approach, which appears to introduce great uncertainty into the legal expression of directors' duties ... Subclause (3) requires directors to have regard to a menu of non-shareholder interests, but gives no guidance as to what form this 'regard' should take, and therefore gives no guidance to directors on what they must do in order to comply.'[199]

While s.172 might have some benefits such as an educational role for directors, it is submitted that it will not make a lot of difference in practice. Directors will continue to be protected by a reliance on acting in good faith in most cases, and it is unlikely that they will disclose major risks of their companies in the Review.

VII. CONCLUSION

It has been argued in this chapter that, while s.172 may have an educational impact, it is not likely to make a lot of difference as far as the corporate governance issues that were problematic in the period leading up to the financial crisis. The Government wanted to ensure, in enacting s.172, that company directors should be more concerned than they have been to take into account long-term consequences of what they do, rather than merely being concerned with the next quarterly figures, and it wanted directors to be more enlightened in their approach to decision-making. It is not clear whether that state of affairs has or will come to pass. The chapter has identified some pressures, such as shareholders' desire for benefits and market demands, that may well militate against directors engaging in more long-term strategy, and it has been submitted here that the legislation might not correct that problem. Whether directors will take into account a broader range of interests than merely share-holders is uncertain. It is likely that the modus operandi employed in the past by directors will continue, that is, considering wider interests to the extent that that action will enhance shareholder interests. And when all is said and done that appears to be the thrust of s.172.

The above conclusions can garner some support from the little empirical evidence we have at the moment. Generally speaking the respondents to the questionnaires and interviews administered by Taylor in a study designed to ascertain the impact of s.172 on companies,

---

[199] *Corporate Responsibility: Managing Risk and Creating Value*, June 2006 at para 4.46 at http://www.aph.gov.au/senate/committee/corporations_ctte/com pleted_inquiries/2004–07/corporate_responsibility/report/index.htm (accessed 16 December 2009).

indicated that directors and others involved in company management were sceptical about the utility of the duty.[200]

It might be argued that s.172 does little more than provide directors with 'a get out of jail free card,' if their actions are challenged, for it permits them to defend a case for breach by asserting that they did what they did because they were considering the interests of non-shareholding stakeholders in deciding what would promote the success of the company. Along with this criticism another that can be levelled is that the legislation provides little or no guidance either to directors who have to make corporate decisions, or to the courts which may be asked to review what directors have done. Neither the ill-fated OFR nor the business review provides much in the way of guidance, nor is the latter likely to require disclosure that will prevent further financial crises.

While the duty provided for in s.172 might be regarded as educational (as far as directors are concerned) it is vague and provides little direction or even guidance. It might well be seen as a general statement of principle, hopefully encouraging directors to aim for the long-term success of the company and to demonstrate enlightenment, but there is certainly an enforcement problem with the provision.

William Sahlmann has asserted that 'managers bear a disproportionate share of the responsibility for what transpired [in the financial crisis] and therefore for what must change.'[201] Will s.172 have any role to play in this change? Sahlmann is sceptical about any corporate governance action making a difference arguing that this 'will do little to decrease the likelihood or magnitude of the next bubble–panic cycle.'[202] It is argued that s.172 is unlikely to have any great impact on company boards and how they transact business, and hence is not really fit for purpose.

The then Conservative Party's spokesman on the Companies Bill, Jonathan Djanogly, said in September 2007 that:

'Ultimately, it will be for the courts to determine how far the new [directors'] duties extend as there is scope for interpretation and differing applications in

---

[200]   P. Taylor, 'Enlightened Shareholder Value and the Companies Act 2006' (unpublished PhD thesis, May 2010), Birkbeck College, University of London, at 189.
[201]   W. Sahlman, 'Management and the Financial Crisis (We have met the enemy and he is us ...)' Harvard Business School, Working Article No. 10–033 at http://www.hbs.edu/research/pdf/10–033.pdf (accessed 15 July 2010).
[202]   Ibid.

practice. But any settled case law will take time to develop – so watch this space.'[203]

We have been watching, Mr Djanogly, and we are still waiting with bated breath.

---

[203] Speech to the Chartered Secretaries Professional Practice Group 6th Annual Technical Conference, 5 September 2007.

3 Narrative reporting and enlightened shareholder value under the Companies Act 2006

Charlotte Villiers

I. INTRODUCTION

'Enlightened shareholder value' (ESV) underpins the business review requirements of the Companies Act 2006 (the Act) with the aims of enhancing shareholder engagement and creating a long-term business culture.[1] Despite the perceived importance of the business review I argue in this chapter that the legislative reporting requirements in the Act fall short of their aim of assisting the goals of ESV. Not only are the legislative requirements too vague, but also the enforcement mechanisms are inadequate. The result is that although the Act 'requires high quality and detailed narrative reporting to shareholders',[2] instead 'few [companies] provide the depth of understanding or a clear and coherent picture of performance ... necessary in the current economic environment ... a compliance mindset is often suppressing effective communication'.[3] These faults let down not only the shareholders but other stakeholders too, as well as the company in the long term. Ultimately, such defects undermine the directors' duty to promote the company's success, and reduce the ability to challenge the directors, with the risk that trust in the UK's corporate governance system will fall.

In the second section, the chapter outlines the connection between the narrative reporting requirements and the directors' duty to promote the

---

[1] ClientEarth, *Referral to the Financial Reporting Review Panel Re: the Rio Tinto Group Annual Report 2008*, July 2010 at http://www.clientearth.org/company-transparency/ at 16.

[2] Ibid.

[3] PriceWaterhouseCoopers, *A snapshot of FTSE 350 Reporting – Compliance Mindset Suppresses Communication*, (London, PwC, 2009) at http://www.corporatereporting.com/snapshot-_FTSE350_reporting.pdf at 1.

company's success, highlighting the ESV objective. The third section identifies the limitations of the legislative provisions and the narrative reporting framework for the purposes of ESV. The fourth section presents evaluations of company business reviews from a number of published surveys and reports as well as a small scale research project carried out by the author. The evidence gathered shows up the limitations of the legislation reflected in company reports. The fifth section highlights the problems by reference to a recent test case referred to the Financial Reporting Review Panel by Client Earth. The paper concludes with a comment on the current consultation by the government on the future of narrative reporting.

II. SECTION 417 OF THE COMPANIES ACT 2006: ITS RELEVANCE TO ENLIGHTENED SHAREHOLDER VALUE

Section 417 of the Act states the business review reporting requirements for all except small companies. The section contains a number of mandatory, broad requirements for all companies and further, more specific contents requirements for quoted companies. It provides that:

(3) The business review must contain:
  (a) a fair review of the company's business, and
  (b) a description of the principal risks and uncertainties facing the company.
(4) The review required is a balanced and comprehensive analysis of:
  (a) the development and performance of the company's business during the financial year, and
  (b) the position of the company's business at the end of that year, consistent with the size and complexity of the business.
(5) In the case of a quoted company the business review must, to the extent necessary for an understanding of the development, performance or position of the company's business, include:
  (a) the main trends and factors likely to affect the future development, performance and position of the company's business; and
  (b) information about:
    (i)   environmental matters (including the impact of the company's business on the environment),
    (ii) the company's employees, and
    (iii) social and community issues,
  including information about any policies of the company in relation to those matters and the effectiveness of those policies; and

    (c)   subject to subsection (11), information about persons with whom the company has contractual or other arrangements which are essential to the business of the company.

If the review does not contain information of each kind mentioned in paragraphs (b)(i), (ii) and (iii) and (c), it must state which of those kinds of information it does not contain.

(6)   The review must, to the extent necessary for an understanding of the development, performance or position of the company's business, include:

    (a)   analysis using financial key performance indicators, and

    (b)   where appropriate, analysis using other key performance indicators, including information relating to environmental matters and employee matters.

'Key performance indicators' means factors by reference to which the development, performance or position of the company's business can be measured effectively.

The purpose of s.417 is clearly stated in subsection (2):

'The purpose of the business review is to inform members of the company and help them assess how the directors have performed their duty under section 172 (duty to promote the success of the company).'

Three immediate observations can be made with regard to s.417 and s.172 of the Act.[4] First, there is an expressly stated link between them. Section 417 demands information that will enable shareholders to assess the performance of directors in the fulfilment of their duty in s.172. Second, there is a close correlation between the factors that directors must consider to meet their duty to promote the company's success and the specific, listed information to be provided by quoted companies in their business reviews. Thus directors must, at least for quoted companies, take into account factors such as employee relationships and relationships with customers and suppliers as well as the company's impact on the community and environment and, correspondingly, information is required on these aspects of the business for quoted companies,[5] though medium-sized companies are not required to supply analysis using non-financial performance indicators relating to employees or environmental matters. Third, both provisions give company directors

---

   [4]   Professor Keay has set out s.172 in full in: A. Keay, 'The Duty to Promote the Success of the Company: Is It Fit for Purpose in a Post-Financial Crisis World?', Chapter 2 of this book.

   [5]   Though not if information relating to 'essential' contractual third parties would be seriously prejudicial to them (s.417(11)).

considerable discretion in how they are to meet the requirements, with, implicitly, the potential for a challenge to be made by the shareholders.[6]

Section 172 encapsulates the ESV principle that now underpins UK company law.[7] In short ESV appears to be an endorsement of shareholder primacy[8] but with an emphasis on the long-term interests of shareholders that necessitates recognition of the contribution and interests of other stakeholders. ESV is a compromise between shareholder primacy and a pluralist – or 'stakeholder' – approach to company law and offers a guide for the application of directors' duties by identifying the matters they must take into account, such as the long-term consequences of decisions taken and their impact upon the environment and the employees' and other interests. ESV was adopted on the basis that it would 'better achieve wealth generation and competitiveness for the benefit of all.'[9] As is explained by Professor Keay, 'this approach was clearly based on shareholder value and involved directors having to act in the collective best interests of shareholders, but it eschewed an exclusive focus on the short-term financial bottom line and sought a more inclusive approach that valued the building of long-term relationships.'[10]

---

[6] Section 417 expressly states that its purpose is to enable shareholders to assess the performance of the directors and s.260 of the Companies Act 2006 provides for the possibility of a derivative claim to be brought in respect of a cause of action arising from an actual or proposed act or omission involving breach of duty by a director.

[7] See for example J. L. Yap, 'Considering the Enlightened Shareholder Value Principle' (2010) 31 *Company Lawyer* 35; D. Fisher, 'The Enlightened Shareholder – Leaving Stakeholders in the Dark: Will Section 172(1) of the Companies Act 2006 Make Directors Consider the Impact of Their Decisions on Third Parties?' (2009) 20 *International Company and Commercial Law Review* 10; A. Keay, 'Section 172(1) of the Companies Act 2006: an Interpretation and Assessment' (2007) 28 *Company Lawyer* 106.

[8] A. Johnston, 'After the OFR: Can UK Shareholder Value Still be Enlightened?' (2006) 7 *European Business Organization Law Review* 817 at 842.

[9] The Company Law Review, *Modern Company Law for a Competitive Economy: The Strategic Framework,* (DTI, London, 1999) para 5.1.12 and the Company Law Review Steering Group, Department of Trade and Industry, *Modern Company Law for a Competitive Economy: Developing the Framework* (DTI, London, 2000) at 15 and para 2.22.

[10] See A. Keay, 'Section 172(1) of the Companies Act 2006: an Interpretation and Assessment' (2007) 28 *Company Lawyer* 106 at 107, and A. Keay, 'Tackling the Issue of the Corporate Objective: An Analysis of the United Kingdom's "Enlightened Shareholder Value Approach"' (2007) 29 *Sydney Law Review* 577 at 590.

Compared to the previous common law duty of directors to act in the company's interests, s.172 appears to be more supportive of a stakeholder perspective. The common law duty did not preclude directors from having regard to various stakeholders as part of their duty to act bona fide in the best interests of the company, but, as Goddard remarks, 'section 172 goes further: it posits a relationship between the pursuit of shareholder wealth maximisation and the obligation to consider the impact of decisions on various stakeholders.'[11] Goddard quotes a government minister who said that s.172 'marks a radical departure in articulating the connection between what is good for a company and what is good for society at large'.[12]

As noted above, s.417 is closely related to s.172: its purpose is to enable shareholders to assess whether the company's directors have fulfilled their duty of promoting the company's success. Indeed ESV, together with improved transparency and shareholder engagement, were regarded as 'fundamental cornerstones' of the Act. Sir Philip Goldenberg described the combination of ESV and greater transparency as 'the key to successful corporate governance'.[13] Professor Keay further remarks that whilst s.172 'was only one part of the concept of ESV that the Government wanted to bring into force', 'the other half was the requirement for companies to prepare and publish an operating and financial review' (OFR).[14] The reporting of qualitative and forward-looking information was to 'enable users to achieve a proper assessment of the performance and prospects of the business' and such information would itself 'enlighten' the shareholder value goal.[15] As Keay discusses, the operating and financial review was ultimately dropped and was replaced by the business review requirement now found in s.417 which would be less prescriptive. Although the business review is not as strong in its requirements as the operating and financial review, nevertheless the

---

[11] R. Goddard, 'Directors' Duties' (2008) 12 *Edinburgh Law Review* 468 at 471–2.

[12] Ibid quoting Margaret Hodge MP, Department of Trade and Industry, *Companies Act 2006: Duties of Directors, Ministerial Statements 2007* at www.berr.gov.uk/files/file40139.pdf.

[13] Quoted by B. Bundock, T. Malloch and J. Thornton in *Environmental and Social Transparency Under the Companies Act 2006: Digging Deeper* (London, ClientEarth, 2010) at 44.

[14] A. Keay, 'The Duty to Promote the Success of the Company: Is it Fit for Purpose?' p. 75 of Chapter 2 of this book.

[15] See A. Johnston, 'After the OFR: Can UK Shareholder Value Still be Enlightened?' (2006) 7 *European Business Organization Law Review* 817 at 828 and 832.

intention behind it is clearly that 'informed, engaged shareholders – or those acting on their behalf – are the means by which the directors are held to account for business strategy and performance.'[16] Professor Lowry suggests that s.417 makes clear that the business review 'is an integral part of the duty of loyalty' and 'the effect of the reporting requirements in s.417 will, at the minimum, focus the minds of directors on stakeholder interests.'[17] The business review, together with best practice codes and shareholder demands for better information, still has the potential to lead to the sort of information that would have been produced under the OFR, and might also promote the enlightened shareholder value approach to corporate management and reporting.[18]

However, despite the stated and perceived intentions behind s.172 and s.417, the likelihood of them leading to the achievement of an enlightened shareholder value approach to company management is open to doubt. This prediction arises because numerous shortcomings in the legislation can be identified. These are considered in the next section.

III. THE PROBLEMS AND LIMITATIONS OF THE LEGISLATION

Professor Lowry argued recently that 'the inter-relationship between s.172 and s.417 does much to further the objective of constructing a disclosure regime which underpins the core duty of loyalty and which is economically efficient in its operation'.[19] This may be a somewhat optimistic view of the legislation. In reality, the legislation is not likely to achieve easily an enlightened shareholder value version of company law because a number of problems are apparent in the concept of ESV and in the legislative provisions themselves and how they might be applied.

---

[16]   Department of Trade and Industry, Company Law Reform, quoted by B. Bundock, T. Malloch and J. Thornton in *Environmental and Social Transparency Under the Companies Act 2006: Digging Deeper* (London, ClientEarth, 2010) at 46.

[17]   J. Lowry, 'The Duty of Loyalty of Company Directors: Bridging the Accountability Gap Through Efficient Disclosure' (2009) 68 *Cambridge Law Journal* 607 at 621.

[18]   C. A. Williams and J. M. Conley, 'Triumph or Tragedy? The Curious Path of Corporate Disclosure Reform in the UK' (2007) 31 *William and Mary Environmental Law Review* 317 at 357.

[19]   J. Lowry, 'The Duty of Loyalty of Company Directors: Bridging the Accountability Gap Through Efficient Disclosure' (2009) 68 *Cambridge Law Journal* 607 at 622.

These problems include: lack of clarity in the meaning of ESV; lack of detail in the legislative requirements; the discretion given to directors in how they are to fulfil the requirements, leading to difficulties for shareholders and other stakeholders in challenging the directors and holding them to account; the problematic assumption that shareholders will be willing to challenge the directors; and, ultimately, the limited potential for enforcement of the related provisions.

(a) The Unclear Concept of ESV

ESV is not a clear concept. There remains a question over who is to be enlightened and who or what is to provide the enlightenment. The concept arguably requires that both the shareholders and the directors must be 'enlightened' but in reality, the directors have discretion about which factors are relevant to the management of the company and how that management is to be reported, and the extent to which such factors are to be taken into account. The input of stakeholders is not indicated. While the directors are required to take into account the impact of the company's activities on stakeholders the legislation does not provide a forum for the stakeholders to express their views. Nor is the business review intended to be for the benefit of those stakeholders. A further problem with the ESV principle is that it could have the effect of making some of the relevant constituents worse off than they were under the previous legislation. In particular, for employees, the disappearance of the earlier s.309 of the Companies Act 1985, which singled them out for consideration by the directors, now means that they must compete with a non-exhaustive list of other stakeholders for recognition by the directors. Indeed, none of the interests listed are to be given primacy since the directors need only to 'have regard to' such interests. Nor does this preclude directors from taking decisions that are inconsistent with any such interests.[20] Furthermore, the non-shareholders are left without any way of ensuring that the directors pay genuine attention to their needs beyond mere lip service since there is no guidance in the legislation about the extent to which their interests are to be considered.

In addition, because of this discretion enjoyed by the directors, it remains difficult for both shareholders and non-shareholders to prove that directors have failed to take their interests into account when conducting

---

[20] This interpretation is suggested by Clifford Chance in a report submitted to the UN Special Representative of the Secretary-General on the Issue of Human Rights: Corporate Law Tools Project, September 2009 at http://www.reports-and-materials.org/Corporate-law-tools-reports-UK-Sep-2009.pdf.

their business decisions. Nor does enlightened shareholder value provide any method of enforcement for non-shareholder constituents even if they have proof that the directors have failed in their duty. In reality, the approach does not really change much from the previous shareholder-focused approach. It still requires directors to prioritize the interests of the shareholders, with other constituent interests to be taken into account only if to do so also would benefit the shareholders collectively in the long term. In addition, such stakeholders are forced by the legislation to rely on the shareholders to make a challenge. This was a criticism of the earlier s.309. Without locus standi to challenge them, the directors had nothing to fear from the employees. If their interests should conflict with those of the shareholders it would be unlikely that the shareholders would make a challenge on their behalf. At the same time, the shareholders face the obstacle of an increased discretion enjoyed by the directors which equips them with a defence against a shareholder challenge. Andrew Keay summarizes the problem:

> 'Arguably, the only enlightened element seems to be found in the recognition that directors may take into account material interests, namely those enumerated in section 172(1), if they wish and not be sued for doing so, but this is only provided that the action that they take promotes the success of the company for the benefit of the members as a whole. It must be noted that directors cannot pursue a course of action that might be good for all material interests, unless it ultimately benefits the members. So, this would appear to rule out the possibility of actions such as directors declining to dismiss employees, unless that would ultimately benefit shareholders. It is submitted that the overall effect of section 172(1) is that ESV can be classified as a "shareholders first interpretation."'[21]

The enlightened shareholder value approach essentially requires shareholders to be enlightened about the company's position beyond a short-term profit-oriented vision. Indeed, shareholders are required to accept this vision and to assess the directors' performance from this perspective. Thus s.172 sets out the basic goal and s.417 sets out the reporting requirements that support the corporate implementation of the goal. The fact that shareholders must rely on information provided to them by the directors makes it difficult for them to assess or to challenge the performance of directors in the fulfilment of their duty to promote the

---

[21] A. Keay, 'Tackling the Issue of the Corporate Objective: An Analysis of the United Kingdom's "Enlightened Shareholder Value Approach"' (2007) 29 *Sydney Law Review* 577 at 592 and see further A. Keay, 'The Duty to Promote the Success of the Company: Is it Fit for Purpose?' Chapter 2 of this book.

success of the company under an ESV focus. They can only act on the information that the directors choose to provide for them. If they are to adopt a more progressive and genuinely enlightened view of the company, the shareholders would need to assert their own externally obtained knowledge about environmental, social and corporate governance issues to engage with and discuss the reports and to seek further information if necessary. So there appears to be something circular about all of this: ESV is shaped by what the directors regard as important from a long-term perspective and shareholders are to assess their efforts also based on the information that the directors choose to give. It is not clear how the directors are to be enlightened beyond having regard to the factors listed in s.172. The extent to which they must regard those factors is left to them to decide. The legislation does not offer them any real guidance in this regard.

(b) Lack of Detail in the Legislative Requirements

Sections 172 and 417 provide only a skeleton of what the directors must consider and provide information upon. The list of interests is non-exhaustive, so directors may expand on them or they may choose to discount such interests if they do not consider them relevant to the company's business prospects or to provide an understanding of the business. Indeed in the reporting requirements under s.417, none of the specified matters to be included is compulsory but if they are not covered the business review must state that fact. Subsection (5) does not require an explanation of why such matters are not covered but, arguably, the investors might expect an explanation if the business review is to be seen as a credible and worthwhile document. Subsection (5) is rather vague on the points it identifies for coverage and what is to be included is left very open. So long as the information given can be considered to help in understanding the company's business development, performance or position then the directors may determine for themselves what information is provided. So long as they decide the issue in good faith their decision will not be open to challenge.[22] Such matters need only be included if necessary for an understanding of the business. The section gives no hint about what degree of understanding is needed nor how directors should decide to what extent such matters are necessary to this understanding of the business. Again, if consideration of different factors

---

[22] Good faith can have the effect of limiting a decision but might also legitimate it: *Charterbridge Corporation Ltd v Lloyds Bank Ltd* (1970) 1 Ch 62.

suggests conflicting courses of action, the directors need only to take their own good faith business decisions to promote the success of the company or to report adequately.[23]

The directors are given power to decide not to disclose information relating to: matters under negotiation; approaching developments; or persons with whom the business has a relationship if they consider that disclosure of such information would be seriously prejudicial to the company's interests or to the third person's and the public interests. Thus according to subs.(10):

> 'Nothing in this section requires the disclosure of information about impend-ing developments or matters in the course of negotiation if the disclosure would, in the opinion of the directors, be seriously prejudicial to the interests of the company.'

Subsection (11) states, in addition:

> 'Nothing in subsection (5)(c) requires the disclosure of information about a person if the disclosure would, in the opinion of the directors, be seriously prejudicial to that person and contrary to the public interest.'

Subsection (11) deals with the opposition expressed by a significant number of business organizations to the requirement to disclose infor-mation relating to suppliers. Not only did the Government try to provide reassurance by saying that it was only necessary to disclose information regarding significant relationships that would be likely to influence the performance of the company's business or its value, but also this exemption is designed to protect those with whom the company has a relationship. The exemption only applies if it is also in the public interest not to disclose the information; it is not concerned with protecting the company's interests.

While the legislation has sparse detail, guidance has been offered by the Accounting Standards Board (ASB) in the form of a Reporting Statement of Best Practice. The ASB originally issued a reporting statement for an OFR in 1993. The statement aimed to provide a framework within which directors could discuss the main factors under-lying the company's performance and financial position. The Statement was revised in 2003. Following the recommendation for an OFR in the Company Law Review and the Government's proposals in 2004 on the

---

[23] Hansard, HC Comm D 11 June 2006 at Cols 591–593, Margaret Hodge MP: See further L. Sealy and S. Worthington, *Cases and Materials in Company Law*, 8th ed (Oxford, Oxford University Press, 2008) at 294.

implementation of a legislative requirement for an OFR, the ASB was granted a statutory power to make reporting standards for the OFR. The intention during the preparations for the OFR legislation was that any such standards published by the ASB would be mandatory for companies under the OFR regime. The ASB issued a Reporting Standard (RS 1) in 2005 to this effect. However, when the OFR legislation was repealed, the ASB's Reporting Standard was formally withdrawn and was converted into a statement of best practice on the OFR, with the intention that the statement would offer guidance and have persuasive, rather than mandatory, force.

The current Statement[24] is non-mandatory, unlike its prior intended Standard, which would have accompanied the OFR. The Reporting Statement covers quite a large range of information to be included where directors consider it necessary for an understanding of the business. For example, it provides, inter alia, detailed guidance on possible key performance indicators and on trends and factors affecting the business as well as details on a company's relationships with different third parties. However its effectiveness is limited to being of guidance status only and so can be ignored or used only partially by the directors without fear of legal challenge.

One reason for the generalized wording of the legislation is to provide sufficient flexibility for the legislation to be able to accommodate different types of company with different circumstances. However over time new corporate, economic, social, political or environmental priorities arise and the legislation appears not to be so flexible as to be able to adapt to radically changing circumstances. Consequently, on matters such as climate change, which are gaining greater recognition as serious issues to be addressed, the government has had to introduce new and separate reporting guidance in order to flesh out the legislative intentions. For example, the guidelines on greenhouse gas emissions[25] fill an important gap in the detail of the legislation and the ASB's Reporting Statement. Thus, in effect, there are other reporting demands that exist alongside the legislation, so that the narrative reporting process has become increasingly complex and difficult.

---

[24] Accounting Standards Board, *Reporting Statement: Operating and Financial Review,* January 2006.

[25] Department for Environment Food and Rural Affairs, *Guidance on How to Measure and Report Your Greenhouse Gas Emissions* (September 2009) at http://archive.defra.gov.uk/environment/business/reporting/pdf/ghg-guidance.pdf.

(c) Directors' Discretion

As already noted, in both s.172 and s.417 the discretion enjoyed by directors is significant. Thus under s.172 directors are to act in good faith and to give regard to such interests in a way that *they* believe will promote the company's success. The courts have shown over time that the good faith element in directors' duties is relatively easy to satisfy[26] and may therefore serve to legitimize the decisions that directors make rather than expose them to further challenge. Within such discretion, the wording of s.172 indicates to the directors that their overriding aim is to satisfy the interests of the members as a whole over the long term. In practice, directors are going to continue to feel constrained to look after the interests of their shareholders, but the discretion within the legislation provides them with a cushion should any challenges be mounted. Similarly, s.417 provides directors with discretion on what they must report. Thus they only need to report those factors listed if they consider them necessary for an understanding of the business. Again it is likely to be difficult to question directors about information not reported.

The point of the review is for directors to indicate the regard which they have had for the factors set out in s.172. Nevertheless, there is nothing to prevent directors making quite neutral statements which give little detail about their thinking and discussions at board level. How useful such reports will be is clearly open to doubt.[27] Moreover directors are likely to provide bland reports in order to avoid legal liabilities for inaccurate statements.

(d) Liability Concerns

Despite the existence of a 'safe harbour' provision in the Act[28] for forward-looking reporting statements, directors, advised by their lawyers, are still worried that they will be held liable for statements that turn out to be incorrect. This causes them to be unwilling to provide detail that they fear could come back to haunt them in a legal challenge.

This fear of liability is arguably exacerbated by the fact that there are no clear standards in the legislation against which directors' actions are to be measured. There are no criteria against which to measure the

---

[26] See for example *Re Smith & Fawcett Ltd* [1942] Ch 304.

[27] See A. Keay, 'The Duty to Promote the Success of the Company: Is it Fit for Purpose?' Chapter 2 of this book.

[28] See s.463 and s.1270, inserting new s.90A into the Financial Services and Markets Act 2000.

company's success. This fact has a double-edged effect. First, the directors fear liability because there is nothing in the legislation to suggest that they will necessarily be treated leniently by a court in a future legal challenge. On the other hand, and more likely, this lack of measurable standards could render directors 'virtually unassailable'[29] and any alleged breach of s.172 will be 'extremely difficult to prove'.[30] It is not clear how the objective 'reasonable care' test required in s.174 would be interpreted in the context of a claim based on s.172, in which the honest, but subjective, beliefs of the directors are given such weight. The relationship between s.172 and s.174 is distinctly unclear.

This position renders a challenge by shareholders, although theoretically possible under s.260(3), unlikely in practice. The history of derivative actions highlights that they are notoriously difficult to pursue, given the level of uncertainty and costs. There is little to suggest that, in the kinds of circumstances being discussed here, there will be any improved chances of success for a derivative claim. Furthermore, to rely on shareholders to pursue such an action might also amount to wishful thinking, given their well-known general lack of willingness to engage meaningfully in corporate governance issues. This point is discussed next.

(e) Lack of Shareholder Engagement

The campaign lawyers, ClientEarth, highlight as the main purpose of the business review legislation shareholder engagement and dialogue.[31] Virginia Ho also highlights the fact that the enlightened shareholder value model that has emerged is 'in part at the behest of major institutional shareholders who are demonstrating a greater willingness to favour long-term investment strategies, sustainable business practices and more

---

[29] D. Arsalidou, 'Shareholder Primacy in Clause 173 of the Company Law Bill 2006' (2007) 28 *Company Lawyer* 67, quoted by D. Fisher, 'The Enlightened Shareholder – Leaving Stakeholders in the Dark: Will Section 172(1) of the Companies Act 2006 Make Directors Consider the Impact of Their Decisions on Third Parties?' (2009) 20 *International Company and Commercial Law Review* 10 at 15.

[30] Fisher, ibid.

[31] See for example, ClientEarth, *Response to the Financial Reporting Council's Draft Plan And Levy proposals 2010/2011*, (March 2010) at 7 at http://www.clientearth.org/reports/environmental-justice-clientearth-response-to-the-financial-reporting-councils-draft-plan-and-levy-proposals-2010.pdf.

of whom are incorporating environmental, social and governance measures in firm portfolio risk analysis.'[32] Shareholders have been increasingly under the spotlight since the financial crisis began, as important corporate governance actors who will challenge directors' actions. But how responsible and engaged are investors in practice?

Institutional investors are increasingly pressurised to act as 'responsible investors' because generically with other shareholders they are identified as the company's owners, particularly for corporate governance purposes. For example, following the corporate scandal resulting in the collapse of the Maxwell corporation, the Cadbury Report, published in 1992, laid the foundations for the UK's corporate governance system. The Report identified shareholders as 'owners'. Paragraph 6.6 makes clear that since shareholders have delegated their responsibilities as owners to the directors who act as their stewards,

> 'it is for the shareholders to call the directors to book if they appear to be failing in their stewardship and *they should use this power*. While they cannot be involved in the direction and management of their company, they can insist on a high standard of corporate governance and good governance is an essential test of the directors' stewardship. The accountability of boards to shareholders will, therefore, be strengthened if shareholders require their companies to comply with the Code.'[33] (emphasis added)

It is clear from this statement that the Cadbury Committee did not envisage shareholders behaving passively but rather that they would actively participate in the corporate governance of their companies. Thus the Code made reference to reports and accounts being put to shareholders and for shareholders to comment and ask questions on them as well as to make use of annual general meetings and other communications with the board to make resolutions and to make use of their votes.

The Institutional Shareholders' Committee (ISC) has periodically updated its *Statement of Principles on the Responsibilities of Institutional Shareholders and Agents*. These have since been largely adopted by the Financial Reporting Council as a UK Stewardship Code for Institutional Shareholders in 2010. This Code requires institutional investors to monitor the performance of, and establish, where necessary, a regular dialogue with investee companies.

---

[32] Virginia Harper Ho, '"Enlightened Shareholder Value": Corporate Governance Beyond the Shareholder-Stakeholder Divide' (2010) 36 *Iowa Journal of Corporation Law* 59 at 62.

[33] Cadbury Committee, *Report on the Financial Aspects of Corporate Governance* (London, Gee, 1992) at para 6.6.

Another view of responsible ownership is much broader than that seen through the corporate governance lens. Whereas the narrower corporate governance expectations are for shareholders to vote and to monitor their directors and hold them to account, 'responsible investors' might also include those who are more willing to act to support sustainability issues. Indeed the ESV model brings with it a more widely encompassing potential role for shareholders. Increasingly, investor standards focus on long-term considerations rather than on short-term success, reflecting the long-term investment horizons of the institutional shareholders whose investments are also highly diversified.[34] There is also an increasing emphasis on social and environmental impacts. The OECD Principles of Corporate Governance and the Global Compact provide prominent examples and more recently the UN Principles for Responsible Investment demonstrate a commitment to sustainable development through the fulfilment by investors of their fiduciary duty.

Despite positive signals, a number of obstacles to effective responsible ownership have also been identified. Hendry et al, for example, highlight various factors that contribute to investors retaining a 'trader' mentality rather than adopting an ownership identity and taking on the responsibilities that go with ownership. They note that the freedom afforded by a liquid stock market to simply sell shares if things look bad weakens the financial justification for shareholder activism. Furthermore, institutional investors compete with each other and that reduces the incentive for activism when other investors are likely to free ride. When investors do meet with executives the purpose is not so much to control or influence management but rather, to use such meetings as a basis for their buying and selling decisions.[35] On the other hand, Hendry et al note that these free-rider problems have been reduced by the re-concentration of share ownership, which also makes it more difficult simply to sell. Engagement then offers the potential to improve returns. In addition, higher voting power and delegated voting rights provide encouragement to be more active, as do the increased opportunities to use votes on matters such as remuneration and reappointment of directors.[36]

---

[34] As noted in the UN Principles for Responsible Investment.

[35] J. Hendry, P. Sanderson, R. Barker and J. Roberts, 'Responsible Ownership, Shareholder Value and the New Shareholder Activism' BRESE Working Paper No 13 (November 2004) at http://www.brunel.ac.u/research/brese/pub/work.htm at 6. See also J. Hendry, P. Sanderson, R. Barker and J. Roberts, 'Owners or Traders? Conceptualizations of Institutional Investors and Their Relationship with Corporate Managers' (2006) 59 *Human Relations* 1101.

[36] Ibid.

Other obstacles to shareholder engagement include the organizational structures of the institutional investors that have affected their cultures vis-à-vis socially responsible investment and also with regard to shareholder activism more generally. Juravle and Lewis, for example, note that 'organizational culture – comprising organizational artefacts, values and underlying beliefs – may be an additional impediment to environmental, social and governance ('ESG') integration in the core investment decision-making process'.[37] They note that the internal environment may be 'dominated by a pull towards short-termism, herding/gravitation towards defensible decisions and a lack of integration of ESG aspects'.[38] Hendry et al note similar problems with regard to more mainstream shareholder engagement.[39]

(f) Enforcement Difficulties

There has been noted above a general difficulty in enforcing the provisions in s.172 and s.417. Shareholders are not keen to exercise their voice in this way and nor are they encouraged to do so by the courts. Yet nor are the stakeholders given a chance to challenge the directors for any perceived breaches of s.172. The business review is not aimed to be for their benefit, so they may find the requisite information to prove their claim difficult to obtain. Moreover, the fact that the legislation does not endow them with locus standi to go to the courts renders them 'toothless' against the directors.[40] Thus the directors have little to fear from such stakeholders legally, although their reputation could be damaged by the noisier stakeholder campaigners.

A further impediment to effective enforcement of the legislation is the fact that liquidators face difficulty in proving that a breach of s.172 led to financial loss, which, at best, would be difficult to calculate.[41] Ultimately, it is little surprise that some commentators have described s.172 as a

---

[37] C. Juravle and A. Lewis, 'Identifying Impediments to SRI in Europe: A Review of the Practitioner and Academic Literature' (2008) 17 *Business Ethics: A European Review* 285 at 299.

[38] Ibid.

[39] J. Hendry, P. Sanderson, R. Barker and J. Roberts, 'Responsible Ownership, Shareholder Value and the New Shareholder Activism' BRESE Working Paper No 13 (November 2004) at http://www.brunel.ac.u/research/brese/pub/work.htm.

[40] J. L. Yap, 'Considering the Enlightened Shareholder Value Principle' (2010) 31 *Company Lawyer* 35 at 36.

[41] D. Fisher, 'The Enlightened Shareholder – Leaving Stakeholders in the Dark: Will Section 172(1) of the Companies Act 2006 Make Directors Consider

right without a remedy.[42] The information requirements do nothing to alleviate this fault.

The Financial Reporting Council (FRC), together with its operating body, the Financial Reporting Review Panel (FRRP), has an important role in monitoring the annual accounts of public companies and large private companies for compliance with the applicable accounting legislation and standards. The FRRP has been authorized by the Companies (Defective Accounts and Directors' Reports) (Authorised Person) and Supervision of Accounts and Reports (Prescribed Body) Order 2008,[43] under s.457 of the Act, for the purposes of s.456 of the Act, to make an application to court for a declaration that the directors' report of a company does not comply with the requirements of the Act and for an order requiring the directors of the company to prepare revised accounts or a revised report.[44] To date the FRRP appears never to have gone to court under these provisions.[45] ClientEarth considers that the environmental and social reporting requirements, which are important to the ESV principle, are not given sufficient priority by the FRRP, which appears to concentrate more strongly on the requirements of International Financial Reporting Standards (IFRS) and Generally Accepted Accounting Principles (GAAP) because these are much more numerous than the legislative environmental and social reporting requirements.[46] Such a response by the FRRP is likely to lead to an emphasis on the financial reports potentially at the expense of supervision of the ESV-orientated aspects of the business review. Indeed, while there is evidence that the FRRP regularly questions companies in relation to the principal *financial* risks and uncertainties aspect of their business reviews, they do not appear to ask questions in relation to the *environmental or social* matters,

---

the Impact of Their Decisions on Third Parties?' (2009) 20 *International Company and Commercial Law Review* 10 at 15.

[42] J. L. Yap, 'Considering the Enlightened Shareholder Value Principle' (2010) 31 *Company Lawyer* 35 at 36 and Fisher, ibid, at 16.

[43] SI 208, No. 623

[44] See ClientEarth, *ClientEarth Response to the Financial Reporting Council's Draft Plan and Levy Proposals 2010/11* (March 2010) at http://www.clientearth.org at 4–5.

[45] ClientEarth makes this observation in its response to the government's recent consultation on the future of narrative reporting in the UK: See *ClientEarth response: The Future of Narrative Reporting*, (2010) at http://www.clientearth.org.

[46] ClientEarth, *ClientEarth Response to the Financial Reporting Council's Draft Plan and Levy Proposals 2010/11*, ClientEarth (March 2010) at 5–7.

or company compliance with the requirements of the Act in this regard.[47] Questions also remain about the capacity and composition of the FRRP membership, especially on the issue of independence from the companies whose activities they are authorized to regulate.[48]

In the next section I draw on evidence provided by numerous surveys and reports as well as empirical evidence of my own that highlight these legislative failings.

IV.   THE EMPIRICAL EVIDENCE OF NARRATIVE REPORTING

It was established above that some observers emphasise the dialogue and engagement function of the narrative report. To be useful a report should facilitate effective communication.[49] Yet the evidence suggests that this is not happening in reality. Rather, companies are reporting in order to comply with the letter of the law, but this does not lead to communication that assists shareholders in engaging with the company.

Numerous surveys have been conducted to test the quality of narrative reports published since s.417 came into force.[50] Those studies focused solely on the analyses of corporate annual reports – archival or documentary data. Quoted companies' directors' report sections were reviewed to see if they met key business review requirements and a quantitative approach was employed to analyse the data. The first observation to note is that s.417 has led to longer annual reports. The ASB, for example,

---

[47]   Ibid at 9.

[48]   Ibid at 10–11, noting the connection one member of the Panel has with the Oil Industry Accounting Committee.

[49]   See C. Villiers, 'Disclosure Obligations in Company Law: Bringing Communication Theory into the Fold' (2001) 1 *Journal of Corporate Law Studies* 181; C. Villiers, *Corporate Reporting and Company Law* (Cambridge, Cambridge University Press, 2006).

[50]   Black Sun plc, *The First 23 – Reporting under the Business Review* (August 2006); Radley Yeldar, *How Does It Stack Up? Narrative Reporting Content in the FTSE 100* (September 2006); Deloitte, *Write to Reason: Surveying OFRs and Narrative Reporting in Annual Reports* (October 2006); The Virtuous Circle, *Preparedness for the New Corporate Reporting Requirements: A Study of FTSE200 Business Reviews and a Consideration of Their Readiness for the New Companies Bill* (October 2006); and PricewaterhouseCoopers, *Show Me More Than the Money: An Assessment of How Prepared Companies are for the Business Review* (November 2006); ASB, *A Review of Narrative Reporting by UK Listed Companies in 2006* (January 2007).

recently claimed that the average size of annual report has passed 100 pages[51] and PricewaterhouseCoopers (PwC) claims that companies' annual reports now average around 149 pages with 60 per cent of such reports dedicated to narrative, contextual and nonfinancial information.[52]

The early reviews of narrative reporting just after the introduction of s.417 found that companies struggled with reporting their key performance indicators. They simply listed many financial performance indicators and failed to identify and state which ones were key indicators. There was also a lack of relevant non-financial performance indicators because companies struggled to identify them. The result was that they stuck to the common two: environment and employees. Similarly companies tended to list every conceivable risk they could think of, and failed to state the principal risks capable of having a negative impact on the health of their companies. Radley Yeldar's report also found that many companies were still struggling to move beyond a tick-box attitude to narrative reporting.[53] The Virtuous Circle noted that despite the fact that the business review requirement is to offer further explanation to the accounts, only about a third of companies did so[54] and they concluded that the production of a comprehensive business review would place new responsibility and workload on UK-listed companies.[55]

More recent reviews from 2009 on the state of UK narrative reporting from various corporate reporting agencies, accounting firms and governmental regulators have also been critical.[56] They suggest that the drive by most FTSE 350 companies to comply with existing regulations is

---

[51]   ASB, *A Review of Narrative Reporting 2008/9*.

[52]   PricewaterhouseCoopers, *Corporate Reporting a Time for Reflection: A Survey of the Fortune Global 500 Companies' Narrative Reporting* (April 2007) at 7.

[53]   See press release at http://ry.com/news/news/?id=4697 accompanying Radley Yeldar, *How Does It Stack Up? Narrative Reporting Content in the FTSE 100* (September 2006).

[54]   The Virtuous Circle, *Preparedness for the New Corporate Reporting Requirements: A Study of FTSE200 Business Reviews and a Consideration of Their Readiness for the New Companies Bill* (October 2006) at 4.

[55]   Ibid at 10.

[56]   ASB, *A Review of Narrative Reporting by UK Listed Companies in 2008/2009* (2009); Black Sun plc, *100/08: Annual Analysis of FTSE 100 Corporate Reporting 2008* (2009); Deloitte, *Written to Order: Surveying OFRs, EBRs and Narrative Reporting in Annual Reports* (2009); Deloitte, *A Telling Performance: Surveying Narrative Reporting in Annual Reports* (2009); FRC and ASB, *Rising to the Challenge: A Review of Narrative Reporting by UK Listed Companies* (2009).

producing stale and incoherent reports which are frustrating both regulators and stakeholders and possibly also leading to new forms of creative compliance. A recent PwC report states that few UK companies provide a clear and coherent picture of performance considered necessary in the current economic environment.[57]

The FRC published a discussion paper in 2009 which highlighted that UK corporate reporting was too complex and needed urgent change.[58] More recently still, a study conducted for the Coalition for Corporate Responsibility has concluded that the business review 'does not appear to be serving the purpose for which it was intended.'[59] That report highlighted the inadequate reporting of what might be widely regarded as principal risks and uncertainties such as CO_2 production and susceptibility to climate change. The report found that human rights issues were in general poorly reported, as were market presence and indirect economic effects so that it could not be said that companies were really providing a 'balanced and comprehensive analysis of their position.' The report further concluded that there was poor correlation between the issues reported and the risk either to stakeholders or to the shareholders.

What comes across strongly in the reviews is that legal and regulatory compliance is important to preparers of annual reports but that this does not necessarily result in clear, useful, or truly informative reports. As Helen Brand, the Chief Executive of the Association of Chartered Certified Accountants observes: 'Today's reporting certainly does hit almost all the notes – but in doing so, creates a cacophony which is deafening its audience.'[60] Playing all the right notes might make a lot of noise but it does not necessarily provide a tune.

My own research, conducted recently with a colleague, Dr Olaojo Aiyegbayo, has consisted of a small scale empirical study in which questionnaires were sent to a number of FTSE 100 companies and investment managers and corporate governance officers of a sample of

[57] PricewaterhouseCoopers, *A Snapshot of FTSE 350 Reporting: Compliance Mindset Suppresses Effective Communication* (2009).

[58] Communication should be focused, open and honest, clear and understandable, interesting and engaging and regulation should be targeted, proportionate, coordinated and clear: see FRC, *Louder Than Words: Principles and Actions for Making Corporate Reports Less Complex and More Relevant* (June 2009).

[59] A. Henriques, 'The Reporting of Non-Financial Information in Annual Reports by the FTSE100' (CORE 2010) at http://corporate-responsibility.org/ftse100-company-reports-reveal-inadequacy-of-companies-act/.

[60] See ACCA and Deloitte, *Hitting the Notes, But What's the Tune?: An International Survey of CFOs' Views on Narrative Reporting* (2010, ACCA, London), in Foreword.

institutional investors were interviewed.[61] In this paper I therefore provide a summary of what we found. Our research findings largely support the surveys detailed above. The themes that emerged included: confirmation that annual reports and directors' reports remain fundamentally important as information sources; preparers have difficulty in identifying and reporting on non-financial key performance indicators and principal risks; a lack of interest in the ASB's Reporting Statement of Best Practice; continued fears of liability for inaccurate statements.

(a) Importance of the Annual Report and Directors' Narrative

Our interviews confirm that the annual report and directors' report are regarded by fund managers as a critical information source. Our interview participants considered that the enhanced business review legislation has had a positive impact on the quality of reporting documents. As one corporate governance director we interviewed stated,

> 'well it is still relatively early days but actually we are pretty positive. We see a number of companies doing a fantastic job in the documents that they are producing. There are some really high quality business reviews that are way beyond the sort of reporting we used to get 5 years ago.'

Another interviewee said, 'the current state is good, better than what we had before.'

The annual report serves as a confirmatory or reference document because fund managers obtain corporate information from various other sources, including broker reports, company presentations, management meetings, and investor relations road shows. The annual report provides assurance that the information fund managers receive during the presentations and road shows is accurate and fund managers might use the annual report to question or challenge management during one-to-one meetings. One participant highlighted the role of the annual report as an indicator of future performance:

> 'it does have statements about what the directors expect to achieve in certain markets and that is something we do find useful. It sets the expectation for that company so if the company has indicated targets that it expects to hit within a time frame then you can check that they are delivering against that. I

---

[61] A more detailed report of our findings in this section has been published in the *Journal of Business Law*: O. Aiyegbayo and C. Villiers, 'The Enhanced Business Review: Has It Made Corporate Governance More Effective?' (2011) *Journal of Business Law* 699.

think it is very helpful to have an historical document to know what management said at a certain time and in certain market conditions.'

(b)   Difficulty in Selecting Non-financial KPIs and Principal Risks

All our interview participants agreed that companies struggle to report effectively their non-financial key performance indicators (KPIs), and principal risks. Participants generally considered that companies do not explain adequately the selection basis of their non-financial KPIs and principal risks and their relevance to the corporate strategy and objectives. Interviewees claimed that many companies simply list their principal risks without justifying their selection. Our review revealed that employee engagement and the environment were cited as the two most important non-financial KPIs. This observation is perhaps not surprising given that the business review legislation requires companies to report on their employee relations and their environmental efforts on a 'comply or explain' basis. Few companies will want to admit that they are not including the required information on the environment so one might expect them to be more likely to insert generic or boilerplate information in order to tick the legal box. Nevertheless, both the investment relations managers we interviewed argued that there is only so far that their companies can go with their environmental efforts after reducing official business trips abroad, using less paper and operating in environmentally efficient offices.

In recognizing the economic benefits of a company having or expressing environmental awareness, one investment relations manager mentioned how the economic benefits and public/political goodwill of monitoring the environmental efforts of their portfolio companies informs their investment decisions:

> 'The only way the environment affects our business is as a fund manager (private equity firm) we deliver services to pension funds and charities which, by legal requirements or ethics, have an interest in working with people who behave according to best practices in this field. We are taking that seriously and also it is recognised within the business that the environment is important and that behaving appropriately is important and that is reflected in our investment policies where we look at the environmental impact of the companies that we invest in. From an ethics point of view, we don't necessarily want to work with polluters, and from a business point of view, we recognise that it will be a business advantage over the long term to operate best practice in that field.'

(c)   The Limitation of the ASB Reporting Statement

As noted above, guidance has been offered by the ASB in the form of a Reporting Statement of Best Practice. The current Reporting Statement provides details about best practices in narrative reporting and what an OFR might contain. Companies are not compelled or required to use it but must state in their annual reports if they do. Our research suggests that the ASB's Reporting Statement does not seem to be gaining much traction with companies because they do not see the importance of it. One of our investor relations managers, for example, told us that he was 'not sufficiently familiar' with the Reporting Statement. Indeed, we spoke to a representative from the ASB during our research and he told us that because companies are not required to follow the reporting statement a lot of them are getting away with just doing the bare minimum. The current ASB's Reporting Statement contains 69 pages which may put off preparers from using it in addition to the compliance burden attached to it. Ambler and Neely suggest that 'companies are more likely to embrace the spirit of the ASB Reporting Statement if they see advantage in so doing. Otherwise they will do the minimum to keep out of trouble.'[62]

(d)   Liability Fears

With regard to the forward-looking statements, the investment relations managers participating in our research expressed the opinion that as a result of the financial crisis, management is cautious about the forward-looking statements which they put in the business review. They worry that a warranty or a misrepresentation will incur financial penalties and reputational damage. The result is that, guided by their lawyers, managers supply carefully worded forward-looking statements in their business reviews aimed at avoiding potential litigation. They avoid committing themselves in print in order to prevent having their statements come back to haunt them in a few years time due to poor reading of industry trends. These behavioural patterns suggest that directors have little faith in the safe harbour provisions that exist in the Act.[63] Paradoxically the problems appear to arise when the lawyers get

---

[62]   T. Ambler and A. Neely, 'Narrating the Real Corporate Story' (2008) *Business Strategy Review*, Summer edition, 29–32 at 30.

[63]   See s.463, Companies Act 2006 and s.1270, inserting new s.90A into the Financial Services and Markets Act 2000.

involved. Lawyers review statements made in the annual reports, particularly the risk sections and the forward-looking statements. One investment relations manager, who prepares the annual report told us

> 'I think the problem is that as soon as you have the risk sections and forward looking statements you will have advisers or legal advisers or lawyers involved in the process and you find that it becomes very sterile because you don't want to say anything that might come back to haunt you.'

The corporate governance directors we interviewed expressed the belief that the influence of the lawyers in the background stifled the voice of the chairman and CEO or management in the narrative disclosure. The shareholders were consequently unable to access the authentic voice of the management because of companies' lawyers vetting their disclosure drafts, especially those containing forward-looking information. In the words of one interviewee:

> 'the more the lawyers get involved and are looking over directors' shoulders, the less we get to see what the directors actually think because what we are hearing are the lawyers' voices instead of the directors. The directors are the people we want to hear from.'

To conclude this section, what comes across strongly is that the legislation has led to some improvements in reporting but, in reality, compliance with the law does not necessarily lead to effective communication. Indeed, to some extent, the worries about compliance actually serve to limit the potential for more useful or effective information that can promote genuine engagement. In the next section I hope to highlight further some of these problems by reference to a test case brought to the FRRP by the campaigning lawyers, ClientEarth.

V. A TEST CASE: CLIENTEARTH, THE RIO TINTO GROUP'S ANNUAL REPORT 2008 AND THE FINANCIAL REPORTING REVIEW PANEL

ClientEarth is an organization of activist lawyers who campaign on social and environmental issues[64] and who review corporate reports and reporting practices with a view to holding to account those companies that fail to report adequately. Following receipt of a draft of its recent publication

---

[64] See their website at: http://www.clientearth.org/.

Digging Deeper[65] in which it reviewed environmental and social transparency under the Act, the FRRP sent a letter in response to ClientEarth. As noted above, the role of the FRRP is to review accounts for compliance with the law and accounting standards. The FRRP enquires into cases where it appears that there is, or may be, a question of whether accounts and reports comply with the requirements of the Act.[66]

In its letter to ClientEarth the FRRP stated:

'The Financial Reporting Review Panel is playing its part in monitoring and enforcing these new legal requirements but, as you will appreciate, our experience of reviewing the enhanced disclosures is limited at this time.

Let me say at once that there is one very important way in which you can help us gain experience in this area. The Panel has always welcomed well informed referrals from the public about companies within our remit whose corporate reporting appears not to comply with the relevant reporting requirements. If you, or your organisation, have cause to believe that any such company is not complying with its reporting obligations we shall be very pleased to hear from you. ...'[67]

Responding to that letter, ClientEarth wrote to the FRRP expressing concerns over what they considered was non-compliance with the legislation by the Rio Tinto Group in its Annual Report of 2008. In short, the claim made by ClientEarth was that Rio Tinto's annual reports did not reflect the reality of its environmental and social impacts and practices, and were not compliant with UK law. The Rio Tinto Group is a globally operating UK and Australian based multinational mining group which had a combined market capitalization of around £38 billion in October 2009. According to ClientEarth, 'reports from government agencies, investigative journalists, non-governmental groups and others suggest many major problems with Rio Tinto's practices' leaving a 'legacy of polluted rivers, community conflicts, indigenous rights problems and corresponding reputational, conflict, regulatory and litigation risk.'[68] ClientEarth further alleged that one of the most widely and strongly

---

[65] ClientEarth, *Environmental and Social Transparency under the Companies Act 2006: Digging Deeper* (ClientEarth: London, 2010) (draft sent May 2009).

[66] See FRC website at: http://www.frc.org.uk/frrp/how.

[67] Letter from Carol Page, Secretary and Director of Panel Operations of the FRRP, to James Thornton of ClientEarth (15 June 2009) quoted in ClientEarth, *Referral to the FRRP Re: the Rio Tinto Group Annual Report 2008* (July 2010, London, ClientEarth) at 5.

[68] See ClientEarth, *Media Briefing: Rio Tinto's Greenwash Challenged in First Big Test of UK's Company Reporting Regulator* (July 2010) at http://clientearth.org.uk.

criticized projects in which Rio Tinto is involved is the Grasberg mine in Papua, Indonesia, a joint venture with US-based Freeport McMoRan Copper & Gold.[69] Among other things, the Norwegian Sovereign Wealth Fund divested from Rio Tinto on account of 'severe environmental damage' at Grasberg; the mine has been subject to bombings and other attacks from local resistance groups; and the mine operators continue to pay for mine security to be provided by the Indonesian military, despite the military's history of human rights violations in Papua.[70]

ClientEarth's complaint to the FRRP was that the picture presented by the independent sources 'is at odds with that presented by the Rio Tinto Group's annual reports, which are also rife with broad and simplified statements that fail to convey the complexity of the challenges that the company faces in reality'.[71] The implication is that Rio Tinto's reports do not comply with UK law.

ClientEarth's submission related to the Rio Tinto Group's Annual Report for the year 2008, and events that occurred during 2008. The main concerns were as follows[72]:

A.   A systemic failure to engage with the apparent facts in a fair, balanced and comprehensive manner.
B.   Apparent omissions and misrepresentations, relating to:
    i.   Problems associated with specific Rio Tinto operations (and their environmental or social impacts), including in particular:
       –   Grasberg, West Papua
       –   QIT Madagascar Minerals
       –   Rössing, Namibia
       –   Bougainville, Papua New Guinea
       –   La Granja, Peru
    ii.   The company's approach to and success in addressing issues with indigenous communities at or around their operations, such as at:
       –   Grasberg, West Papua
       –   The Upper Peninsula of Michigan
    iii.   Problems in exploration and development phases, in particular

[69]   Ibid.
[70]   Ibid.
[71]   Ibid.
[72]   ClientEarth, *Referral to the Financial Reporting Review Panel Re: the Rio Tinto Group Annual Report 2008* (July 2010, London, ClientEarth July 2010) at http://www.clientearth.org/company-transparency/ at 10–11.

information regarding the way that Rio Tinto manages relationships with exploration partners, to ensure that they conduct their work in a manner consistent with the long-term success and social licence to operate of the company, and details of relationships which appear to be compromising the company's position, such as that with:

–   Muriel Mining in Colombia

iv.   Operations in countries with concerns of State human rights violations, particularly in connection with Rio Tinto operations or where military or State-provided security forces have been associated with Rio Tinto operations.

v.   Problems associated with specific products (and their environmental or social impacts), particularly with reference to:

–   Uranium

ClientEarth sought an investigation by the FRRP and that the FRRP should pursue court action if Rio Tinto is failing to meet its legal obligations. This referral was the first time that the FRRP had been called on directly to discharge its statutory role to enforce the business review legislation. In the view of ClientEarth, if these laws are not enforced, shareholders and investors face a major obstacle to taking a proactive role in shaping company practice and performance.[73]

The Rio Tinto Group chose not to comment on ClientEarth's complaints and left it to the FRRP to decide the outcome.

Recently the FRRP published its decision:[74]

'In discussions with Rio Tinto the Panel has been considering whether additional information about some of the company's operations referred to in the 2008 business review ought to have been included in the review in order to comply with the Act's requirement for a balanced analysis.

Following these discussions, in their report and accounts for the year ended 31 December 2010, published today, the directors of Rio Tinto include more information about environmental matters, social and community issues and related reputational risk.

---

[73]   ClientEarth, *Media Briefing: Rio Tinto's Greenwash Challenged in First Big Test of UK's Company Reporting Regulator* (July 2010) at http://www.clientearth.org.uk.

[74]   FRRP, *Statement by the Financial Reporting Review Panel in Respect of the Report and Accounts of Rio Tinto Plc* (FRRP PN 131) (15 March 2011) available at http://www.frc.org.uk/frrp/press/pub2539.html.

The Panel welcomes the action taken by the directors and regards its enquiries as concluded.'

This was an astonishingly brief statement by the FRRP, although it had included with the statement a note to editors which indicated the new information that had been provided by Rio Tinto in its 2010 Directors' Report. That note reads as follows:

'Additional information included in the Rio Tinto Annual Report following discussions with the Panel comprises details of the potential health risks posed by exposure to workers and communities surrounding uranium mines; details of the sensitivities the group faces in dealing with local communities, such as the La Granja copper development in Peru and the Eagle project in Michigan in the United States; an example of the potential for the group's projects to impact on biodiversity, with information relating to biodiversity projects associated with the group's activities in Madagascar; additional details of the group's non-managed Grasberg mine in Indonesia and the nature of the environmental, social and reputational issues relating to that mine.'

It is clear from this press release that the FRRP was of the view that Rio Tinto had not supplied adequate information to be legally compliant in its 2008 business review, and that its additional information provided in the 2010 report, following discussions with the FRRP, was enough to conclude the matter. Rio Tinto, indeed, pointed out in its 2010 directors' report that it had been in discussions with the FRRP and indicated the information it had added in three other sections of its Annual Report:

'Following discussions with the UK Financial Reporting Review Panel (FRRP), Rio Tinto has agreed to include certain additional information in the 2010 Annual Report at the FRRP's request. This information includes on page 32, additional details of the potential health risks posed by exposure to workers and communities surrounding uranium mines; on page 34 details of the sensitivities the Group faces in dealing with local communities, such as at the La Granja copper development in Peru and the Eagle project in Michigan in the United States; on page 37, an example of the potential for the Group's projects to impact on biodiversity, with information relating to biodiversity projects associated with the Group's activities in Madagascar; on page 38, additional details of the nature of the Group's interests in the non-managed Grasberg mine in Indonesia, the nature of the environmental risks and social issues relating to that mine; and reference to the sale of shares by the Norwegian Government Pension Fund in 2008 as an example of the possible impact of the reputational risks faced by the Group in relation to its non-managed operations.'

In a report of 284 pages, it could be argued that Rio Tinto supplied minimal information in response to the complaint made by ClientEarth. The information dealing with the aspects raised by ClientEarth amounts to five paragraphs on the social well-being issues, two paragraphs on the environmental stewardship issues, and six paragraphs on the economic prosperity issues. These are provided in an appendix to this chapter. These had to be unearthed by the author from other issues on each of the indicated pages.

Could one be satisfied with the outcome of this case? Whilst it might be said that the FRRP did persuade Rio Tinto to provide the information sought by ClientEarth, it would be difficult to say that the presentation of that information really provided ultimately a fair and balanced view of the business. One might indeed describe Rio Tinto's response as grudging and minimal, given the gravity of the matters raised. The FRRP's press release also appears rather thin. Whilst it points us to the relevant information in the Annual Report and expresses satisfaction with the outcome, the FRRP does nothing to guide companies in the future on how to present their accounts and reports so that they actually comply with the spirit of the legislation. There is nothing in the press release to explain to socially-orientated investors what had gone wrong with the earlier accounts, nor what they should be able to expect from compliant companies. Of course the FRRP faces issues of costs and of commercial sensitivity that will inevitably limit what it can do or say publicly, but one might perhaps hope for more openness than is witnessed in this case.

Client Earth responded in a press release of its own that stated:[75]

- '• The FRRP shies away from making a statement about whether or not Rio Tinto's reports complied with the law.
- • The FRRP states that it closed its inquiry after Rio Tinto's directors "agreed" to include some, but not all, of the information called for in ClientEarth's complaint in their latest annual report.
- • The FRRP makes no statement as to whether or not this information is required by law, as asserted by ClientEarth.

A number of key issues that ClientEarth raised with the FRRP have not been addressed in Rio Tinto's new report, yet the FRRP has not made it clear how it was decided that these should not be included in the new report. The inquiry was conducted entirely behind closed doors.'

---

[75] ClientEarth, *First Test of UK's New Corporate Environmental and Social Law Falls Short*, 24 March 2011 at http://www.clientearth.org.

In the same press release, Ben Bundock, legal adviser on company transparency, ClientEarth, added:

'The closed-door and consensual manner of this investigation and its conclusion don't provide any clarity as to what this law means for all UK companies. It fails to send a strong message to other companies that to comply with the law they must report about their environmental and social impacts with detailed and balanced information. Unless there is a change of approach, we won't see the goals of the Companies Act achieved.'

This story highlights many of the problems identified earlier in this paper. The legislation does not ensure that companies will provide a balanced and comprehensive analysis of their position. The legislation is insufficient for effective communication with shareholders or other stakeholders and, whilst the role of the FRRP is important, the enforcement mechanisms are inadequate. Companies are still able to present themselves in a way that does not necessarily correspond with their actions or with the obstacles that they face in reality. Indeed, for some companies, the presentation of fair and balanced reviews remains an uphill challenge. The results hardly sit comfortably with the intention behind the ESV model of company law.

VI. CONCLUSION: THE FUTURE OF NARRATIVE REPORTING IN THE UK

In this chapter, I have explored the relationship between two important and controversial provisions in the Act. Sections 172 and 417 represent a model of company law based on the principle of enlightened shareholder value. The two provisions are closely connected, the narrative reporting aspect intended to support the goal of the directors' duty to promote the success of the company in an enlightened way.

It appears that ESV is applicable both to the actions of the directors in their management of the company and also to the demands of the shareholders and their responses to the actions of the directors. What is unclear, however, is how either of those parties is actually to be enlightened. The legislation provides hints in its skeletal lists of factors to be taken into account but the directors enjoy extensive discretion in how they are to treat those factors. So long as they act honestly they have little to fear from the shareholders or the courts.

Although there is an implication that the legislation aims to encourage shareholder engagement, assisted by the information they are given by the directors, in reality shareholders are unwilling or unable to engage effectively. Often the information with which they are supplied is not sufficient to inform them of the company's true situation or it supplies them with meaningless noise and clutter. The legislation lacks sufficient detail to guide directors and preparers of the business review and the ASB's Guidance Statement remains unattractive as a reporting device. Directors continue to fear liability for the things that they say in their company reports despite the existence of legislative safe harbours.

The empirical evidence supports these negative conclusions, as does the recent test case referred by ClientEarth to the FRRP. This uncomfortable state of affairs leaves open to question the future of the legislation. For s.172, it is still too early to make a meaningful judgment. Arguably, the same could be said for s.417. However, it might be predicted that the ability of s.417 to support the aims of s.172 appears to be doomed if the legislation and reporting practices remain as they are. Andrew Johnston saw the replacement of the OFR as a lost opportunity to encourage and enable the capital markets to take a longer-term view of the relationships that make up UK public companies.[76] In its Coalition Agreement document the present government stated its intention to reinstate the OFR 'to ensure that directors' social and environmental duties have to be covered in company reporting, and investigate further ways of improving corporate accountability and transparency'.[77] More recently, the Department of Business Innovation and Skills consulted on the future of narrative reporting.[78] The objective of the consultation was 'to look at ways to drive quality of company reporting to the level of the best and thereby enable stronger and more effective shareholder engagement'. At the time of writing, the government has not responded to the consultation although the responses of the consultees would indicate that probably there will be little change to the legislation. In the Summary of Responses Document[79] it is suggested that the changes made by the business review legislation are still bedding down and other new corporate governance provisions such as the Corporate Governance Code and the Stewardship Code are too new to have had an impact. The document suggests that 'further regulatory change might be premature'

---

[76] A. Johnston, 'After the OFR: Can UK Shareholder Value Still be Enlightened?' (2006) 7 *European Business Organization Law Review* 817 at 843.

[77] *The Coalition: Our Programme for Government*, (Cabinet Office, May 2010) at 10.

[78] Department for Business, Innovation and Skills, *The Future of Narrative Reporting in the UK – A Consultation* (August 2010).

[79] Department for Business, Innovation and Skills, *Summary of Responses to The Future of Narrative Reporting – A Consultation* (December 2010).

although some streamlining of the reporting framework to reduce the complexity and overlapping requirements might be advantageous.[80]

However, if a genuine ESV model of company law is to be achieved, it might be argued that, for the long-term success of the company, many more matters should be taken into account by directors in their corporate activities and in their reporting and that the legislation should make coverage of such information mandatory. ClientEarth expands the matters listed in s.172 and s.417 to include, as ClientEarth states:

> '*amongst many other matters* (emphasis retained), a company's approach to climate change; water or air pollution resulting from a company's activities; a company's human rights impacts or policies; disputes experienced by a company with communities in the UK or beyond; a company's provision of healthcare to employees in high risk positions; or a company's approach to diversity in the workforce or the gendered impacts of its activities.'[81]

It is also arguable that these should be compulsory information matters, rather than 'comply or explain' or voluntary, which do not provide companies with the incentives to provide relevant or sufficient information other than to present themselves as positively as possible. Part of the reporting process should include an explanation by the directors of the process they have used, and that might include explaining how they have determined material issues. Obviously in this regard there needs to be further clarification of the issue of materiality in company reporting in light of ESV, so that directors can be guided meaningfully about what and how they must report if shareholder engagement and long-term success are to be achieved.[82] This could be given by the FRC and that might help to strengthen its oversight and monitoring function.

A major weakness of the narrative reporting framework for the purposes of ESV noted above is the poor monitoring and enforcement of compliance with the reporting requirements. Whilst directors fear liability for inaccurate statements, such fear leads to them not saying enough. However, effective monitoring requires reports that are reliable, relevant, understandable and comparable and that present a balanced and comprehensive analysis of the company's position. A more rigorous enforcement regime might pave the way towards more useful reports. That may well be a prerequisite also to more genuine shareholder engagement. What

---

[80]   Ibid at 5.
[81]   See ClientEarth, *ClientEarth Response to the Financial Reporting Council's Draft Plan and Levy Proposals 2010/11* (March 2010) available at http://www.clientearth.org at 1, footnote 1.
[82]   Ibid at 12–16.

this paper shows is that the roles of the FRRP and the FRC are potentially pivotal to the development of a real ESV approach to company law. Their record so far has been uninspiring. It was suggested by numerous consultees in the government's recent consultation on the future of narrative reporting that the FRRP's role should be better promoted and resourced.

There is still a very long way to go in narrative reporting. It is still, in many ways, at a young stage and there is much that can be done to develop it into a clear and effective system. While the starting points might be a strengthening of the monitoring and verifying aspects of the framework, more detail needs to be provided to guide the directors on their reporting activities. A reinstatement of the Reporting Standard that accompanied the OFR would be a progressive step, though it might need further revisions to clarify the link to ESV. Only with such preliminary steps are shareholders, and other stakeholders, likely to be able to engage effectively with the directors, for the long-term success of companies and of society.

APPENDIX: INFORMATION EXTRACTED FROM RIO TINTO'S ANNUAL REPORT 2010 IN RESPONSE TO DISCUSSIONS WITH THE FINANCIAL REPORTING REVIEW PANEL

From Rio Tinto 2010 Directors Report

Page 113

UK Financial Reporting Review Panel

Following discussions with the UK Financial Reporting Review Panel (FRRP), Rio Tinto has agreed to include certain additional information in the 2010 Annual Report at the FRRP's request. This information includes in the Social wellbeing section, additional details of the potential health risks posed by exposure to workers and communities surrounding uranium mines and details of the sensitivities the Group faces in dealing with local communities, such as at the La Granja copper development in Peru and the Eagle project in Michigan in the United States; in the Environmental stewardship section, an example of the potential for the Group's projects to impact on biodiversity, with information relating to biodiversity projects associated with the Group's activities in Madagascar; in the Economic prosperity section, additional details of the nature of the Group's interests in the non-managed Grasberg mine in Indonesia, the nature of the environmental risks and social issues relating to that mine; and reference to the sale of shares by the Norwegian Government Pension Fund in 2008 as an example of the possible impact of the reputational risks faced by the Group in relation to its non-managed operations.

Social Wellbeing

Page 32 Rio Tinto operates two uranium mines, Ranger in Australia and Rössing in Namibia. When not appropriately managed, exposure to ionising radiation from uranium mines can pose potential health risks for workers or surrounding communities and we understand there may be some concern that those working or living near our uranium mines could be at risk.

Page 34 The introduction of a mining, smelting or refining operation can be disruptive and concerning to local communities, particularly where resettlement, land rights or areas of spiritual value are concerned. We apply leading industry practice in dealing with such matters and try to minimise and mitigate negative impacts and gain broad-based community support for our activities.

Page 34 However, people can validly have differing opinions about a development. For example, some sections of the community around the US-based Eagle project in Michigan have requested broader access to Eagle Rock, notwithstanding the understandings we have reached with other sections of the community to address safety and other considerations.

Page 34 Community action may also affect our ability to conduct our operations, such as our 2008 decision to temporarily suspend pilot project construction work at the La Granja copper development in Peru. Development of this project was subsequently scaled back as a result of the global financial crisis.

Page 34 Even when the broader community is supportive, individuals or NGOs may continue to have concerns about or oppose our activities and they may commence legal action to challenge it. We seek to respond to such actions, whilst respecting the views of those people who disagree with us. We accept that we cannot meet everybody's concerns and expectations, but wherever we operate we seek to do so with broad-based community support.

Environmental Stewardship

Page 37 The potential for impact on biodiversity makes our projects sensitive for external stakeholders and employees. Rio Tinto's future success depends on our ability to manage these issues, and our biodiversity strategy provides the management framework with an industry leading goal to have a "net positive impact" (NPI) on biodiversity.

Page 37 An underlining principal of our biodiversity work is to ensure that biodiversity conservation activities are community based. For example in Madagascar, we have negotiated legal agreements with local communities to manage avoidance zones for conservation. Whilst it may never be possible to obtain unanimous support for these programmes, and some sections of the community continue to have objections, we believe that it has the support of the majority of those affected in the local community.

Economic Prosperity

Page 38 Rio Tinto holds interests in companies and ventures it does not manage. However, we engage as members of the boards of directors, operating committees and/or technical committees. Because we believe that the principles in the way we work are universal, in our dealings with joint venture partners and non-controlled companies we make every effort to ensure that those standards of conduct are respected at all times.

Page 38 Examples of our non managed operations include the Escondida copper mine in Chile and the Grasberg copper-gold mine in Indonesia. The operator of the Grasberg mine manages complex social, community and environmental issues and has faced opposition from time to time. There have also been instances of violence in areas near the mine, including a series of shooting incidents along the road leading to the mining and milling operations that have resulted in three fatalities in 2009.

Page 38 The Grasberg mine has used a controlled riverine tailings management programme throughout its long history. This programme was approved by the government of Indonesia following numerous technical studies to identify the appropriate tailings management plan for the site.

Page 38 The practice of riverine tailings disposal has been subject to scrutiny for many years by a range of stakeholders, including certain Indonesian governmental authorities and some NGOs. We recognise that riverine tailings disposal has been criticised and that the World Bank does not consider it as good industry practice, in accordance with the International Finance Corporation's (IFC) 2007 Environmental, Health, and Safety Guidelines for mining.

Page 38 However, we continue to believe that the use of riverine tailings disposal at the Grasberg operation is appropriate given the extremely rugged topography, high rainfall and high seismic risk that makes construction of more conventional tailings management facilities technically challenging. We remain actively engaged in supporting the mine's operator, PT Freeport Indonesia, in reducing the impact of waste rock management and tailings disposal.

Page 38 PT Freeport Indonesia has implemented a number of significant improvements in tailings management at the Grasberg mine.

Page 38 We seek to ensure that investors understand the actions we are taking in relation to sustainable development issues and we are aware that the decision to buy or sell our shares may be influenced by their understanding of these issues. For example, the 2008 sale of a 0.6 per cent interest in Rio Tinto by the Norwegian Government Pension Fund was stated to be a result of concerns in relation to the environmental practices at the Grasberg mine.

4 Think again: how good leaders can avoid bad decisions

Andrew Campbell

I. INTRODUCTION

Events in global finance have provided an abundance of examples of how capable leaders can get it wrong. But the problem is not limited to the financial sector. Other companies, regulators and politicians make bad decisions as well. Take the decision by Bush and Blair to invade Iraq; the decision to base a new global airline alliance in Zurich that led to the bankruptcy of Swissair; and the delay in deploying the Interagency Incident Management Group while Hurricane Katrina lashed New Orleans, due to a continuing belief that the levees were holding out.

In the financial sector credit ratings agencies judged some financial instruments to have low risk, when they proved to be high risk. The regulators judged that banks, wholly dependent on the wholesale capital markets, like Northern Rock plc, were stable. Sir Fred Goodwin and his board judged that the value of ABN AMRO's assets were as stated by the auditors even after the crisis had demonstrated that it was impossible to value many derivative products. Managers at Barclay's decided that it was acceptable to submit false data into the process for calculating LIBOR. Looking back, these judgments seem incredible – what could they have been thinking? This chapter is about what goes on in the brain of someone making a decision and about why otherwise capable managers make flawed decisions.

II. HOW OUR BRAINS CAN LET US DOWN

Our brain processes were evolved to cope with the pressures facing humankind over the last million years. These processes have strengths and weaknesses. Flawed judgments are a result of the weaknesses.

According to neuroscientists the brain depends primarily on two hard-wired processes for decision-making: pattern recognition and emotional tagging.[1]

(a) Pattern Recognition

Pattern recognition is a complex process that integrates information from many parts of the brain (for vision, apparently, the brain uses 30 different parts).[2] Pattern recognition draws on previous experiences and judgments that have been stored in the memory and enables the brain to make sense of new situations. Let's consider Hurricane Katrina. Brigadier General Matthew Broderick, chief of Homeland Security Operations Center, had learned from his experiences in military operations in Vietnam and in previous hurricanes, that early reports surrounding a major event are often false. It is better to wait for a 'ground truth' from a reliable source before acting. Despite 17 reports of major flooding and levee breaches some 12 hours after Katrina struck, Broderick believed counter-information from two sources.[3] The Army Corps of Engineers reported that there were no breaches, and CNN reported residents celebrating in the French Quarter (one of the few parts of the city above sea level) who had escaped unscathed.

Broderick's pattern-recognition process told him that these sources were the 'ground truth' he had been waiting for. So he issued a situation report concluding that the levees had not been breached and went home for the night. Moreover his brain was so confident of this judgment that, the following morning, he countermanded a report issued by his subordinates in the early hours. His subordinates concluded overnight that the levees had been breached. Broderick, when he arrived at work, sent an email suggesting that his subordinates could be over-reacting and that no action should be taken until further information had come in. He did

---

[1] C. Camerer, G. Loewenstein and D. Prelec, 'Neuroeconomics: How Neuroscience Can Inform Economics' (2005) 43 *Journal of Economic Literature* 9; A. Damasio, *Descartes' Error: Emotion, Reason and the Human Brain* (New York: Putnam Publishing, 1994).

[2] V. S. Ramachandran and S. Blakeslee, *Phantoms in the Brain, Human Nature and the Architecture of the Mind* (London: Fourth Estate, 1998).

[3] R. Block and C. Cooper, *Disaster: Hurricane Karina and the Failure of Homeland Security,* (Time Books, 2006); US Congress Senate Committee, *Hurricane Katrina: The Roles of DHS and FEMA Leadership* (10 February 2006).

not alert the Interagency Incident Management Group of the disaster in New Orleans for another six hours.

Broderick's pattern-recognition process let him down. He thought he recognized ground truth. But his brain let him down in a second way. It told him to take no action until he had reliable reports of levee breaches. Unfortunately he had not experienced a hurricane in a city built below sea level. In Florida, where most hurricanes hit, floods caused by storms rapidly retreated back to the sea. Waiting for ground truth is a good strategy. In a city below sea level a different strategy is needed.

Many leaders will have had experiences similar to Broderick's. In moving to a new organization, they instinctively resorted to solutions and approaches that were successful in their previous organization and with their previous teams, only to discover that they simply don't work this time round. In conflicts, it is well known that 'generals fight the last war'. So we should expect managers to do the same. Goodwin's greatest achievement prior to ABN AMRO was the acquisition of NatWest. It should not have been a surprise to his chairman or his board that Sir Fred's pattern-recognition process locked on to ABN AMRO as another NatWest, another large poorly run bank that he could re-energize.[4]

(b) Emotional Tagging

Emotional tagging is the process by which emotional information attaches itself to the thoughts and experiences stored in our memories.[5] This emotional information tells us whether to pay attention to something or not, and it tells us what sort of action we should be contemplating (immediate or postponed, fight or flight). If parts of our brain controlling emotions are damaged, even though we retain the capacity for objective analysis, we become slow and incompetent decision makers. Emotional tagging was at play in the case of Wang Laboratories, the most successful company in the word-processing industry in the 1980s. Founder An Wang believed he had been cheated by IBM over a new technology he had invented early in his career. His dislike of IBM led him to create a proprietary operating system even though the IBM PC was clearly

---

[4] See FSA, *The Failure of the Royal Bank of Scotland* (December 2011) at 160–161, 228, 235 discussing the influence of the NatWest acquisition on the board and the CEO.

[5] A. Bechera, H. Damasio and A.R. Damasio, 'Emotion, Decision Making and the Orbitofrontal Cortex' (2000) 10 (3) *Cerebral Cortex* 295; J. LeDoux, *The Emotional Brain* (London, Simon and Schuster, 1996).

becoming the dominant standard in the industry. This flawed decision led to the company's demise in the 1990s.

Broderick was probably also misled by his emotional tags. He was schooled in the military and would, therefore, have trusted information coming from the Army Corps of Engineers more than from other sources. This positive emotional tag may well have caused him to focus on the Army Corps' report rather than the 15 or more conflicting reports.

Emotional tags will also have influenced many of the poor financial judgments. Goodwin reputedly disliked the CEO of Barclays, whose bid for ABN AMRO put the bank in play. The negative emotions derived from this would have caused him to feel good about winning the prize. The credit rating agencies were generating large revenues from rating derivative products. These positive emotions would have made them feel good about ratings that expanded the market for derivatives. Even regulators will have suffered from emotional tags. Concerns they may have had about the wholesale market will have sat alongside a recognition that they would meet fierce resistance from banks and politicians if they placed restrictions on growth.[6] We all experience the same emotional struggle when we are faced with a difficult choice, such as talking to a subordinate about poor performance. Our brain gives us many excuses, and over time, if the situation is not critical, can persuade us to do nothing.

III. THE INSTINCTIVE ROUTE TO DECISION-MAKING

Faced with a decision, our brains assess the situation using pattern recognition and arrive at a plan of action using emotional tags. Decision-making, or rather judgment forming, is, according to neuroscientists, primarily an emotional process.[7] Our unconscious weighs the emotional tags related to the situation and different action plans to arrive at a judgment of which is the best plan. This conclusion is then surfaced to

---

[6] See FSA, *The Failure of the Royal Bank of Scotland* (December 2011) at 29: 'Within this context, it is likely that, if the FSA had proposed before the first signs of the crisis (that is, before summer 2007) the measures that in retrospect appear appropriate, such proposals would have been met by extensive complaints that the FSA was pursuing a heavy-handed, gold-plating and unnecessary approach.'

[7] N. Naqvi, B. Shiv and A. Bechara 'The Role of Emotion in Decision Making' (2006) 15(5) *Current Directions in Psychological Science* 260.

our conscious brain for examination, but only after it has passed through our amygdala, the source of negative feelings, and our nucleus accumbens, the source of our positive feelings. In other words, by the time our conscious mind starts to assess the situation, our unconscious has already made a judgment and flooded our brain and our physique with feelings associated with that judgment.

It is for this reason that we are bad at spotting the distortions of our own thinking. First we cannot audit the process our unconscious used to arrive at its judgment. Second, our brains and our bodies are already flooded with feelings related to that judgment. Hence our conscious mind is often fully engaged in developing a rationale for the feelings we have, rather than exploring why the judgment we appear to have made might be wrong.

This is not to say that we are entirely powerless in the face of our unconscious. We do engage in rational thought. We consider what will happen if the plan is implemented.[8] We engage our imagination. If we encounter no problems, we will decide to follow the plan. If we spot a flaw in the plan, we will cycle back looking for another plan that fits the feelings we have. One of the benefits of the advice 'sleep on it' is that it gives an opportunity for the feelings to subside.

Our brains apparently do not naturally lay out options and evaluate alternatives. We rely on unconscious processes to bring a plan of action to our consciousness and then assess that plan to see if it makes sense. So our brains work in a 'one plan at a time' process.[9] This makes managers especially bad at reconsidering their initial pattern recognition. In fact they often do not reconsider their initial assessment of the situation unless they have cycled through two or three plans and found none that fit. Only then do they challenge their initial framing, as they look for an alternative explanation that might enable them to find a workable plan.[10]

This explains why Goodwin and his board colleagues never reconsidered the decision they had made to acquire ABN AMRO if at all possible. According to one board member, the ABN AMRO deal was discussed at more than a dozen board meetings. But each discussion was about how to do the deal rather than whether to do the deal. The initial pattern recognition that the deal was a good one was never challenged.[11]

---

[8]   G. Klein, *Sources of Power* (Cambridge, MA, MIT Press, 1999).

[9]   S. Finkelstein, J. Whitehead and A. Campbell, *Think Again* (Cambridge, MA, Harvard Business School Press, 2009).

[10]   G. Klein, *Sources of Power* (Cambridge, MA, MIT Press, 1999).

[11]   FSA, *The Failure of the Royal Bank of Scotland* (December 2011) at 178–180.

IV. RED FLAG CONDITIONS

This understanding of how the brain makes decisions enables us to identify four conditions under which flawed decisions are probable. We call these 'red flag conditions.'[12] The first condition arises when our brains may be drawing on *misleading experiences.* We may have some previous experience that is similar to the current situation, yet different in important areas that we may overlook.

William D. Smithburg became CEO of Quaker Oats Company in 1981 where he executed the successful acquisition of Gatorade – the sports drink company – in 1983. In 1994, the expanding company sought to repeat the success by acquiring another successful but underexploited drinks company – Snapple. Smithburg failed to recognize that whereas Gatorade was promoted and distributed in a traditional fashion and a rising star in its market, Snapple was a drink that was promoted in quirky, entrepreneurial ways and was already losing market share. The acquisition was disastrous, leading to the downfall of both Smithburg and Quaker itself.

Another red flag condition arises when our thinking has been primed before we begin to evaluate the situation, by previous judgments or decisions we have made that connect with the current situation in a misleading way. We refer to these as *misleading prejudgments.*

Steve Russell, the CEO of Boots UK Limited between 2000 and 2004, had a potentially misleading and strong prejudgment that Boots needed to grow and that healthcare services were an attractive opportunity. In his own words, 'I had been formulating this ambition for Boots since I was merchandising director of Boots the Chemist in the late 1980s. So, when I became CEO, I was determined to make it happen.' With hindsight, he commented: 'We did not have the know-how to make these services work. We should not have tried to do so much of it ourselves.' Other managers suggested that many of the services Boots tried to enter were inherently low-margin businesses. The decision had to be reversed in the face of significant losses and contributed to Russell's resignation.

The third red flag condition is *conflicts of interest.*

On his appointment as Head of the World Bank, Paul Wolfowitz identified to the Ethics Committee that he had indirect supervision over his lover, Ms. Shahah Ali Riza, and offered to excuse himself from any personnel decisions relating to Riza. However, over the course of the next

---

[12]   S. Finkelstein, J. Whitehead and A. Campbell, *Think Again* (Harvard, MA: Harvard Business School Press, 2009).

few months he repeatedly involved himself in decisions about her career, resulting in his eventual dismissal.

The fourth red flag condition is *inappropriate attachments*, such as the attachment we might feel to colleagues or a business when considering cost reductions.

A striking example of inappropriate attachments is that of Sir Derek Rayner, who acquired Brooks Brothers – the iconic US retail chain famous for its button-down shirts – when he was CEO of Marks and Spencer (M&S) in the 1980s. In the four years of his leadership, M&S had modernized, transformed itself from a family-run company, doubled earnings per share, and grown revenues from £2.9 billion to £4.6 billion. And yet, he paid $750 million for Brooks Brothers even though his team said it was worth only $450 million. When he announced the deal, M&S's share price fell sharply. Why did he do it?

As Judi Bevan describes in her book *The Rise and Fall of Marks & Spencer*,[13] Rayner '… was enamored with Brooks Brothers clothing, which was in large part aimed at men of Rayner's age and taste.' Although his advisers had presented six possible acquisition targets, Rayner ignored all the others and 'went straight for the preppy, upmarket Brooks Brothers chain'.

These iconic examples make good text. But we can all cite examples from our professional and personal lives in which red flag conditions have distorted our own judgments. So how can we help protect the leaders of our large organizations from making decisions based on these red flag distortions? How could we have helped Goodwin, the rating agencies or the Financial Services Authority?

V. SAFEGUARDS

The first step in reducing the number of flawed decisions is to identify red flag conditions. We are all familiar with identifying conflicts of interest. It is necessary to get equally good at identifying experiences and previous judgments that could be misleading and attachments that could be inappropriate and then put in place safeguards which will reduce the risk of a bad decision.

There are many 'safeguards', that is, additions to a decision process that can counterbalance the effects of distorted thinking. Most safeguards are well known: the challenge is to pick the right ones given our

---

[13]   J. Bevan, *The Rise and Fall of Marks & Spencer … And How It Rose Again*, 2nd edn (London, Profile Books, 2007).

understanding of the likely cause of the distortion. For example, a presentation from an expert consultant might be a suitable safeguard for a decision maker who has misleading experiences about a new market entry. However, if that decision maker is the chief executive who has strong prejudgments and self-interest, the situation will need a stronger safeguard – perhaps robust challenge from the Chairman or Board.

Safeguards can be grouped into four categories:

Experience, data, and analysis. In business, there are many ways data can be collected and experience broadened. A discussion with a key customer can provide valuable feedback on a proposed new product. Market research might evaluate the risks of entering a new market. Consultants could be brought in, partly for their expertise and readily available manpower, but also because they are more objective. BP plc, under John Browne, sometimes employed two firms of lawyers for very important decisions, such as major acquisitions, in order to get contrasting opinions.

Debate and challenge. Creating a debate amongst the decision makers which challenges assumptions and forces options onto the table can be a powerful safeguard. It need not involve elaborate processes. It could mean simply chatting through an issue with a friend or colleague. But in large organizations a typical approach is to form a decision group. The membership of the group, the leader of the group and the process the group follows are all important choices that can be adjusted depending on the red flags. For example, groups can split the authorizer, evaluator, and proposer roles to promote more debate. Members can be allocated 'hats' representing different debating styles (as suggested by the lateral thinker, Edward de Bono)[14] or the group can appoint a devil's advocate whose job is to produce arguments against the emerging consensus.

Governance. The decision group will debate options and develop a point of view. But above the decision group there are often further levels of management or governance. If not, they can be created. This is the main role of the supervisory board in the European governance system, the non-executive directors in the UK system and the House of Lords in Britain's democracy. These extra layers act as a long stop: to catch the flawed proposal before the final decision is made.

---

[14] See 'Six Thinking Hats' at http://www.debonothinkingsystems.com/tools/6hats.htm

Monitoring. If all else fails, there is one final safeguard: monitoring the decision after it has been made. By setting clear milestones and monitoring performance against these milestones a bad decision can be quickly spotted and corrective action taken. Clearly, this safeguard is not effective for some decisions, such as an acquisition or a declaration of war. But it was monitoring that enabled Matthew Broderick to change his judgment, even if late; and it was monitoring that caused Boots to reverse its health and wellbeing diversifications.

While it might be discouraging to discover that the brains of our leaders (and us) are predisposed to make errors of judgment under certain conditions, it is a reality we need to come to terms with. Most organizations already recognize this reality when dealing with conflicts of interest. In fact, in law, directors are required to avoid conflicts of interest.[15] But we are less aware of the other red flag conditions, and we have not developed governance processes to effectively deal with the reality.

While the Walker review calls for more challenge in boardrooms,[16] it fails to deal with the reality that challenge is largely avoided by non-executives, not least for reasons of self-interest. It is uncomfortable challenging an expert (the CEO) who is supported by other experts (the executive directors) when all the information available for debate is provided by those selling the proposal. If we are to face up to the insights that decision neuroscience has given us, we need more radical proposals. For example we could require that every significant board decision comes with an analysis of red flag conditions, a description of the process the decision has been through and why this process is likely to have balanced out any probable distortions. We could also require that all significant decisions are presented to the board alongside the case against. Warren Buffet has proposed that acquisition proposals involving payment with equity should be accompanied by a consultant report arguing against the deal, and that the consultant compensation should depend on the deal not going ahead.

For most managers, these suggestions smack of absurd bureaucracy. But I suspect that the same criticism was made when finance academics suggested the use of discounted cash flow analysis or when governance

---

[15] Companies Act 2006 s.175 and s.177.
[16] D. Walker, *A Review of Corporate Governance in UK Banks and Other Financial Industry Entities: Final Recommendations* (26 November 2009) (The Walker Review), Recommendation Six.

experts first argued for independent chairmen. Until we face up to the causes of bad decisions, we are unlikely to make much advance in reducing them.

5 Shareholder activism and litigation against UK banks – the limits of company law and the desperate resort to human rights claims?

Roman Tomasic and Folarin Akinbami*

I. INTRODUCTION

Any study of shareholder litigation against directors of listed companies risks concluding almost as soon as it has begun. A major reason for this is the general lack of such cases, especially when a comparison is made with other common law jurisdictions such as the US and Australia.[1] In contrast there has been much more shareholder litigation in regard to UK private companies. Most shareholder derivative claims in the UK and Australia involve private companies and not public companies.[2] One

* We are grateful for funding from the Leverhulme Trust (project: Tipping Points project). We would also like to thank the British Academy for funding some data collection under the Stakeholders and Gatekeepers in Corporate Governance project funded under Co-Reach Project 64–033. An earlier version of this chapter was presented at the Conference on 'Directors Duties and Shareholder Litigation in the Wake of the Financial Crisis', The Centre for Business Law and Practice, University of Leeds, 20 September 2010. We would like to thank the participants at this conference for comments and feedback. We would also like to thank Ms Natalie Etchells LLB (Durham) for her assistance in collecting the statistics in the empirical section of the chapter.
1 See generally J. Armour, B.S. Black, B.R. Cheffins and R. Nolan, 'Private Enforcement of Corporate Law: An Empirical Comparison of the UK and the US' (2009) 6 *Journal of Empirical Legal Studies* 687; M. Legg, 'Shareholder Class Actions in Australia: The Perfect Storm' (2008) 31 *University of New South Wales Law Journal* 669.
2 See generally J. Loughrey, A. Keay and L. Cerioni, 'Legal Practitioners, Enlightened Shareholder Value and the Shaping of Corporate Law' (2008) 8 *Journal of Corporate Law Studies* 79; R. B. Thompson and R. S. Thomas, 'The

might have expected to find that the recent financial crisis might have provided opportunities for legal actions to be brought against directors of loss-making banks and other financial institutions, but this has not happened.

Bank depositors have been reassured by an enhanced depositor protection scheme and have returned to the prevailing level of trust that they tended to have for banks before the crisis. The crisis facing highly leveraged financial institutions was triggered by a liquidity crisis. This liquidity crisis saw banks refuse to lend to each other because of their fears concerning the quality of the securities being offered – this crisis of trust between banks continues to some extent today. So, what are the prospects for further litigation? Banks are unlikely to sue each other for the failures that have occurred as they all have similar stories to tell and their relationships with each other are too important to be damaged by public litigation.[3] What then are the prospects for shareholder litigation in response to misconduct or breach of duties in UK banks? The short answer is that shareholder litigation is unlikely, reflecting a broader failure of corporate law in the Anglo-American world.[4]

II. SOME CORPORATE LAW THEORIES ON SHAREHOLDER ACTIVISM

Those who study organizations have noted that a number of options are available to those who are dissatisfied with the way in which their organisation is operating. Hirschman famously referred to the options

---

Public and Private Faces of Derivative Lawsuits' (2004) 57 *Vanderbilt Law Review* 1747; R. B. Thompson and R. S. Thomas, 'The New Look of Shareholder Litigation: Acquisition-Oriented Class Actions' (2003) 57 *Vanderbilt Law Review* 133; and I. Ramsay and B. Saunders, 'Litigation by Shareholders and Directors: An Empirical Study of the Australian Statutory Derivative Action' (2006) 6 *Journal of Corporate Law Studies* 397.

[3] This pattern was identified some years ago by Macaulay in regard to business litigation in general; see further S. Macaulay, 'Non-Contractual Relations in Business: A Preliminary Study' (1963) 28 *American Sociological Review* 55.

[4] See generally K. Greenfield, *The Failure of Corporate Governance: Fundamental Flaws and Progressive Possibilities* (Chicago, University of Chicago Press, 2006); T. Frankel, *Trust and Dishonesty: America's Business Culture at a Crossroad* (Oxford, Oxford University Press, 2006).

which he described in the title of his book as 'Exit, Voice and Loyalty'.[5] In the context of shareholder action a variety of combinations of these strategies is available. Thus, the resort to the 'exit' option may see shareholders simply sell their shares and exit the company.

At the other end of the spectrum from the exit option is the 'loyalty' option under which shareholders remain docile and hold on to their shares for the long term. However, a small group of loyal shareholders may voice their concerns, but they are usually a small minority, as most make a rational calculation that any action upon their part will be too costly. Thus some bank shareholders may simply have high levels of trust in their banks and banks often emphasize the importance of trust for their business. Many people have a high degree of trust in their banks, even though they may distrust individual bankers.[6]

Exclusive resort to the 'voice' option may see shareholders seeking to engage with directors and senior management of the company to voice corporate governance concerns. As we have seen, voice may also be associated with either exit or loyalty decisions. Voice may take a variety of forms; one of these is the resort to litigation against the company or its officers. However this litigation option encounters another general obstacle in the form of what Olson referred to as 'the logic of collective action'.[7] Individual rational calculations regarding the cost of litigation will dissuade some shareholders from taking action on their own unless their costs are significantly lower than those of others. In this context it is interesting to note that action against BAE Systems in regard to bribery allegations was taken by a public interest group, Corner House, and not by its larger shareholders.[8] It may be that public money would be well spent funding similar public interest actions against banks.

Reviewing the nature of legal claims that shareholders might make is important in the context of the dominance of the director primacy model in managing companies. This model promotes maximizing shareholder

---

[5]   A.O. Hirschman, *Exit, Voice and Loyalty: Responses to Decline in Firms, Organizations, and States* (Cambridge, Harvard University Press, 1970).

[6]   P. Sapienza and L. Zingales, 'Financial Trust Index the Results: Wave IV' Chicago Booth/Kellogg School, at: http://www.financialtrustindex.org/results wave4.htm; M. Knell and H. Stix, *Trust in Banks? Evidence from Normal Times and from Times of Crises,* (Working Paper 158), Vienna, Oesterreichische Nationalbank, 2009.

[7]   M. Olson, *The Logic of Collective Action: Public Goods and the Theory of Groups* (Cambridge, Harvard University Press, 1971).

[8]   See further *R (on the Application of Corner House Research Campaign) v Director of the Serious Fraud Office and BAE Systems plc* [2008] EWHC 714 (Admin*)*.

wealth, but leaves all critical business decisions in the company to the board and the company's management. This need not be a bad thing if directors are well-qualified and are not subject to constant pressure to achieve short term performance goals. These pressures, to a large degree, come from institutional investors themselves.[9] So rather than being seen as the solution, short-term oriented institutional investors may actually be part of the problem.

There are many ways of looking at the roles that are uppermost in the minds of shareholders; the approach shareholders take to their role in the company will indicate what response can or should be expected of them with regard to the enforcement of their legal rights and claims; the particular perspective adopted may not lead to litigation and might simply lead to the use of the 'exit' option of sale of shares. Thus, insofar as public companies are concerned, Jennifer Hill pointed out that there has been a massive movement away from the nineteenth century view of shareholders as owners, even if the nexus of contracts view points to a principal-agent relationship between shareholders and directors.[10]

This saw a move to Berle's view of shareholders as beneficiaries for whom managerial powers were held by directors in trust, but where shareholders were not to participate in corporate governance.[11] With the rise of large corporations this trust-orientated view has been discredited by judges in more recent times. Another view of shareholders was that of 'bystanders' to managerial power in the ascendancy; this view continued into the twentieth century. On some occasions, shareholders have been seen as participants in a system of private government within the corporation which has seen the advocacy of corporate constitutionalism by writers such as Bottomley.[12]

A variation of the view of the shareholder as bystander is that of shareholders as investors who merely contribute capital without wanting to have a role in managing the company, as Henry Manne had articulated

---

[9]   See for example L. E. Mitchell, 'The Board as a Path Toward Corporate Social Responsibility' in D. McBarnet, A. Voiculescu and T. Campbell (eds), *The New Corporate Accountability: Corporate Social Responsibility and the Law* (Cambridge, Cambridge University Press, 2007).

[10]   J. Hill, 'Visions and Revisions of the Shareholder' (2000) 48 *American Journal of Comparative Law* 39.

[11]   A.A. Berle, 'Corporate Powers as Powers in Trust' (1931) 44 *Harvard Law Review* 1049. The contrary view was expressed by Dodd in M.E. Dodd, 'For Whom are Corporate Managers Trustees?' (1932) 45 *Harvard Law Review* 1145.

[12]   S. Bottomley, 'From Contractualism to Constitutionalism: A Framework for Corporate Governance' (1997) 19 *Sydney Law Review* 277.

it.[13] Yet another version of the shareholder role identified by Hill is that of the shareholder as guardian or monitor of managerial decision-making.

Finally, Hill points to an emerging and somewhat disturbing image of the institutional shareholder as a 'Managerial Partner' with management in the task of controlling the company's decision making. Hill notes that this partnership between institutional investors and management helps to legitimize managerial power and maximize outcomes for shareholders. The dark side of this phenomenon is that it is occurring at the same time as labour interests are being 'decollectivised' which has seen a decline in employee wages whilst executive remuneration has skyrocketed.[14]

In such a situation of proximity between institutional shareholders and corporate management, the prospects for institutional shareholder litigation against management are probably much reduced. This is especially so because the managers of institutional investment funds are themselves rewarded in the same way as managers of the companies in which they invest. In the US Lawrence Mitchell has noted that:

> 'The problem is that institutions had their own short-term pressures. In particular, their compensation systems were structured in a manner that rewarded fund managers for their quarterly performance. If the institutions – or those who managed them – were to use their power for anything, the natural financial incentive would be for them to use their power to increase their own compensation. And so they did.'[15]

It would be surprising if similar tendencies were not evident in the UK.

III. IN THE SHADOW OF THE WALKER REVIEW

One of the findings from official inquiries into the global financial crisis and its effects in the UK is that shareholders were remarkably docile during the height of the market euphoria, with little if any effort being made by them to constrain banks from their more risky business

---

[13] H. Manne, 'Our Two Corporation Systems: Law and Economics' (1967) 53 *Virginia Law Review* 259 at 260–261.

[14] See J. Hill, 'Visions and Revisions of the Shareholder' (2000) 48 *American Journal of Comparative Law* 39, text around footnotes 171 to 184.

[15] L. E. Mitchell, 'The Board as a Path Toward Corporate Social Responsibility' in D. McBarnet, A. Voiculescu and T. Campbell (eds), *The New Corporate Accountability: Corporate Social Responsibility and the Law* (Cambridge, Cambridge University Press, 2007) at 301. Also see L. E. Mitchell, *Corporate Irresponsibility: America's Newest Export* (New Haven, Yale University Press, 2001).

strategies; this applied to small shareholders as well as to larger institutional investors. The final report of the *Walker Review into Corporate Governance in UK Banks and Other Financial Institutions* noted that 'there appears to have been a widespread acquiescence by institutional investors and the market in the gearing up of the balance sheet of banks as a means of boosting returns on equity'.[16] In other words banks were allowed to assume significantly increased indebtedness by shareholders who hoped for greater dividends or rises in the value of shares. Shareholder greed therefore played a part in explaining their docility. This had the effect of aggravating various problems experienced by banks.

Traditionally, it is believed that shareholders should be able to deal with many of the internal problems of the corporation by using internal mechanisms, such as the election and dismissal of directors and the passage of resolutions at general meetings. However, these tools are not as effective as our legal theory of self-regulating corporations would assume. It is therefore left to other market mechanisms, such as price signals and the threat of takeover, to challenge directors or to gain their attention in listed companies.

However the theory that poor corporate governance in a company will lead to a new management team seeking to take over the company is often questionable as many other reasons usually drive takeover activity (as with the Cadbury takeover by Kraft) and companies that have been the subject of a takeover are not necessarily any more efficient and often fail. Takeover rules may also constrain shareholders and directors to a large extent.[17]

Walker approached this problem in terms of failures in the responsibility of shareholders as owners; he noted that they would often simply sell their shares if they had concerns about the company, and he therefore

---

[16]   D. Walker, *A Review of Corporate Governance in UK Banks and other Financial Industry Entities: Final Recommendations* (26 November 2009) at para 5.10. This can be contrasted with the view that it is not reasonable to expect institutional investors to shoulder the bulk of the burden of corporate governance since regulators, auditors and professional bodies also have a role to play in the corporate governance of banks and other financial companies, see F. Curtiss, I. Levine and J. Browning, 'The Institutional Investor's Role in Responsible Ownership' in I. MacNeil and J. O'Brien (eds) *The Future of Financial Regulation* (Oxford, Hart Publishing, 2010).

[17]   See generally D. Kershaw, 'The Illusion of Importance: Reconsidering the UK's Takeover Defence Prohibition' (2007) 56 *International and Comparative Law Quarterly* 267.

called for a more effective stewardship role for major shareholders. He explained that:

'As a matter of public interest, a situation in which the influence of major shareholders in their companies is principally executed through market transactions in the stock cannot be regarded as a satisfactory ownership model, not least given the limited liability that shareholders enjoy.'[18]

In some respects this was a repeat of a call by the Hampel Committee to bring about an increased governance role for institutional investors.[19] Similar efforts were also made in the subsequent Myners report.[20] However, this strategy has not been without its critics.[21]

Often, fund managers and senior management of companies have been more concerned with short-term share prices than with longer term performance of their companies. Walker therefore urged that fund managers consider adopting a 'commitment to a stewardship obligation' where this could be done within the terms of their mandate so as to more effectively hold company management to account. As he observed:

'Some governance by owners is essential, at least in respect of the selection, composition and performance of boards, if boards and the executive of listed companies are to be appropriately held to account in discharge of their agency role to their principals. Shareholders who do not exercise such governance oversight are effectively free-riding on the governance efforts of those that do.'[22]

Not surprisingly, Walker found that the failure of institutional investors to seek to engage with management of banks and other financial institutions

---

[18] D. Walker, *A Review of Corporate Governance in UK Banks and other Financial Industry Entities: Final Recommendations* (26 November 2009) at para 5.7.

[19] R. Hampel, Committee on Corporate Governance *Report of the Committee on Corporate Governance*, (London, Gee, 1998).

[20] P. Myners, *Institutional Investment in the UK: A Review* (London, HM Treasury, 2001).

[21] See for example R. Webb, M. Beck and R. McKinnon 'Problems and Limitations of Institutional Investor Participation in Corporate Governance', (2003) 11 *Corporate Governance: An International Review* 65.

[22] D. Walker, *A Review of Corporate Governance in UK Banks and other Financial Industry Entities: Final Recommendations* (26 November 2009) at para 5.8.

meant that they had 'little impact in restraining management before the recent crisis phase.'[23] He observed generally that:

'Company performance will be influenced, directly or indirectly, actively or passively, by the initiatives and decisions that shareholders or their fund management agents take or choose not to take.'[24]

This observation applies as much to internal efforts to engage with management as to external efforts, such as the pursuit of litigious strategies, although Walker would no doubt frown upon the use of the latter. As already noted, often disgruntled shareholders may simply decide to sell their shares if they are unhappy with the way that a company is being managed. This might be a 'blunt' means of communicating discontent of a major shareholder to the board, but it may also be justified by institutional investors in view of the fiduciary duties owed by fund managers.[25] Thus while the exit option is a blunt form of market signalling, it is also necessary to examine what internal mechanisms are available to discontented shareholders who are prepared to take action of this kind.

The Walker Report strongly advocates use of the 'engagement option' and takes the view that such early intervention will save money in the long run.[26] Walker urged the adoption of ideas found in the Code of Responsibility of Institutional Investors (prepared by the Institutional Shareholders' Committee in 2009) and the reissue of these principles, almost unchanged, by the Financial Reporting Council as a Stewardship Code. Principle 5 of the Code states that 'Institutional investors should be willing to act collectively with other investors where appropriate.'[27]

The Stewardship Code also uses the familiar 'comply or explain' model; fund managers would be required to clearly state on their websites whether they adhered to the Stewardship Code, or to some other business model if the Stewardship Code is seen as being too onerous, and

---

[23]   Ibid at para 5.10.

[24]   Ibid at para 5.2.

[25]   Ibid at para 5.2; also see generally the discussion in G. Stapledon, 'Institutional Investors: What are their Responsibilities as Shareholders?' in J. Parkinson, A. Gamble and G. Kelly (eds) *The Political Economy of the Company* (Oxford, Hart Publishing, 2000).

[26]   D. Walker, *A Review of Corporate Governance in UK Banks and other Financial Industry Entities: Final Recommendations* (26 November 2009) at para 5.31.

[27]   Financial Reporting Council (FRC), *The UK Stewardship Code* (July 2010) (the Stewardship Code) at Principle 5.

requiring those institutions that are committed to this form of engagement to 'participate in a [FRC] survey to monitor adherence to the
Stewardship Code'.[28]

The Stewardship Code proposals are relatively modest and, judging on
past performance with soft law codes, are of doubtful effect. The one
area where there are prospects for greater activism by institutional
investors is in regard to foreign institutions but these will not be subject
to the Code.[29] This raises serious questions regarding the potential
efficacy of the Stewardship Code.[30] While the UK's efforts to foster soft
law codes of conduct made considerable progress in the 1990s and were
widely adopted in other parts of the world,[31] the limits of these codes
have been increasingly recognized over the last decade.[32] The fact
that foreign institutions will not be subject to the Code and the fact that
the Code is soft law are both potential constraints on shareholder
activism.

Another constraint on shareholder activism is the 'free rider' problem.
In a country like the UK where share ownership is not concentrated
among a few shareholders but is instead widely dispersed, an activist
shareholder incurs substantial costs relative to the size of its shareholding
while other shareholders share in the rewards without incurring any
costs.[33] As Walker admitted, fund managers may be reluctant to spend
their members' funds on actions which may have significant free-rider
benefits to those who do not contribute to the cost of such action; Walker

---

[28] D. Walker, *A Review of Corporate Governance in UK Banks and other
Financial Industry Entities: Final Recommendations* (26 November 2009) at
Recommendations 18, 19 and 20.

[29] See further, M. M. Siems, *Convergence in Shareholder Law* (Cambridge,
Cambridge University Press, 2008) at 118.

[30] B. R. Cheffins, 'The Stewardship Code's Achilles Heel' (2010) 73
Modern Law Review 985 at 1017–1023.

[31] Cheffins has noted that Britain was something of an exporter in so far as
Codes were concerned: B. Cheffins, 'Corporate Governance Reform: Britain as
an Exporter' at http://ssrn.com/abstract=215950.

[32] See generally, E Wymeersch, 'Corporate Governance Codes and Their
Implementation' (2006) at http://ssrn.com/abstract=931100; for another general
study see R. V. Aguilera, and A. Cuervo-Cazurra, 'Codes of Good Governance'
(2009) 17 *Corporate Governance: An International Review* 376.

[33] I. MacNeil, 'Activism and Collaboration Among Shareholders in UK
Listed Companies', (2010) 5 *Capital Markets Law Journal* 419 at 428.

listed this as the first reason why there was unwillingness among fund managers to use resources on enhanced engagement efforts.[34]

A more significant constraint is that any individual fund manager will have spread their funds around a number of firms so that it will by itself not have sufficient shareholdings in any one firm to have much influence if it decides to place pressure upon the company internally. Fund managers invest in several companies in order to minimise risk, diversify income streams for their funds and sometimes to comply with legal requirements, and in so doing, generate increased profits for their funds. This means that their holdings in any one company are relatively small.[35] It has, however, been argued that such fragmented share ownership poses a major stumbling block to shareholder activism by institutional investors and therefore significantly limits the chances of the Stewardship Code being a success.[36]

Institutional shareholders' capacity for concerted action is also seriously handicapped by, for example, rules regulating the activities of shareholders if they act in concert.[37] Where institutional shareholders hold more than ten per cent of a company's shares, they face regulatory constraints when they seek to collaborate and so cannot easily be involved in collective negotiation and engagement efforts with other shareholders without triggering some regulatory (takeover) rules.[38] Walker saw the need for the introduction of 'safe harbour' rulings to facilitate such collective actions by shareholders.[39] Very conveniently, both the Takeover Panel and the FSA issued guidance notes to deal with cases such as this.[40] The complexity of these arrangements nevertheless

---

[34] D. Walker, *A Review of Corporate Governance in UK Banks and Other Financial Industry Entities: Final Recommendations* (26 November 2009) at para 5.16.

[35] See generally, M.M. Siems *Convergence in Shareholder Law* (Cambridge: Cambridge University Press, 2008) at 288–289.

[36] B. R. Cheffins, 'The Stewardship Code's Achilles Heel' (2010) 73 *Modern Law Review* 985 at 1020–1023.

[37] F. Curtiss, I. Levine and J. Browning, 'The Institutional Investor's Role in Responsible Ownership' in I. MacNeil and J. O'Brien (eds) *The Future of Financial Regulation* (Oxford, Hart Publishing, 2010) at 309–310.

[38] D. Walker, *A Review of Corporate Governance in UK Banks and other Financial Industry Entities: Final Recommendations* (26 November 2009) at para 5.44.

[39] Ibid at para 5.45.

[40] The Takeover Panel noted these concerns and issued Practice Note 26 on 9 September 2009 to clarify circumstances in which collective initiatives by shareholders would be seen as being 'control seeking'; see further at http://www.

raises further obstacles to effective collective action against unresponsive boards.[41] However, these regulatory constraints do not apply to litigation against the company, unless the actions are taken in a takeover context.

On the other hand, the problems faced by individual small shareholders seeking to take action within the company are even greater than those facing larger shareholders. Thus, Walker noted that:

'individual shareholders acting alone face almost insuperable barriers to successful participation in engagement activity, while the costs of gathering information and co-ordinating large numbers of small investors make it impossible for them to have any meaningful impact on governance.'[42]

It was for this reason that Walker urged that a new engagement model be adopted by institutional shareholders in UK companies. Yet while individual shareholders face considerable obstacles to initiating effective litigation against their companies, institutional investors are not necessarily in a superior position. Siems points to research showing that institutional investors 'are typically more informed and experienced than private investors ... [but] ... institutional investors are regarded as more risk-averse and conservative than other shareholders.'[43]

Although institutions may seem to have more resources, they are also subject to their mandates and they often usually adopt a short-term or quarterly view of stock prices. As a result, they may not be the solution to corporate governance problems that Walker suggests. These handicaps also apply to litigious actions that shareholders may contemplate.

---

takeoverpanel.org.uk/wp-content/uploads/2008/11/PS26.pdf. The EU Acquisitions Directive (Directive 2007/44/EC) also requires that persons who act in concert notify the FSA where there is an intention to acquire more than ten per cent of shares in a company. The FSA has sought to provide some flexibility in this regard with guidance (issued on 19 August 2009) as to how it would deal with such activist shareholder actions; see further D. Walker, *A Review of Corporate Governance in UK Banks and other Financial Industry Entities: Final Recommendations* (26 November 2009) at 152.

[41]   In Annex 7 of his Final Recommendations, Walker referred to the obstacles created by Rule 9 of the Takeover Code which seek to regulate collective initiatives by shareholders which may lead to a degree of control over a company on an on-going basis: see Walker ibid at 151.

[42]   D. Walker, *A Review of Corporate Governance in UK Banks and other Financial Industry Entities: Final Recommendations* (26 November 2009) Ibid at para 5.16.

[43]   M. M. Siems, *Convergence in Shareholder Law* (Cambridge, Cambridge University Press, 2008) at 118.

In any event, Walker's suggested engagement between institutional shareholders and their companies is a somewhat benign form of interaction. For example, one form of institutional activism in the use of voting powers occurs in narrow and somewhat contentious circumstances, such as the appointment and remuneration of directors, board composition and strategic issues affecting the rights of shareholders.[44] Walker however cautions against institutional shareholders organizing negative votes against management proposals because of the 'potential embarrassment and tension that may surround negative voting'.[45] Surely this should not be the criterion which influences the way in which institutional investors exercise their duties as shareholders.

It is interesting to contrast this attitude with the approach taken by a number of institutional investors when News Corporation sought to relocate to Delaware and to strengthen managerial power vis-à-vis shareholders; in that situation a group of institutional investors commenced legal proceedings against News Corporation in the Delaware courts.[46]

But for Walker a negative vote should only be used 'as a last resort'.[47] This cautious attitude mirrors previous practices by institutions as the situations in which they were likely to take such negative action before the financial crisis were relatively rare, and one doubts that a rebranded Stewardship Code will be likely to lead to more strident action on the part of fund managers.[48] Walker acknowledges that:

> 'The limited institutional efforts at engagement with several UK banks appear to have had little impact in restraining management before the recent crisis

---

[44] See further C. Mallin, 'Institutional Investors: The Vote as a Tool of Governance' (2010) *Journal of Management and Governance* 1.

[45] D. Walker, *A Review of Corporate Governance in UK Banks and other Financial Industry Entities: Final Recommendations* (26 November 2009) at para 5.48.

[46] See further *UniSuper Ltd v News Corporation* (2005) WL 3529317 (Del Ch)); this case is discussed at length in J. Hill, 'The Shifting Balance of Power between Shareholders and the Board: News Corp's Exodus to Delaware and Other Antipodean Tales' Sydney Law School Research Paper No. 08/20 at http://ssrn.com/abstract=1086477; J. Hill, 'Subverting Shareholder Rights: Lessons from News Corp's Migration to Delaware' (2010) 63 *Vanderbilt Law Review* 1.

[47] D. Walker, *A Review of Corporate Governance in UK Banks and Other Financial Industry Entities: Final Recommendations* (26 November 2009) at para 5.49.

[48] I. MacNeil, 'Activism and Collaboration Among Shareholders in UK Listed Companies' (2010) 5 *Capital Markets Law Journal* 419.

phase, and it is noteworthy that levels of voting against bank resolutions rarely exceeded 10 per cent.'[49]

If this continues to be the case we will need to look outside the corporation to see if more effective intervention might be available in the event of failure of internal mechanisms.[50] However apart from resort to the FRC's Codes, Walker appeared reluctant to urge greater legalization of corporate governance responses. As his report noted:

'The implicit preference embedded in the current UK corporate governance model is to focus principal attention on key matters such as the qualities of directors, the functioning of boards and appropriate incentive structures, with primary legislation and black letter regulation reserved for a limited array of prescriptive rules related to explicit obligations relating to disclosure and fiduciary duties.'[51]

The strong conservative message that is implicit in the approach adopted by Walker is consistent with his background as a banker and helps to explain the support that his report has received from successive UK governments. He preferred to see improvements made to strengthen 'an overall culture of good governance' and opposed any resort to refining provisions of the Companies Act 2006 as being likely to undermine this culture and introduce a legalistic culture.[52] In these circumstances Walker warned of the dangers of litigation if his preferred model was not followed and he argued that:

---

[49]   D. Walker, *A Review of Corporate Governance in UK Banks and Other Financial Industry Entities: Final Recommendations* (26 November 2009) at 5.10.

[50]   The EU Commission announced in June 2010 that it intended to undertake a corporate governance review which would include an examination of institutional investors' adherence to 'stewardship codes' of best practice': see EU Commission, Green Paper on Corporate Governance in Financial Institutions and Remuneration Policies (COM(2010) 285) (June 2010) at http://ec.europe.eu/internal_market/company/docs/modern/com2010_284_en.pdf. It is obviously too soon to know what these outcomes will be, but these stewardship ideas are not new.

[51]   D. Walker, *A Review of Corporate Governance in UK Banks and Other Financial Industry Entities: Final Recommendations* (26 November 2009) at para 1.17.

[52]   Ibid at para 2.23.

'Migration from this model to a wider statutory approach would have profound implications, including not least the possibility that it would increase the vulnerability of boards to litigation.'[53]

He therefore emphasized that new legislation or regulations should not be pursued as these '… may have little or no comparative advantage or relevance' when seen in the context of 'the powerful influence exerted by the FSA Handbook and the Combined Code process'.[54] This was of course a very narrow view as it ignores the fact that both kinds of approaches are required if there is to be adequate accountability.[55] It also ignores the vast body of academic research literature on litigation that emphasizes the value of 'bargaining in the shadow of the law' and which sees it as a powerful tool; most cases of such bargaining do not lead to cases getting into the courtroom. But Walker effectively rejected the use of legal rules and litigation and instead placed a high degree of faith in informal codes and the somewhat erratic comply or explain approach to corporate governance that has been adopted.[56]

Walker's championing of institutional investor engagement as the primary method of securing improved corporate governance and account-ability largely ignores the counter-tendency that is so often discussed in the corporate law literature, namely, the rise of powerful boards and chief executives, or what has come to be accepted as the Director Primacy model of the corporation.[57] Under this 'nexus of contracts' inspired model the participation rights of shareholders are limited, but re-emerge in the form of the stated commitment of directors to seek to maximize shareholder welfare. In this way, shareholders are seen as beneficiaries, but are expected to remain on the sidelines or as 'bystanders'.[58] The

---

[53]   Ibid at para 1.18.

[54]   Ibid at para 1.20.

[55]   See generally: D. McBarnet, A. Voiculescu, and T. Campbell (eds), *The New Corporate Accountability: Corporate Social Responsibility and the Law* (Cambridge, Cambridge University Press, 2007); also see J. Braithwaite, *Regulatory Capitalism: How it Works, Ideas for Making it Work Better* (Cheltenham, Edward Elgar, 2008).

[56]   This is not the place to engage in a more detailed discussion of the reliability of Codes like the UK Code of Corporate Governance.

[57]   See further S. Bainbridge, 'Director Primacy and Shareholder Disempow-erment' (2006) 119 *Harvard Law Review* 1735. Also see S. Bainbridge, *The New Corporate Governance in Theory and Practice* (Oxford, Oxford University Press, 2008).

[58]   J. Hill, 'Visions and Revisions of the Shareholder' (2000) 48 *American Journal of Comparative Law* 39, especially references at footnote 152.

managerial powers given to directors and the operation of the 'business judgment' rule makes it very difficult for shareholders to effectively challenge the dominance of directors in company decision making.[59] Our last line of defence in the UK seems to be the introduction of 'enlightened shareholder value' policies.[60] This approach offers the potential to be successful but whether or not it will ultimately be successful remains to be seen.

So where are we to go from here? The above discussion of the potential for shareholder activism within the corporation helps to identify the constraints that may be placed upon shareholder activism were it to be expressed in the form of litigation against the company or its officers; one can only suspect that there would not be much enthusiasm amongst institutions for this given the difficulties of generating action within the company itself.

The financial press has long played a significant role in shining light upon corporate governance failures. A good example of this is the criticism in the financial press of Sir Stuart Rose's continued role as Chairman at Marks and Spencer after his service as CEO. But despite its value, the press has its limits in monitoring the complex internal affairs of large listed companies.

Another means of external action is the use of more strident regulatory techniques, such as the FSA's fines on Northern Rock officers for actions taken in selling products prior to the onset of the crisis. A more active regulator is much to be welcomed, after the FSA's unsatisfactory experience with light-touch regulation.[61] This strident regulatory approach would apply especially in regard to regulated financial institutions, but the funding resources available to regulators for litigation are limited and sometimes need to be supplemented by government in high profile cases.[62]

---

[59]   See however A. Keay, 'Company Directors Behaving Poorly: Disciplinary Options for Shareholders' (2007) *Journal of Business Law* 656 and J. Hill, 'The Rising Tension Between Shareholders and Director Power in the Common Law World' (2010) 18 *Corporate Governance: An International Review* 344.

[60]   See generally S. Kairie, 'At the Crossroads: Shareholder Value, Stakeholders and Enlightened Shareholder Value: Which Road Should the UK Take?' (2006) 17 *International Company and Commercial Law Review* 329.

[61]   See generally R. Tomasic, 'Beyond "Light Touch" Regulation of British Banks after the Financial Crisis' in I. MacNeil and J. O'Brien (eds), *The Future of Financial Regulation* (Oxford, Hart Publishing, 2010).

[62]   For example, in the largest corporate prosecution in Australia following the collapse of the insurance company HIH, the Commonwealth Government made special allocations of funds to the Australian Securities Investments

This leaves resort to the courts by shareholders. However as we have seen the courts are reluctant to deal with corporate matters until all internal avenues have been exhausted by litigants. This perhaps explains why so many cases have been brought by liquidators after the failure of companies. Shareholder actions, such as litigation, involve significant costs and have uncertain outcomes. There are also the wider collective action problems in widely held companies which discourage disparate smaller shareholders from organizing themselves in order to challenge entrenched management teams, either through internal processes of the company, such as the general meeting, or through external processes, such as resort to the courts.

IV. AN OVERVIEW OF SHAREHOLDER LITIGATION IN ENGLAND AND WALES SINCE 2000

It is interesting to undertake a somewhat limited analysis of the contours of company litigation under the UK Companies Act over the last decade. Using the Westlaw internet database, cases from 2000 to 2010 which were concerned with shareholders were examined. Excluded from the count were Scottish cases, European Court of Justice cases and Privy Council cases. A total of 115 relevant cases were revealed in this search; of these, 107 cases (or 93 per cent) were brought by individual shareholders and eight cases (or 6.9 per cent) were brought by institutions.

It is notable that litigation rarely concerns public companies; thus, over this period, 92.2 per cent of cases (106 cases) concerned a private limited company, one case involved a foreign corporation whilst the remainder (eight cases or 6.9 per cent) concerned a UK public limited company. A total of 59.1 per cent (or 68 cases) were successful.[63]

Commission (ASIC). Additional funds were also allocated to ASIC to fund high profile corporate prosecutions against James Hardy, OneTel and Offset Alpine. The preparedness of governments to fund unexpected corporate actions of this kind is essential if regulators are to be effective. See further Parliament of Australia, Joint Committee on Corporations and Financial Services, *Statutory Oversight of the Australian Securities and Investments Commission* (May 2005), Ch 2 at: http://aph.gov.au/senate/committee/corporations_ctte/asic/asic_05/c02. hym at paras 2.32 to 2.40.

[63]   It might be argued that this pattern reflects what McQueen has described as the 'colonisation' of UK company law by partnerships and small firms in the late nineteenth century, so that company law mainly serves the needs of smaller

The basis of the claims made in these company related cases varied, with the most common grounds involving claims of unfair prejudice (32.2 per cent) and membership or share related issues (24.3 per cent); these two areas covered more than half of all claims made. Also, some 14.8 per cent of cases involved shareholders' agreements; derivative claims arose in eight (or 6.9 per cent) cases. Table 5.1 sets out these claims.

Table 5.1: *Type of legal claims litigated in England and Wales since 1 January 2000*

Type of legal claim	Number of cases	Percentage of total cases
Unfair prejudice (s.994 and old s.459)	37	32.2%
Membership or share issue	28	24.3%
Shareholder agreements	17	14.8%
Derivative claims	8	7.0%
Human rights or judicial review	2	1.7%
Other claims	23	20.0%
TOTAL cases	115	100%

Of the above 115 cases (there were 153 defendants in total), fewer than half of the total defendants were shareholders (43.8 per cent), although 12.4 per cent of defendants were both shareholders and directors. Companies constituted 29.4 per cent of defendants.

Most cases involved solvent companies (88.7 per cent or 102 cases) and most were applications or first instance petitions (74.7 per cent), and 25 cases (or 21.7 per cent) were on appeal; four cases involved preliminary issues.

Unfair prejudice cases: A total of 37 unfair prejudice cases were brought either under the new s.994 of the Companies Act 2006 (10 cases) or under s.459 of the Companies Act 1985 (27 cases). Only two of these cases involved public companies.[64]

---

companies: see further, R. McQueen, *A Social History of Company Law: Great Britain and the Australian Colonies 1854–1920* (Farnham, Ashgate Publishing, 2009).

[64] *Rock (Nominees) Ltd v RCO (Holdings) plc (in members' voluntary liquidation)* [2004] EWCA Civ 118; [2004] BCC 466, in which case the alleged unfair prejudice in breach of s.459 was not substantiated; and *CAS (Nominees)*

Shareholders were involved in a large proportion of these cases, with 43.3 per cent (or 23 cases) of defendants being shareholders; a third of defendants were companies (33.9 per cent) and eight directors (15 per cent) were defendants.

Membership or share issue cases: All of the membership or share issue cases involved private companies, with 96.4 per cent of these cases (or 27 cases) being brought by an individual; most of these cases were brought against other shareholders (52.9 per cent) and six defendants were shareholders/directors (17.6 per cent of defendants). The issues arising in these membership or share related claims are set out in Table 5.2 (below).

Shareholder agreement cases: Of the less than 15 per cent of cases (17) involving shareholder agreements, only one case concerned a public company,[65] and institutional shareholders were involved in making two claims, with the remaining claims being made by individuals. Of the 17 claims, 13 were successful (76.4 per cent), suggesting that the courts are more relaxed in dealing with these claims than with derivative actions (see below).

Derivative actions: Of the eight derivative action claims, only one of these involved a public company.[66] Seven cases involved individual shareholders with the remaining case being brought by an institutional shareholder. Of these cases, 37.5 per cent were successful, 25 per cent were adjourned and 37.5 per cent failed. Seven companies comprised defendants (or 46.6 per cent of defendants), with directors forming 2 per cent of defendants (or three defendants); the remaining defendants were shareholders (20 per cent) and shareholders/directors (13.3 per cent). These figures reflect a wider critique of the limited utility of derivative action proceedings.[67]

Ltd v Nottingham Forest FC plc [2002] BCC 145 in which case the alleged breach of s.459 was dismissed.

[65]   See further *Holt v Faulks*; [2000] 2 BCLC 816. In this case a shareholder applied to the court to implement a clause in a shareholder agreement and sought summary judgment against a company's former executive director seeking a transfer notice for his shares in the company.

[66]   See further *Harley Street Capital Ltd v Tchigirinsky (No 2)* [2005] EWHC 1897 (Ch); [2006] BCC 209. The court refused the application that involved claims of breaches of fiduciary duty and a dilution of the fourth defendant company's interest in a joint venture. A freezing injunction was discharged.

[67]   See generally A. Reisberg, 'Derivative Claims under the Companies Act 2006: Much Ado About Nothing?' in J. Armour and J. Payne (eds), *Rationality in Common Law: Essays in Honour of DD Prentice* (Oxford, Hart Publishing, 2009). Also see A. Keay and J. Loughrey, 'Something Old, Something New,

Human rights cases: This category is particularly interesting, bearing in mind the fact that there has been a rise in human rights cases concerning company-related matters. There were two human rights and judicial review cases initiated by shareholders during the period since 2000, both involving public companies.[68]

Both cases were defended by a government agency. The first case involved the Treasury Commissioner and arose in relation to the claims by former Northern Rock plc (Northern Rock) shareholders who challenged the basis upon which they had been compensated when Northern Rock had been nationalized. In the other case, shareholders in the Railtrack group brought an action against the Secretary of State for Transport claiming misfeasance by the Secretary for his plan to place the company into administration on the grounds of insolvency.

In both cases, the key ground relied upon by the shareholders was the claim that their property rights had been infringed in contravention of human rights provisions. It seems that all possible company law causes of action were found wanting. In the case involving Railtrack it was argued that the proposed plan infringed Article 1 of Protocol 1 of the European Convention on Human Rights contained in the Human Rights Act 1998 Schedule 1 Part II Article 1. The case involving Northern Rock shareholders also involved claims that there had been a contravention of Article 1 of Protocol 1 of the European Convention on Human Rights. The Northern Rock case will be discussed more fully in the next section.

Other cases: Of the remaining 23 cases (20 per cent of all cases), two involved public companies,[69] 20 cases concerned UK private companies and one case concerned a company that was not incorporated in the UK. Of these 23 cases, 15 involved solvent companies; four were insolvent,

---

Something Borrowed: An Analysis of the New Derivative Action under the Companies Act 2006' (2008) 124 *Law Quarterly Review* 469.

    [68]   See further *R (on the application of SRM Global Master Fund LP) v Commissioners of HM Treasury* [2009] EWCA Civ 788; [2010] BCC 558 and *Weir v Secretary of State for Transport (No 2)* [2005] EWHC 2192 (Ch).

    [69]   See further *Hall v Cable and Wireless plc* [2009] EWHC 1793 (Comm); [2011] BCC 543. In this case the shareholders claimed that the company had wrongfully failed to disclose material information to the market thereby causing loss to the shareholders. In finding for the company the court held that the defendants did not have a cause of action for breach of the listing rules or for the alleged market abuse. The second case was *Thakrar v Ciro Citterio Menswear plc (in administration)* [2002] EWHC 1975 (Ch) in which the claimant sought a declaration that the defendant company was bound by the terms of a settlement agreement. The court found in favour of the claimant ordering specific performance of the agreement.

two were under administration, one had ceased trading and one was in receivership.

One case involved an institutional shareholder and all other cases involved individual shareholders. Table 5.3 sets out the types of claims made in each of these cases, showing that the first three categories of case, winding up cases, cases involving procedural issues and administration proceedings, comprised 52.1 per cent of cases.

Table 5.2:   Membership or share-related claims in England and Wales since 1 January 2000

Type of legal claim	Number of cases (out of 28)	Percentage of total membership or share cases
• Share transfer, sale, purchase or acquisition of shares	11	39.2%
• Meeting, resolution, articles of association claim	3	10.7%
• Valuation claim	3	10.7%
• Register of members issue	3	10.7%
• Entitlement to shares issue	5	17.8%
• Entitlement to funds or assets issue	2	7.1%
• Board of directors issue	1	3.6%

Table 5.2 shows that out of the 28 membership or share related claims, 11 (39 per cent) were related to share transfers, sales, purchases or the acquisition of shares. This represents by far the largest cause of action for membership or share related claims. Interestingly only one claim (3.6 per cent) concerned an issue relating to the board of directors, suggesting that shareholders are perhaps more interested in their own personal interests as shareholders rather than their responsibilities, as owners, to hold directors to account.

The residual category of 'other claims' reported in Table 5.3 shows that winding up proceedings, administration proceedings and procedural issues comprise over half of the remaining cases. The remainder deal with a variety of legal breaches. The numbers are too small to allow for any generalizations to be made about them.

Table 5.3: *Types of legal claims made in the residual category of 23 cases*

Type of legal claim	Number of cases (out of 23)	Percentage of total cases
• Winding up proceedings	5	21.7%
• Procedural issues	5	21.7%
• Administration proceedings	2	8.7%
• Breach of agreement/deed	2	8.7%
• Negligence	2	8.7%
• Breach of Listing Rules	1	4.3%
• Deprivation of assets issue	1	4.3%
• Breach of fiduciary duty	1	4.3%
• Disqualification	1	4.3%
• Fraud	1	4.3%
• Misapplication of assets	1	4.3%
• Deceit	1	4.3%

V. THE NORTHERN ROCK PLC SHAREHOLDER APPEAL[70]

When the House of Commons Treasury Committee undertook its inquiry into the failure of Northern Rock, it focused attention primarily on the business model used by the bank and the conduct of its regulators and directors. It did not delve too deeply into the position of the Northern Rock shareholders, although it did take a fairly negative view as to their prospects when it observed that:

'It is unfortunate that the shareholders who acquired their shares as part of demutualisation and the staff of Northern Rock have suffered significantly from the fall in the value of Northern Rock shares. However, it is not possible to make a distinction between types of shareholders in the circumstances of Northern Rock. In a market environment, shareholders as a whole must be viewed as taking a risk from which they sought a reward and for which they are now paying a price.'[71]

---

[70] The following section draws upon R. Tomasic, 'Shareholder Litigation and the Financial Crisis: The Northern Rock Shareholder Appeal Considered' (2009) 262 Company Law Newsletter, October 29 2009, at 1–5.

[71] The House of Commons Treasury Committee, *The Run on the Rock* (HC 56–1) (January 2008) at 20–21.

This would not have been a comforting observation for the shareholders. The decision of the Court of Appeal in the appeal by Northern Rock shareholders following the nationalization of Northern Rock and the subsequent compulsory acquisition of their shares is an important statement of the role of legal mechanisms in periods of major financial crises. The Court's rejection of the appeal in *R (on the application of SRM Global Master Fund LP) v Commissioners of HM Treasury*[72] identified key drivers of the legal response and highlighted the relatively weak position of shareholders of banks, such as Northern Rock, that failed during the global financial crisis.

These key drivers included the legislative framework which was put in place by the UK Parliament following the passage of the Banking (Special Provisions) Act 2008. This hastily passed enactment laid down the assumptions that should be followed by the Treasury – appointed independent valuer when deciding on the amount of compensation that should be paid to former shareholders of nationalized banks.[73] In the end this meant that the resolution of the appeal largely became a matter of statutory interpretation. Also driving the legal response was the knowledge of central banks which act as lenders of last resort (LOLR) in times of crisis. The Court of Appeal was to turn to this body of economically-inspired principles to provide the basis for its decision when it accepted the importance of this body of thought, as expressed by the former Governor of the Bank of England Lord Eddie George.

Reference was made by Lord George to earlier statements regarding the LOLR that had been made by Walter Bagehot following the collapse and subsequent run on Overend, Gurney & Co in 1866. A 1993 speech delivered by Lord George served to set out the principles that the Court of Appeal regarded as fundamental in this case. In doing so, the Court of Appeal was prepared to recognise the importance of economic concepts such as 'moral hazard' as providing a basis for the policy that had been adopted by the Bank of England and the UK government.[74]

---

[72]   [2009] EWCA Civ 788; [2010] BCC 558.

[73]   See further R. Tomasic, 'The Rescue of Northern Rock: Nationalisation in the Shadow of Insolvency' (2008) 1(4) *Corporate Rescue and Insolvency* 109.

[74]   Moral hazard in banking refers to the tendency of banks to take on more risk by, for example, increasing leverage or investing in riskier assets, at the expense of the public safety net: see T. Padoa-Schioppa, *Regulating Finance: Balancing Freedom and Risk* (Oxford, Oxford University Press, 2004) at 99. Interestingly, governments were prepared to ignore this constraint when they offered financial assistance to failing firms as the concept of moral hazard was seen as less important than maintaining the stability of the banking system.

Another notable feature of this appeal is that the principal legal foundations of the shareholders' action were not found in insolvency law or in company law principles, but in the application of European human rights law concepts as developed by the European Court of Human Rights. In particular, the decision of the Court of Appeal rested on the interpretation of Article 1 of the First Protocol (A1P1) of the European Convention on Human Rights which guarantees the protection of private property.[75] The case law under this provision developed the principles to be applied in the payment of compensation following the compulsory acquisition of property by the State.[76] This meant that little room remained for the application to this case, by way of analogy or otherwise, of commercial law principles from other areas, such as the law of salvage and principles of unjust enrichment.[77]

(a) Legal and Economic Background Factors

In August 2007 Northern Rock experienced difficulties in sourcing funds to support its lending; it had grown rapidly to become the fifth largest UK mortgage lender, but relied upon an unsustainable business model that depended upon the continued availability of short term funds. The collapse of the sub-prime mortgage bubble in the US had a direct effect upon the ability of the bank to continue to operate.[78]

The failure of Northern Rock is notable in that it was seen as potentially jeopardizing the stability of the entire UK financial system.

---

[75] Article 1 provides: 'Every natural or legal person is entitled to the peaceful enjoyment of his possessions. No one shall be deprived of his possessions except in the public interest and subject to the conditions provided for by law and by the general principles of international law. The preceding provisions shall not, however, in any way impair the right of a State to enforce such laws as it deems necessary to control the use of property in accordance with the general interest or to secure the payment of taxes or other contributions or penalties.'

[76] See further T. Allen, *Property and the Human Rights Act 1998* (Oxford, Hart Publishing, 2005); also see generally R. P. Malloy, *Private Property, Community Development and Eminent Domain* (Farnham, Ashgate, 2008).

[77] *R (on the application of SRM Global Master Fund LP) v Commissioners of HM Treasury* [2009] EWCA Civ 788; [2010] BCC 558 at [64]-[66].

[78] See further R. Tomasic, 'Corporate Rescue, Governance and Risk-taking in Northern Rock: Part 1' (2008) *Company Lawyer* 297 and R. Tomasic, 'Corporate Rescue, Governance and Risk-taking in Northern Rock: Part 2' (2008) 29 *Company Lawyer* 330.

News that the company had sought financial support from the Bank of England led to a run on the bank after 13 September 2007. Thereafter the Chancellor of the Exchequer authorized the Bank of England to provide emergency support as lender of last resort (LOLR).

This support was aimed at injecting stability and confidence into the banking system and the Chancellor also sought to guarantee deposits to quell the bank run. This eventually led the Bank of England to lend some £27 billion to Northern Rock. This temporary relief was primarily aimed at stabilizing the UK banking system and avoiding contagion. Nationalization became necessary as a suitable private sector solution had not been forthcoming. Nationalization took place immediately after the passage of special legislation, the Banking (Special Provisions) Act 2008, on 21 February 2008; this enactment was replaced a year later by the Banking Act 2009.[79]

The Banking (Special Provisions) Act 2008 allowed for the making of compensation orders on designated terms. Critically, s.5(4) of this Act required an independent valuer, when making a valuation, to assume that 'all financial assistance provided by the Bank of England or the Treasury to the deposit-taker in question has been withdrawn ...' and that 'no financial assistance would in future be provided by the Bank of England or the Treasury to the deposit-taker ...'.[80]

Furthermore, the Northern Rock Plc Compensation Scheme Order 2008 (made under s.5 of the 2008 Act) provided that the amount of compensation that would be payable would be 'an amount equal to the value immediately before the transfer time of all shares in Northern Rock'[81] and that the valuer must assume that Northern Rock was 'unable to continue as a going concern' and that it was in administration.[82]

The case brought by the Northern Rock shareholders was first heard by Burton LJ and Silber J in the Queen's Bench Division, who handed down their judgment on 13 February 2009 in *R (on the application of SRM Global Master Fund LP) v Commissioners of HM Treasury*.[83] The appeal

---

[79] See further R. Tomasic, 'Creating a Template for Banking Insolvency Law Reform After the Collapse of Northern Rock: Part 1' (2009) 22(5) *Insolvency Intelligence* 65 and R. Tomasic, 'Creating a Template for Banking Insolvency Law Reform After the Collapse of Northern Rock: Part 2' (2009) 22(5) *Insolvency Intelligence* 81.

[80] Banking (Special Provisions) Act 2008 s.5(4).

[81] Northern Rock plc Compensation Scheme Order 2008 (SI 2008/718) Sch 1 Part 2 para 3.

[82] Ibid para 6.

[83] [2009] EWHC 277 (Admin); [2009] BCC 251.

was heard in June 2009 and the decision handed down on 28 July 2009.[84] Laws LJ, with whom the Master of the Rolls and Waller LJ agreed, delivered the judgment dismissing the appeal.

The shareholders bringing the appeal comprised two hedge funds (SRM and RAB) that respectively held 11.5 per cent and 8.18 per cent of the shares in Northern Rock, although these shares had been acquired after the Government announced that it would provide financial assistance to the bank. Perhaps this was the last gasp of hedge fund activism.[85] The remaining party bringing the action represented small shareholders: there were some 150,000 small shareholders at the date of the nationalisation. It is interesting to note that prior to September 2007 institutional investors had been docile and largely content to allow bank boards to engage in highly risky business strategies of the kind pursued by Northern Rock, Halifax Bank of Scotland plc (HBOS) and the Royal Bank of Scotland plc (RBS).

The Bank of England, the FSA and the Treasury, known as the Tripartite Authorities, had previously entered into a Memorandum of Understanding (MOU) regarding their respective roles in a situation of crisis. This MOU included the Bank's role as LOLR aimed primarily at reducing 'the risk of a serious problem causing wider financial or economic disruption' so as to 'minimise both moral hazard in the private sector and financial risk to the taxpayer ...'.[86]

The Court of Appeal noted that the 'precise purpose of LOLR, and the conditions under which it may be made available, are of great importance for the issues in this appeal'.[87] The court went on to quote at length from a speech by Lord George in which he explained the nature of the LOLR function of seeking to protect the system from 'contagion' and the principles that the Bank applied in exercising this function. The court quoted Lord George's statements that:

---

[84]   *R (on the application of SRM Global Master Fund LP) v Commissioners of HM Treasury* [2009] EWCA Civ 788; [2010] BCC 558.

[85]   See further J. Armour and B.R. Cheffins, 'The Rise and Fall (?) of Shareholder Activism by Hedge Funds', ECGI – Law Working Paper No 136/2009. Also see A. Klein and E. Zur, 'Entrepreneurial Shareholder Activism: Hedge Funds and Other Private Investors' (2009) 64 *Journal of Finance* 187.

[86]   Memorandum of Understanding between the Bank of England, the Financial Services Authority and HM Treasury at http://www.bankofengland.co.uk/financialstability/mou.pdf at para 15.

[87]   *R (on the application of SRM Global Master Fund LP) v Commissioners of HM Treasury* [2009] EWCA Civ 788; [2010] BCC 558 at [6].

'Our support, whatever form it takes, is directed to safeguarding the financial system ... Beyond that, there are various rules we apply. *First*, we will explore every option for a commercial solution before committing our own funds ... *Second*, central banks are not in the business of providing public subsidy to private shareholders. If we do provide support, we will try to structure it so that any losses fall first on the shareholders and any benefits come first to us ... *Third*, we aim to provide liquidity: we will not, in normal circumstances, support a bank that we know at the time to be insolvent ... *Fourth*, we look for a clear exit.'[88]

Lord George had also noted that in order to avoid 'moral hazard' (or the expectation that banks will be rescued when they act recklessly) when liquidity support is provided under a LOLR facility, the support is provided 'on terms that are as penal as we can make them'.[89] As the Court of Appeal summarized this central bank instrument: '[t]he constraints and conditions described by Lord George – last resort, selectivity, unpredictability, no comfort for the shareholders, clear exit – are all fashioned, in part at least, to avoid the hazard'.[90]

The Court of Appeal found that these principles were applied to the handling of Northern Rock. In doing so it rejected the view that the Bank of England was seeking to profit from its intervention in Northern Rock; indeed, financial modelling conducted for the government by its external advisers cast doubt upon any such profit being forthcoming.[91]

(b)   Legal Issues Before the Court of Appeal

One major and two minor legal issues dominated argument by the appellants before the Court of Appeal. The principal issue argued by the appellants was that they had been deprived of their shares for little or nothing as a result of the assumptions that had been imposed on the valuer by the Parliament. It was argued (by Lord Pannick QC) that this was in conflict with the property rights of the shareholders under A1P1 of the European Convention on Human Rights.

It was also argued that the Government was well rewarded for the financial assistance that it had provided to Northern Rock. In response, it was argued (by Jonathan Sumption QC) that the aim of the Banking (Special Provisions) Act 2008 was quite clear in seeking to put the shareholders in the same position that they would have occupied if Northern

---

[88]   Ibid at [8].
[89]   Ibid at [9].
[90]   Ibid at [11].
[91]   Ibid at [26].

Rock had not received financial support from the Government; in other words, that the business was worthless without Government support.

In finding in favour of the respondents, the Court of Appeal identified three governing principles that had emerged out of the European case law on the protection of property rights under A1P1 of the Convention. These three key principles were: '(1) the need for a fair balance to be struck between public interest and private rights; (2) the principle of proportionality; (3) the doctrine of margin of appreciation'.[92]

According to Laws LJ, the first principle requiring that a balance be struck between the public interest and private rights is the overarching principle. The next two principles provide the means by which such a balance is to be struck.[93] As for the second principle, proportionality 'allows for controlled intrusions into a right in question in pursuance of a legitimate aim; but in every case the intrusion must be proportionate to the aim'.[94] As earlier European cases have shown, there must be a 'reasonable relationship of proportionality between the means employed and the aim to be realised.[95] This would apply to the compensation terms that were offered and would ordinarily require the payment of an amount reasonably related to the value of the property taken.[96]

However these first two principles must be read with the third principle, that of the 'margin of appreciation'. This doctrine had previously been summarized by Lord Hope of Craighead in *R v DPP ex parte Kebilene*[97] and had been applied in *James v UK*,[98] which gave it a very broad meaning. It assumes that national governments are in the best position to evaluate local needs and conditions and implies that the balance between the private interest and the public interest will not be uniformly struck across every case. As the Court of Appeal stated, for example, citing *Lithgow v UK*,[99] nationalization is quite different from a compulsory purchase order given the complexity of nationalization and its objectives, and the standard of compensation payable may differ.[100]

---

[92]   Ibid at [43].
[93]   Ibid at [55].
[94]   Ibid at [46].
[95]   Ibid at [47].
[96]   Ibid at [55].
[97]   [2000] 2 AC 326 at 380.
[98]   (1986) 8 EHRR 123.
[99]   (1986) 8 EHRR 329.
[100]   *R (on the application of SRM Global Master Fund LP) v Commissioners of HM Treasury* [2009] EWCA Civ 788; [2010] BCC 558 at [52] citing *Lithgow v UK* (1986) 8 EHRR 329 at [121].

Any application of the margin of appreciation doctrine under the European Convention on Human Rights will be driven by a democratic imperative. As a result, the judiciary will defer to the opinion of the elected legislature and only interfere with its decision as to nationalisation and the level of compensation payable if the judiciary concluded that the State's judgment was manifestly unreasonable.[101] The Court of Appeal accepted that this would lead one to ask whether the assumptions in s.5(4) of the 2008 Act were 'manifestly without reasonable foundation?'[102]

As to this the court held that the assumptions in the legislation regarding the making of compensation orders were reasonable. It found that the assumptions put the shareholders in the position they would have occupied had no LOLR support been provided.[103] It concluded:

'If the shareholders had received more favourable treatment than was furnished by these arrangements, the LOLR operation would ... have been the source of a specific benefit conferred on them. That would not be consistent with a governing principle of LOLR, namely its deployment only in the interest of the financial system as a whole.'[104]

The court rejected arguments that the rescue involved no risk to the Government and that it was motivated by the desire for profit.[105] It accepted testimony from a senior Government official (Kingman) and from the Government's advisers (Goldman Sachs) that these were not the motives behind the rescue.[106] It was seen to be particularly telling that no private sector party was prepared to come to the assistance of Northern Rock, illustrating the level of perceived risk that the Government was assuming in this rescue.[107] The court also rejected arguments to the effect first that the FSA (and the Bank of England) had a duty to protect Northern Rock shareholders[108] and second that there was a failure to provide procedural safeguards to protect A1P1 rights, finding that the availability of judicial review provided such a safeguard.

The Court of Appeal adopted the view expressed in the court below that the primary responsibility for the insolvency of Northern Rock lay

---

[101] Ibid at [59] and [75].
[102] Ibid at [60] and [62].
[103] Ibid at [77].
[104] Ibid at [62].
[105] Ibid at [68]-[69].
[106] Ibid at [69].
[107] Ibid at [72].
[108] Ibid at [80]-[81].

with its management, and that its management was answerable to its shareholders, who could ultimately have removed the directors. Yet under normal circumstances the directors of Northern Rock would not have owed a legal duty to their shareholders – their duty was to the company. The inadequate state of the law on the duties of directors meant that little joy could be had from shareholder actions (whether derivative suits or otherwise) against the directors of Northern Rock. This meant that a human rights claim was something of a last resort for the appellants.[109] Overall the outcome of the Northern Rock shareholder appeal illustrates the limited scope that bank shareholders have in seeking to rely upon normal company law remedies and other avenues of redress in banking crises.

VI. CONCLUSIONS

This chapter has sought to deal with an area of some concern to company law scholars, namely, the extent to which company law is actually enforced. The traditional Holmesian view would see law as an expression of what courts do.[110] This is certainly a prevailing American and Realist view, although it is less prevalent in the UK with its long tradition of laissez faire approaches to company law.[111]

In more recent times, the emergence of institutional investors as powerful parts of the corporate landscape has raised questions about their capacity to contribute more to corporate governance and to monitor and even control aberrant management. For the last two decades the UK has sought to use soft law as a means of dealing with managerial conduct, despite the legislative codification and extension of common law rules regarding the duties of directors of UK companies. The Walker Review has been embraced by government representatives in the UK and as such we are likely to see a continuation of a voluntary soft law approach, even though its effectiveness may be questioned.

The presence of some company law litigation maintains the myth that the courts have a role to play in the enforcement of company law. To a

---

[109]   See generally R. Tomasic, 'Raising Corporate Governance Standards in Response to Corporate Rescue and Insolvency' (2009) 2 *Corporate Rescue and Insolvency* 5.

[110]   For a discussion of this theme of differences between US and UK approaches to law see W. Twining, *Globalisation & Legal Theory* (London, Butterworths, 2000).

[111]   Ibid.

certain extent the enforcement of company law does take place through the involvement of lawyers and the advice that they give to their clients. Lawyers have, however, also shaped company law in such a way that the prospects for successful litigation against directors of large public companies, such as directors of failed UK banks and financial institutions, are somewhat remote.

There is clearly a major divide in the way the courts are used by shareholders in the US and in the UK. In many ways we have tended to follow American legal ideas and it may be that (perhaps through the influence of US investment funds) we might see more company law litigation against banks and financial institutions in the UK. However the prospects for this are really quite remote.

Finally as the Northern Rock shareholder appeal has shown, even where actions are brought before the courts, it has been difficult to find causes of action that are likely to lead to successful outcomes for litigants; instead we have seen a failed resort to human rights arguments. This is, in part, a desperate attempt to overcome the difficulties associated with bringing successful shareholder actions based on more traditional company law principles. It can also perhaps be attributed to the development of public law principles of accountability which has not been contained by a market driven laissez-faire approach.

6 Recent cases on the winding-up of hedge funds on treasure islands

Robin Hollington

I. BACKGROUND AND INTRODUCTION

Lehman Brothers filed for Chapter 11 bankruptcy protection on 15 September 2008. While the aftershocks of that cataclysmic event are still being felt, one of its immediate effects was that many open-ended investment funds for sophisticated investors experienced a very high level of redemption requests by members who had completely lost confidence in their fund's investment model, at the very same time that the fund's liquidity collapsed.

Two popular jurisdictions for the establishment of such funds, or feeder funds to such funds, were the low tax off-shore financial services centres in the Caribbean, particularly the Cayman Islands and the British Virgin Islands (BVI). The laws of both jurisdictions draw heavily on the law of England, including its company and insolvency law, although there are significant differences in some respects. For example, the Cayman Islands does not have the unfair prejudice remedy, although since 2009,[1] the courts there, once satisfied that there are sufficient grounds for winding up a company on the just and equitable basis, have the same wide range of powers in a petition for such a remedy as an English court would have in an unfair prejudice petition. The BVI laws are closer to the UK: there is an unfair prejudice remedy, as well as a statutory derivative action, but the details of their respective insolvency laws diverge.

The Cayman Islands is popular with funds set up by US investment managers. Frequently, there will be an on-shore, usually Delaware-based, fund for US investors, with the Cayman Islands vehicle acting as an off-shore feeder for non-US investors. The funds may take the form of limited companies or limited partnerships: for present purposes, the main

---

[1] Section 95(3) of the Companies Law (2009 Revision).

difference between the two is that, in the latter case, it may be easier to argue that general duties of good faith are owed by the management, going beyond the usual fiduciary duties of directors of companies.[2] One feature common to all the funds would have been the generous terms upon which the investment manager was remunerated. Typically the investment manager would be entitled, together with a success fee, to receive a flat fee, say 2 per cent based on the net asset value of the investments from time to time. So, a cynic would say, the investment manager had a vested interest in delaying or defeating redemption requests from members, at least where there was little prospect of attracting new investors to replace the outgoing investors.

Best practice would ensure that there was a divide between the management of the fund itself and the management of the investments in the fund: the former being the responsibility of an independent board of directors (or the equivalent in limited partnerships, that is, general partners) whose principal focus would be the protection of the interests of investors as a group, the latter being the responsibility of the investment managers, whose principal focus would be the maximization of the value of the investments. Best practice would also ensure that the investors had voting rights and could thereby influence the management.

Best practice was not, however, always achieved. Thus, in many cases the same people had responsibility for both the interests of investors and the maximization of the value of the investments. The investors might also be effectively powerless under the fund's constitution to exercise real control over the board or the investment manager.

A further issue was that even where best practice was followed it could not avoid dissent arising between investors. In any fund, there might be different groups of investors with widely diverging interests. For example, one group might prefer to wait for a turnaround in the market before selling investments, while another group preferred cash now. How were these divergent interests to be reconciled, particular in the exceptionally bad market conditions which prevailed in September 2008 and thereafter?

II. THE PROBLEM

In most cases, the funds, faced with the high level of redemption requests, had an armoury of means at their disposal under the relevant

---

[2]   But see *F&C Alternative Investments (Holdings) Ltd v Barthelemy* [2012] 3 WLR 10

constitutional and contractual documentation to delay and in effect defeat the redemption requests which were flooding in from the members. The funds could 'gate' redemptions, which meant that they could limit the amount they had to meet. They could also 'suspend' redemptions and redemption payments, often indefinitely. They also frequently had the power compulsorily to redeem members, thus turning the tables on their members and taking control into their own hands of the pace of the redemption process. The powers were usually expressed to give the directors (or general partners in the limited partnerships) the widest discretion as to how they exercised these powers.

The circumstances would vary hugely from fund to fund. Some funds would become mired in allegations of misconduct by the directors and/or the investment managers. In many cases, and these were the facts of the Caribbean cases discussed below, the funds had commenced an informal 'wind-down' process of the realization of the investments and the return of capital to members by way of redemptions, compulsory or otherwise. One thing that the funds' constitutional documents did not make express provision for, unsurprisingly, was what should happen in such circumstances.[3]

From the point of view of the investors, the vast majority of whom would have submitted redemption requests, the problem was the fact that they did not control the process by which their investments were to be redeemed. And they and their lawyers turned their attention to the obvious remedy available to them, namely winding up on the just and equitable basis. The shareholders wanted their capital back. This was on the basis that the company might be substantially solvent on a balance sheet basis (i.e. the assets were greater than the liabilities) but, from a broad commercial perspective, was insolvent on a cash-flow basis in the sense that it would have been clearly insolvent on that basis if one ignored the wide discretionary[4] powers the company invariably had under its constitution to restrict or negate an investor's right to require the redemption of its shareholding.

It is a moot point as to the point in time where anybody could or should have anticipated the circumstances that arose in September 2008: some would say that they were all part of the usual capitalist cycle of

---

[3] Funds established since September 2008 may well contain express provision for this eventuality with a view to influencing the approach of the courts if such circumstances were to recur.

[4] There have been disputes as to the limits of such powers: see *Culross Global SPC Ltd v Strategic Turnaround Master Partnership Ltd* [2010] UKPC 33.

boom and bust; others would deny this. In *Rubenstein v HSBC Bank plc*[5] an investor sought to recover damages from his financial adviser as a result of losses suffered from the collapse in September 2008 in the value of the fund that had been recommended by the adviser in 2005. It was held that, whilst the advice had been negligent, the losses claimed were too remote to lead to damages:

> 'What happened to the [fund] on 15 September 2008 and the days following was wholly outside the contemplation of ... any competent financial adviser in September 2005 ...
>
> If it had not been for the extraordinary and unprecedented financial turmoil which surrounded the collapse of Lehman Brothers, Mr. Rubenstein would probably have suffered no loss at all.'[6]

But judicial comments of this nature are neither self-evident nor based on empirical evidence.[7] Economists and other experts are still trying to work out the causes of the events leading up to and flowing from the collapse of Lehman Brothers. The judge in *Rubenstein* was of the opinion in this context that the events in September 2008 were 'outside the contemplation' of the parties, thus denying the investor the relief he sought against his adviser. As will be seen below, the fundamental basis for ordering a winding up of a company on the just and equitable basis is the emergence or existence of a state of affairs 'outside the contemplation' of the shareholders, that is, analogous to the frustration of the joint venture viewed in contract terms. If the judge's description of the events in September 2008 were applied in that context, then it would follow that a winding up of the fund in question should in general be granted as a result of the circumstances surrounding the collapse of Lehman Brothers, as has been held to be the case, albeit for different reasons, in the Cayman Islands, as discussed below.

---

[5] [2011] EWHC 2304 (QB); reversed [2012] EWCA Civ 1184.

[6] Ibid per HH Honour Judge Havelock Allan QC, sitting as a Judge of the High Court at [114] and [116].

[7] On appeal Rix LJ, while not expressly disagreeing with how the trial judge had put it, observed: 'And in truth, although the Lehman Brothers collapse was both a symptom and a contributory cause of market turmoil, the underlying causes of that turmoil went infinitely beyond Lehman Brothers' difficulties. It stretched to a failure of confidence in marketable securities in which there had previously been greater confidence. And what is new about that?': [2012] EWCA Civ 1184 at [117].

This chapter considers how the courts of these Caribbean Islands have responded to the challenges raised where shareholders have sought to have these funds wound up and examines whether traditional principles enunciated in English cases, decided in different circumstances and economic times, have proved fit for purpose.

III. WINDING UP ON JUST AND EQUITABLE GROUNDS: THE GENERAL PRINCIPLES

In his seminal speech in the leading case on winding up on the just and equitable basis, *Re Westbourne Galleries Ltd*,[8] Lord Wilberforce famously said that it was wrong to try to categorize the cases where the courts will make such an order. He stated:

> 'First, there has been a tendency to create categories or headings under which cases must be brought if the (remedy) is to apply. This is wrong. Illustrations may be used, but general words should remain general and not be reduced to the sum of particular instances. Secondly, it has been suggested, and urged upon us, that (assuming the petitioner is a shareholder and not a creditor) the words must be confined to such circumstances as affect him in his capacity as shareholder. I see no warrant for this either. No doubt, in order to present a petition, he must qualify as a shareholder, but I see no reason for preventing him from relying upon any circumstances of justice or equity which affect him in his relations with the company, or, in a case such as the present, with the other shareholders.'

He went on to describe how the words 'just and equitable' appeared in s.25 of the Partnership Act 1892 as a ground for dissolution of a partnership and then stated that 'the importance of this is to provide a bridge between cases under s.222 (*f*) of the Companies Act of 1948 and the principles of equity developed in relation to partnerships.'

When Lord Wilberforce cautioned against the categorization of circumstances which enabled the court to make a winding up order on the just and equitable basis, he was echoing the reminder that every court gives itself when applying general equitable principles, namely:

> 'Rules of equity have to be applied to such a great diversity of circumstances that they can be stated only in the most general terms and applied with particular attention to the exact circumstances of each case.'[9]

---

[8] [1973] AC 360 at 374–375.

[9] *Phipps v Boardman* [1967] 2 AC 46 per Lord Upjohn at 123.

Nevertheless, the well-known four-fold categorization of just and equitable winding-up cases has survived, if only because it remains indispensible for the purposes of explanation, namely:

(1) Loss of substratum;
(2) Deadlock;
(3) Loss of confidence in management;
(4) Expulsion from management.

Although this categorization is useful, it is essential to bear Lord Wilberforce's comments in mind and not to lose sight of the width of the court's jurisdiction under the just and equitable remedy. In fact, if there is an underlying principle applicable to all of the above categories, it is that a company may be wound up on the just and equitable ground if there exists a state of affairs which is 'entirely outside what can fairly be said as having been in the contemplation of the parties when they became members'.

Thus in *Re Westbourne Galleries*[10] Lord Wilberforce stated that although it was often argued that winding up on just and equitable grounds would only apply in cases of 'true deadlock' this was incorrect and the words 'just and equitable' need not be restricted to such cases.[11] Referring to *Re Yenidje Tobacco Co Ltd*[12] as the leading case on winding up in a deadlocked company, Lord Wilberforce approved the dicta of Lord Cozens-Hardy that the remedy would be available where the circumstances are such that we ought to apply, if necessary, the analogy of partnership law and to say that this company is now in a state which could not have been contemplated by the parties when the company was formed.[13]

Lord Hoffmann expressed the matter in the following way in *O'Neill v Phillips* which, though an unfair prejudice case, was one where he explicitly adopted the principles applied in just and equitable winding up cases:

'[T]here may be some event which puts an end to the basis upon which the parties entered into association with each other, making it unfair that one

---

[10] [1973] AC 360 at 376. See also *Re Tivoli Freeholds Ltd* [1972] VR 445 at 468 para (4).
[11] *Re Wondoflex Textiles Ltd* [1951] VLR 458 per Smith J.
[12] [1916] 2 Ch 426.
[13] *Re Westbourne Galleries* [1973] AC 360 at 376 citing *Re Yenidje Tobacco Co Ltd* ibid at 42.

shareholder should insist upon the continuance of the association. The analogy of contractual frustration suggests itself. The unfairness may arise not from what the parties have positively agreed but from a majority using its legal powers to maintain the association in circumstances to which the minority can reasonably say it did not agree: *non haec in foedera veni*. It is well recognised that in such a case there would be power to wind up the company on the just and equitable ground (see *Virdi v. Abbey Leisure Ltd* [1990] BCLC 342).'[14]

Bearing in mind the width of the remedy there are nevertheless two categories of case on just and equitable winding up that are particularly pertinent in the context of the present discussion, namely loss of sub-stratum and loss of confidence in management. The next section will examine relevant English developments addressing these categories before considering their application in the BVI and the Cayman Islands.

(a) Loss of Sub-stratum and Open-ended Investment Funds

The classic case of loss of substratum is where a company has been formed, on the proper construction of its constitution, on the footing that it is going to carry out some particular object and then wishes to carry on some quite different object.[15] In those circumstances, even a minority shareholder, against the wishes of the majority, is prima facie entitled to a winding up.

Nowadays, limited companies and partnerships have widely defined objects. Such is invariably the case with open-ended investment funds. However 'loss of substratum' cases are not confined to ones where, on the true construction of the objects clause in the company's memorandum of association, the company is pursuing an object outside that defined in its objects clause. But beyond the broad principle outlined above it is very difficult to state when the 'substratum' of the company has gone.

The essence of the cases involving open-ended investment funds is that the company is in a process akin to an informal winding-up. Could this justify members seeking winding up on just and equitable grounds on the basis that the company, being in the process of an informal winding up, is no longer functioning to achieve the objects for which it was established and has lost its sub-stratum?

---

[14] [1999] 1 WLR 1092 at 1100F-H, 1101H-1102B.

[15] *Re German Date Coffee Company* (1882) 20 Ch D 169. There is an excellent review of the loss of substratum cases in the judgment of Jenkins J in *Re Eastern Telegraph Co Ltd* [1947] 2 All ER 104.

It is not easy to find English precedents which bear a close resemblance to this situation. The most recent English decision[16] is that of Scott J (as he then was) in *Re Perfectair Holdings Ltd*.[17] The facts of that case were complex. In essence the warring factions reached heads of agreement that their joint enterprise should be wound up and the assets realized and distributed amongst them.[18] The heads of agreement, however, led to further litigation between the parties. In particular, one faction caused the company to commence proceedings for damages against its former subsidiary, which was now owned by another faction. That faction sought the winding up of the company on the just and equitable basis. In making a winding up order Scott J held:

> 'The directors were not put into office and cannot claim to be maintained in office for the purpose of liquidating the company. That is not the function of managers. That is the function of a liquidator. If all the shareholders of a company are content that the board of management should sell assets and prosecute actions not for the purpose of advancing any principal object but for the purpose of liquidating, so be it. There is nothing ultra vires in that. But the purpose, in my opinion, of the various powers and privileges conferred on managers is for the serving and furthering of the principal objects of the company of which they are directors and is not for the purpose of liquidating and winding up.
>
> ... Prima facie, in my judgment, a member of a company which has decided to liquidate and has decided not to carry on any of the principal objects for which it was incorporated and for the pursuit of which the incorporator entrusted his money to the company, is entitled to have the liquidation of the company carried out in accordance with one or other of the legislative frameworks that have been provided by statute.'

He added that, although it was not necessary for him to go so far for the purposes of deciding the case before him, he was of the view, if shareholders were agreed that:

> 'the company should cease to carry on any of its principal objects and should liquidate but where the liquidation is being conducted not by means of voluntary liquidation or compulsory liquidation but simply by management from the board of directors, that it would be just and equitable for the

---

[16]   Apart from *Tower Taxi Technology LLP v Marsden* [2005] EWCA Civ 1503, where on the facts the Court of Appeal did not need to consider the authorities.

[17]   [1990] BCLC 423.

[18]   Ibid at 428.

purposes of s.122(1)(g) of the Insolvency Act 1986 for the company to be wound up.'[19]

This decision would appear to lend support to the view that members of open-ended investment funds would be able to seek winding up on just and equitable grounds for loss of sub-stratum where the fund is in the process of an 'informal' winding up, thus potentially accelerating the return of their funds, but it is difficult to draw too close a parallel with this decision because the expectations of investors in open-ended investment funds are far removed from the expectations of the shareholders in *Perfectair Holdings Ltd.*

(b)   Loss of Confidence in Management

The leading case in this category is *Loch v. Blackwood*[20] where it was held by the Privy Council that:

> '[The] lack of confidence must be grounded on conduct of the directors, not in regard to their private life or affairs, but in regard to the company's business. Furthermore the lack of confidence must spring not from dissatisfaction at being outvoted on the business affairs or on what is called the domestic policy of the company. On the other hand, *wherever the lack of confidence is rested on a lack of probity in the conduct of the company's affairs, then the former is justified by the latter, and it is under the statute just and equitable that the company be wound up*' (emphasis added).[21]

The Privy Council went on to approve Neville J's judgment in *In re Blériot Manufacturing Aircraft Co (2)*[22] in which a winding up order was made on the basis that the substratum of the company was gone but also on the additional ground that there was 'proved misconduct by the directors'.[23] The Privy Council considered Neville J's comments on this second ground for winding up to be particularly apt, namely that:

> 'It is truly said by [counsel] that the mere fact of misconduct is no ground for winding up. The words 'just and equitable' are words of the widest significance and do not limit the jurisdiction of the Court to any case. *It is a question of fact, and each case must depend on its own circumstances. ... I think the moneys of the company have been misapplied, and that the company*

---

[19]   Ibid at 437.
[20]   [1924] AC 783.
[21]   Ibid at 788.
[22]   (1916) 32 Times LR 253.
[23]   [1924] AC 783 at 791.

is so constituted that it is deprived of its usual remedies. This is again sufficient for a winding up (emphasis added).'[24]

IV. THE RECENT CARIBBEAN EXPERIENCE

How are the above principles relating to winding-up on the just and equitable basis to be applied in the context of distressed hedge funds which are in informal wind-down mode and where there may also be allegations of misconduct against the directors? There has been a marked difference of approach in the Cayman Islands, in decisions of Justice Jones QC, as compared with the BVI, in decisions of Justice Bannister QC. No case in point has yet reached the Court of Appeal, so the differences are at present unresolved.

(a) Cayman Islands

In two recent decisions, Justice Jones QC has applied a broad-brush approach, in what might be called an 'individual investor friendly' direction.

The first case was *Re Belmont Asset Based Lending Ltd.*[25] In that case, the directors were pursuing a programme of realising the investments and returning the monies realized to shareholders. He held:

'13 ... I question whether it is sensible to adopt terminology invented in the context of England's nineteenth century economy ... [I]t can be said that it is just and equitable to make a winding up order in respect of an open ended corporate mutual fund *if the circumstances are such that it has become impractical, if not actually impossible, to carry on its investment business in accordance with the reasonable expectations of its participating shareholders,* based upon representations contained in its offering document. If such a company, organized as an open ended mutual fund, has *ceased to be viable for whatever reason,* the Court will draw the inference that it is just and equitable for a winding up order to be made.

16. Wherever it is proved that a company established as an open ended mutual fund is *no longer viable as such for whatever reason,* the Court will ordinarily conclude that it is just and equitable to make a winding up order ... There are sound policy reasons for making a winding up order in respect of *non-viable*

---

[24] (1916) 32 Times LR 253 at 255.
[25] [2010] (2) CILR 194 at pp 788–89 This decision has been followed by other judges of the Cayman Islands: see for example Foster QC J in *Re Freerider Ltd,* [2010] (1) CILR 486.

mutual funds, in spite of the fact that this situation has arisen without fault on the part of its management (emphasis added).'

On the face of it, this goes significantly further than existing English case law. It seems to follow that as soon as an open-ended investment fund ceases to be 'viable' in the sense that it decides, or has no choice but, to realize its assets and return capital to its shareholders, any shareholder is entitled to a winding up order regardless of the views of other shareholders.

The second case was *Re ICP Strategic Credit Income Fund Ltd.*[26] In that case, Jones J followed his earlier *Belmont* decision but went further by holding that '[t]he *need for investigation* into the affairs of a company can constitute a freestanding basis for making a winding up order on the just and equitable basis' (emphasis added).[27]

Again this seems to go significantly further than existing English authority. It may be sufficient for a minority shareholder to obtain a winding up order on this basis on its own where the company is already in liquidation and the liquidator should be seen to be independent,[28] but not where the company is otherwise a going concern. On existing English authority, the petitioner was required to establish wrongdoing, not just the need for investigation, and that there was no other way of obtaining redress. Justice Jones QC appeared to be treating the company as already in liquidation and finding that independent liquidators needed to be appointed.

(b) British Virgin Islands

In two judgments in the case of *Citco Global Custody v Y2K Finance,* Bannister QC J has adopted a narrower, arguably less investor-friendly, approach. The facts were that the directors were realizing assets and returning capital to those shareholders who had submitted redemption requests.

In his judgment dated 18 September 2009, he held that in the case of a sophisticated investment vehicle such as an open-ended mutual fund, as opposed to a closely-held company with a small number of shareholders who may be related (such as in *Loch v Blackwood*),[29] it was no ground for winding up on the just and equitable basis that even a cast-iron claim

---

[26] Unreported judgment dated 10 August 2010.
[27] Ibid para 8.
[28] See for example *Re Lowerstoft Traffic Services Ltd* [1986] BCLC 81.
[29] [1924] AC 783.

lay against the directors for breach of their duties. To hold otherwise would make serious inroads into the *Foss v Harbottle* principle of majority rule.

Subsequently, in a judgment dated 25 November 2009, he stated that a 'redemption of those investors who wish to redeem is not a distribution by way of ad hoc liquidation, of the sort which Scott J ... so deplored in' the *Perfectair* case. He held that there had been no loss of substratum since the company remained 'in a position to carry out its last commercial functions for the benefit of those of its investors who have requested that it should do just that.'[30] He went on to hold that, even if there had been a loss of substratum, it would be right to take into account the views of other shareholders as to whether a winding up order should be made.

(c) Subsequent Cases

In subsequent cases, Jones J and Bannister J have each had the opportunity to re-consider the issues in the light of the other's judgments in the above cases.

That opportunity first fell to Jones J in *Re Wyser-Pratte Eurovalue Fund Ltd*.[31] Without specifically addressing the reasoning of Bannister J, he declined to apply it. He seemed to regard it as 'highly artificial and [ignoring] the commercial realities.'[32] He held that 'there is no basis upon which it can be said that it should have been within the reasonable contemplation of the shareholders, at the time they subscribed for shares, that any liquidation would be carried out informally by the Investment Manager'.[33]

Subsequently in *Aris Multi-Strategy Lending Fund Ltd v Quantek Opportunity Fund Ltd*,[34] Bannister J reconsidered the matter in the light of the above decisions of Jones J. He began by distilling the following principle from the old English cases:

'[a] minority seeking a winding up on the grounds that the business life of a company has come to an end will only be permitted to overcome the will of

---

[30]   Unreported judgment dated 25 November 2009 at para 24.
[31]   [2010] (2) CILR 194.
[32]   Ibid at para 20. Jones J in fact was describing the author's submissions (as counsel for the company in that case) in these terms, but the author was relying upon the reasoning of Bannister J in the *Citco Global Custody v Y2K Finance* case.
[33]   Ibid at para 24.
[34]   Unreported judgment dated 15 December 2010.

the majority if they can show that further conduct of the company's business is impossible.'[35]

In reaching this conclusion, he had the support of the English Court of Appeal in *Tower Taxi Technology LLP v Marsden*.[36] Bannister J went on to consider and reject the reasoning of Jones J in the *Belmont* case stating that 'the concept of "non-viability" is too uncertain to ensure consistency of application.'[37] He added that there was 'no principle justifying the Court in appointing liquidators on the grounds that the activities of a company at any particular stage of its career are such that they would, in the opinion of the Court, be better carried out by a liquidator than the current management.'[38]

Just as Bannister J rejected the reasoning of Jones J so, in a subsequent case, Jones J repeated his lack of enthusiasm for the reasoning of Bannister J. In *Re Heriot African Trade Finance Fund Ltd*,[39] Jones J felt driven merely to observe that the law of the British Virgin Islands is not the same as that of the Cayman Islands![40] The learned judge even made a winding up order despite the opposition of a majority of investors, both in number and value.

V. CONCLUSIONS

The above cases disclose a remarkable and most unusual difference of judicial approach. It is difficult to see how the two approaches of Jones J and Bannister J can be reconciled, or how the conflicting decisions can be distinguished on their facts. Three comments may be made.

First, the approach of Justice Jones with regard to allegations of misfeasance on the part of the management appears to go significantly beyond English authority. If his approach is correct, it is much easier to obtain a winding up order based on mere allegations of misfeasance.

Second, so far as concerns 'loss of substratum', it is permissible respectfully to ask whether both Jones J and Bannister J are not missing the point when they apply their respective tests of 'non-viability' or 'impossibility' as to the future trading of the company. On the authority

---

[35]   Ibid at para 28.
[36]   [2005] EWCA Civ 1503.
[37]   Unreported judgment dated 15 December 2010 at para 35.
[38]   Ibid at para 36.
[39]   [2011] (2) CILR 34.
[40]   Ibid at para 35.

of *Re Perfectair Holdings* discussed above, it may be argued that grounds for winding up on the just and equitable basis exist if the commercial reality of the company's position, either by reason of agreement between all the shareholders or by force of outside circumstances, is that the company's affairs are being wound up informally. As Scott J held:

> 'The directors were not put into office and cannot claim to be maintained in office for the purpose of liquidating the company. That is not the function of managers. That is the function of a liquidator.'[41]

If that is correct, then perhaps if an investment fund's main objectives have failed because of a fundamental change in market conditions, and the management insist on controlling the realization of its assets and the distribution to investors, then any investor may seek a court-appointed liquidator.

Third however, even if grounds exist for winding up, a petitioning shareholder is never entitled as a matter of right to such an order, the court retaining in particular a discretion as to the appropriate time when such an order should be made, a discretion which it would exercise having regard to the views of shareholders generally. In that respect, the approach of Justice Bannister would seem to be more in keeping with English authority.

To return to the broad principle which underlies all the grounds upon which a court may make a winding up order on the just and equitable basis, was it beyond the reasonable contemplation of the investors at the time that the fund was formed that, due to exceptionally difficult market conditions, the underlying investment objectives of the fund have totally failed, requiring the fund's assets to be realized and distributed to investors fairly? As the decisions of Jones J and Bannister J show, it is quite possible for one judge to disagree with another about the answer to such a question.

---

[41]   [1990] BCLC 423 at 437.

7 An assessment of the present state of statutory derivative proceedings

Andrew Keay and Joan Loughrey

I. INTRODUCTION

On 1 October 2007 a significant portion of the Companies Act 2006 ('the Act') became operative. Included in the provisions put into force on that day was Part 11 of the Act, which provides for a derivative proceedings regime. Part 11 was enacted in response to the recommendations of both the Law Commission[1] and the Scottish Law Commission.[2] The regime effectively overhauls the common law position which required a shareholder who wished to bring proceedings to enforce the rights of his or her company to establish an exception to the rule in *Foss v Harbottle*.[3]

The rule in Foss provided essentially that if a company was prejudiced in some way it, and it alone, had to bring proceedings against those who had committed the harmful action against it. The shareholders did not have standing to take action. If the wrongdoers were in control of the company, as directors or majority shareholders, usually the company would refrain from taking any legal action, for obvious reasons. Shareholders were left to instituting a derivative action on behalf of their company, and most often shareholders, in bringing such actions, would rely on the 'fraud on the minority' exception. This provided that if a shareholder could establish that the action harming the company constituted a fraud on the minority and the wrongdoers controlled the company,

---

[1] Law Commission, *Shareholder Remedies: Report on a Reference under section 3(1)(e) of the Law Commissions Act 1965* (Law Com, No 246, Cm 3769) (London, Stationery Office, 1997). There have been some adjustments to the original recommendations in England and Wales.
[2] The recommendations of the Scottish Law Commission largely followed those of the Law Commission.
[3] (1843) 2 Hare 461; 67 ER 189.

he or she would be permitted to take derivative proceedings. The proceedings derived from the rights of the company.

In its examination of shareholder remedies the Law Commission considered the common law derivative regime unsatisfactory for a number of reasons: the rules governing standing to bring the action were complicated, inaccessible, overly rigid, and unwieldy; the criteria governing when leave would be granted, such as the concept of wrongdoer control, were unclear; and there was a risk of the preliminary stage being excessively lengthy and expensive because shareholders had to show that they had a prima facie case on the merits.[4] Furthermore it considered that the common law had ossified and was unable to develop in a principled manner to allow shareholders to bring claims in new situations, where the company was being improperly prevented from complaining about a wrong.[5]

The Law Commission intended reforms to take account of six principles: First, the proper claimant in respect of a wrong done to the company was the company itself. Second, individual shareholders should not be able to pursue proceedings on behalf of a company about matters of internal management which could be addressed by the majority by ordinary resolution. Third, courts should generally not interfere with the good faith commercial judgment of directors. Fourth, shareholders should be held to the statutory contract embodied in the company's constitution. Fifth, companies should be protected from unnecessary shareholder litigation; and sixth, shareholder remedies should be efficient and cost effective.[6]

The Law Commission recognized that the introduction of a statutory regime may lead to some increase in litigation because claims could be brought in a wider range of circumstances than at common law and because a streamlined procedure might encourage shareholders to use the derivative claim rather than the unfair prejudice remedy in appropriate

---

[4] Law Commission, *Shareholder Remedies: Consultation Paper* (Law Com, Consultation Paper No 142) (London, Stationery Office, 1997) at paras 14.1–14.4; Law Commission, *Shareholder Remedies: Report on a Reference under section 3(1)(e) of the Law Commissions Act 1965* (Law Com, No 246, Cm 3769) (London, Stationery Office, 1997) at paras 1.4 and 6.14.

[5] Law Commission, *Shareholder Remedies: Consultation Paper* (Law Com, Consultation Paper No 142) (London, Stationery Office, 1997) at para 4.35.

[6] Law Commission, *Shareholder Remedies: Report on a Reference under section 3(1)(e) of the Law Commissions Act 1965* (Law Com, No 246, Cm 3769) (London, Stationery Office, 1997) at paras 1.49–1.10.

cases. However it did not anticipate the increase to be significant.[7] Moreover the reforms were not intended to encourage derivative claims.[8] Rather the Law Commission considered that the policy underlying the common law was sound and that a shareholder's ability to bring an action on the company's behalf should be strictly limited and occur only in 'exceptional' cases.[9] The Government agreed, indicating that derivative claims were 'a weapon of last resort'.[10]

Thus while the reforms were designed to make the action simpler, more efficient and flexible and reduce the cost and length of preliminary proceedings, it was also intended that they should contain safeguards to protect companies from disruptive litigation which was contrary to the company's interests, including litigation over matters of internal management and challenges to the directors' reasonable commercial judgment. Tight judicial control through the leave procedure, and effective case-management subsequently, was considered essential to ensure that these objectives were met.[11]

The legislation therefore provides that in England and Wales and Northern Ireland once a shareholder has initiated derivative proceedings he or she must seek the permission of the court to continue the proceedings. In Scotland permission must be obtained before proceedings are instituted. The provisions that apply to England and Wales and Northern Ireland are similar in operation to those applying in Scotland. For the purposes of this article, the former provisions will be referred to, except when dealing with Scottish cases. Section 261 of the Act provides that, after the issue of derivative proceedings, the shareholder must obtain

---

[7] Ibid at paras 6.12–6.13.

[8] A. Reisberg, 'Derivative Claims under the Companies Act 2006: Much Ado About Nothing?' in J. Armour and J. Payne (eds), *Rationality in Company Law: Essays in Honour of DD Prentice* (Oxford, Hart Publishing, 2009) at 20.

[9] Law Commission, *Shareholder Remedies: Report on a Reference under section 3(1)(e) of the Law Commissions Act 1965* (Law Com, No 246, Cm 3769) (London: Stationery Office, 1997) at para 6.4.

[10] Hansard HL Vol 679 (Official Report) (27 February 2006) Cols GC4– 5 (Lord Goldsmith) at para 6.4.

[11] Law Commission, *Shareholder Remedies: Report on a Reference under section 3(1)(e) of the Law Commissions Act 1965* (Law Com, No 246, Cm 3769) (London, Stationery Office, 1997) at para 1.9 and 1.12; A. Reisberg, 'Derivative Claims under the Companies Act 2006: Much Ado About Nothing?' in J. Armour and J. Payne (eds), *Rationality in Company Law: Essays in Honour of DD Prentice* (Oxford, Hart Publishing, 2009) at 19–20.

the court's permission to continue with the claim. This is a two-stage procedure involving separate hearings before the courts.[12]

Since Part 11 became operative there have been several cases in England and Scotland which have considered it in varying depths. Any cases on new legislation are always eagerly awaited by practitioners and academics alike because there is often some doubt as to how the new legislation will be interpreted and applied by the courts. This article seeks to ascertain, from a critical examination of the cases, what a court has to consider at each stage of the permission process and if any clear guidelines have developed in relation to the interpretation and operation of Part 11.

The article takes the view that while some issues have been settled by the cases, overall, the cases have not clarified the operation of the legislation in many respects. Rather, they have made the situation somewhat confusing. The article focuses on the two-stage process laid down in the legislation and the way in which the courts have interpreted the criteria which they are to consider when evaluating an application for permission. It then considers the lack of clarity that exists in relation to the role that the company and the wrongdoing directors should play during the permission process, and the implications of this. The article finishes with some concluding remarks.

II. THE FIRST STAGE

The aim of the first stage of the permission process is to assess whether the company and the defendant should be put to the expense and inconvenience of considering and contesting the application for permission.[13] In *Langley Ward Ltd v Trevor*[14] the deputy judge said that to enable the court to do this it is incumbent on the applicant:

'to set out clearly and coherently the nature and basis of each claim together with the supporting evidence and legal basis. It must also draw the attention of the court squarely to any legal and evidential difficulties and to any fact at odds with its contentions. The same open, clear and frank approach must be adopted by the applicant as regards the factors which the court is required or

---

[12]   The Law Commission only recommended one stage: *Shareholder Remedies: Report on a Reference under section 3(1)(e) of the Law Commissions Act 1965* (Law Com, No 246, Cm 3769) (London: Stationery Office, 1997).
[13]   *Langley Ward Ltd v Trevor* [2011] EWHC 1893 (Ch) at [62].
[14]   Ibid.

may reasonably be expected to take into account in deciding whether it must, or ought to, refuse permission.'[15]

The first stage involves a court being satisfied that the shareholder has a prima facie case that warrants the court granting permission to bring proceedings,[16] namely that there is a prima facie case that the company has a good cause of action and that the cause of action arises out of a director's default, breach of duty, etc.[17] If the court is not satisfied the claim will be dismissed. If the shareholder succeeds, the application for permission will proceed to the second stage when the court will direct the company to file evidence indicating why permission to proceed should be refused,[18] and the court must decide whether the application should actually be granted.[19] The first stage will usually simply be a hearing on the papers filed at court, with the court making a decision based on the evidence filed.[20] But if the court dismisses the application at this stage the applicant can seek a review by way of an oral hearing.

The prima facie test is familiar to lawyers and was the primary test in applications for interim injunctions in most cases during much of the twentieth century,[21] and is still invoked in some injunction hearings today. At common law it was also the case that to be able to proceed with a derivative action the claimant had to establish a prima facie case as a preliminary matter.[22] Despite the prima facie case test being well-known, the meaning of the concept is elusive.[23] Neither in applications for leave at common law, nor in injunction applications in the UK, have the courts discussed in detail the meaning of the term, or what exactly an applicant must do to establish a prima facie case.[24] It has been suggested that what is required is that a substantial chance of success at the final hearing can

[15] Ibid.
[16] Companies Act 2006 s.261(2).
[17] *Iesini v Westrip Holdings Ltd* [2009] EWHC 2526 (Ch); [2010] BCC 420 at [78].
[18] Companies Act 2006, s.261(3).
[19] *Wishart* [2009] CSIH 65; 2009 SLT 812 at [33].
[20] Civil Procedure Rules 1998 r.19.9A(4)(a).
[21] For example, see *Hoffman-La Roche (F) & Co v Secretary of State for Trade & Industry* [1975] AC 295 at 338, 360; *Cavendish House (Cheltenham) Ltd v Cavendish-Woodhouse Ltd* [1970] RPC 284 (CA).
[22] *Prudential Assurance Co Ltd v Newman Industries Ltd (No 2)* [1982] Ch 204 at 221.
[23] *American Cyanamid Co v Ethicon Ltd* [1975] AC 396 at 404.
[24] C. Gray, 'Interim Injunctions Since American Cyanamid' (1981) 40 *Cambridge Law Journal* 307 at 307.

be demonstrated.[25] This might suggest that it is inevitable that there is some consideration of the ultimate merits of the case. Certainly in injunction hearings the application of the test led to a focus on the relative strengths of the parties' cases and in many instances meant a virtual trial within a trial. In order to establish a prima facie case an applicant in injunction applications had to establish a greater than 50 per cent chance of success.[26]

The test of a prima facie case in common law derivative actions was less strict than that which applies in interim injunction applications, and there is little evidence from the case law that the test at common law presented a significant obstacle to minority shareholders in the past. The number of reported judgments on leave applications is small but of these there are few in which a shareholder had failed to establish a prima facie case.[27]

It has been asserted in a past article that the need to show a prima facie case on the merits set a low threshold for shareholders to meet at common law and all 'the courts will require is for the applicant to demonstrate: a credible case; a substantive claim; a genuine triable issue; or that his case is worthy of being heard in full' (footnotes in the original are omitted).[28]

We now turn to the cases dealt with under the new regime. The cases so far have not been clear or consistent regarding what exactly the first stage of the process requires. On appeal in the Scottish case of *Wishart*,[29] the court seemed to require only a low threshold for the applicant to achieve. The court said that 'the question is not whether the application and supporting evidence disclose a prima facie case against the defenders to the proposed derivative proceedings, but whether there is no prima facie case disclosed for granting the application for leave [permission in

[25]   J. Heydon and P. Loughlan, *Cases and Materials on Equity and Trusts* 5th edn (Sydney, Butterworths,1997) at 978.

[26]   *American Cyanamid Co v Ethicon Ltd* [1975] AC 396 at 406–407.

[27]   A. Keay and J. Loughrey, 'Something Old, Something New, Something Borrowed: An Analysis of the New Derivative Action Under the Companies Act 2006' (2008) 124 *Law Quarterly Review* 469 at 482. Also see A. Reisberg, *Derivative Actions and Corporate Governance* (Oxford, Oxford University Press, 2007).

[28]   A. Keay and J. Loughrey, 'Something Old, Something New, Something Borrowed: An Analysis of the New Derivative Action Under the Companies Act 2006' (2008) 124 *Law Quarterly Review* 469 at 482.

[29]   [2009] CSIH 65; 2009 SLT 812 at [31]. See [2009] CSOH 20; 2009 SLT 376 for the decision at first instance. While the appeal court disagreed with the approach taken at first instance, it came to the same result.

England].' The court went on to say that the applicant should not carry the burden of satisfying the court that he or she has a prima facie case, but rather the court should refuse if it is not satisfied that there is a prima facie case. The court specified the matters which it thought must be taken into account.[30] It first dealt with some formal elements with which the court must be satisfied, namely ensuring that the applicant is a member of the company involved, whether the application relates to derivative proceedings, and that the application specified the cause of action and facts on which the derivative proceedings are based.[31] But it also added that the courts should consider the factors set out in s.268(1)(2) and (3) in order to determine whether the application should be granted. These provisions are equivalent to s.263(2) and (3) of the Act applying elsewhere in the UK. This means that the first stage could be more difficult to get through than the legislation seems to provide for, and more difficult than was the case at common law.

The above cannot be seen as a Scottish interpretation only, for in the case of *Stimpson v Southern Landlords Association*,[32] HH Judge Pelling QC (sitting as a judge of the High Court) appeared to take virtually the same view. The judge said that a court is bound to consider the factors in s.263(3) and (4),[33] being equivalent to s.268(2) and (3) in the Scottish provisions, in determining whether the applicant has a prima facie case.

The few other cases that we have available at the moment do not address what factors, if any, are to be considered by the court. It must be noted that in *Franbar Holdings Ltd v Patel*,[34] in which the two stages of the derivative proceedings process were effectively conflated into one, William Trower QC (sitting as a deputy judge of the High Court) said that the applicant had not sought to establish a prima facie case for permission to continue the proceedings, and yet this comment does not appear to be in accordance with the view of the court in *Wishart* where, as we saw above, the court said that no burden was placed upon the applicant to satisfy the court that he or she has a prima facie case, but rather there should be refusal if the court is satisfied that there is not a prima facie case.[35] It might be that as he did not have to consider specifically the first stage the deputy judge did not turn his mind to it as

---

[30]   [2009] CSIH 65; 2009 SLT 812 at [31].
[31]   The last requirement is peculiar to the provisions applying in Scotland: see s.266(2).
[32]   [2009] EWHC 2072; [2010] BCC 387.
[33]   Ibid at [46].
[34]   [2008] EWHC 1534 (Ch); [2008] BCC 885 at [24].
[35]   [2009] CSIH 65; 2009 SLT 812 at [31].

carefully as he would if he had considered the application at the first stage. But Lewison J in *Iesini v Westrip Holdings Ltd*[36] took an even stricter approach to the first stage than the deputy judge in *Franbar Holdings* as he said that the applicant had to make out a prima facie case that the company has a good cause of action and that it arose out of a director's breach, etc.[37] He said that this was the decision that the Court of Appeal required in *Prudential Assurance Co Ltd v Newman Industries Ltd*.[38] That is certainly true, but the latter case was a decision based on the common law approach to this kind of action. Notably, the Lord Ordinary at first instance in *Wishart*[39] relied on *Prudential*, and the appeal court in *Wishart*[40] said that he had adopted a wrong approach to the matter.

While neither court in *Wishart* or *Stimpson* made its ultimate decision on the application before it on the basis of whether it was satisfied that the applicant had a prima facie case, the comments that were made in each case are rather worrying. They appear to set the bar far higher than would have been envisaged. There is nothing in the legislation either applying to England and Wales and Northern Ireland on the one hand and Scotland on the other, that suggests that the factors in s.263 (in England) must be addressed at the first stage. There is no connection in the legislation between s.261 on the one hand and s.263 on the other. Furthermore, the Law Commission only recommended one stage, which is the second stage provided for in the legislation. The Law Commission in fact expressed concern 'at the way in which a member was required to prove standing to bring an action as a preliminary issue by evidence which shows a prima facie case on the merits'.[41] The main reason for the Law Commission not recommending a preliminary stage was that 'the inclusion of an express test would increase the risk of a detailed investigation into the merits of the case taking place at the leave stage, and that such a "mini-trial" would be time-consuming and expensive'.[42]

---

[36]   [2009] EWHC 2526; [2010] BCC 420 at [79].
[37]   Ibid at [78]. The court permitted the applicant to get through the first stage in *Cinematic Finance Ltd v Ryder* [2010] EWHC 3387 (Ch) at [2].
[38]   *Prudential Assurance Co Ltd v Newman Industries Ltd* [1982] Ch 204.
[39]   [2009] CSOH 20; 2009 SLT 376.
[40]   [2009] CSIH 65; 2009 SLT 812.
[41]   The Law Commission only recommended one stage: *Shareholder Remedies: Report on a Reference under section 3(1)(e) of the Law Commissions Act 1965* (Law Com, No 246, Cm 3769) (London, Stationery Office, 1997) at para 6.4.
[42]   Ibid at para 6.71.

At the second stage where the company can appear and produce evidence, a court must take into account the s.263 factors. But suggesting that they are relevant at the first stage makes the first stage far more substantial than it should be, particularly when one considers the position that existed before the enactment of the statutory derivative regime.

It seems that the interpretation given to the regime is that there will be substantial hearings at both stages of the process. While one might expect this at the second stage hearing, which is inter partes, this is not desirable at the first stage which is held ex parte. This increases costs and could well act as a deterrent to members instituting a derivative action. It also causes one to ask what the difference is between the two stages, because the factors in s.263(2)(3) and (4) have to be considered at the second stage. In fact if there is a difference it would appear that the first stage is tougher than the second for a court must, at the first stage, consider the issue of 'prima face case' besides those matters set out in s.263(2)(3) and (4), if the *Wishart* approach applies. It might be thought that the reference to 'prima facie case' in s.261 is otiose for if a court takes the view that the applicant succeeds under the s.263 factors he or she clearly would have a prima facie case. It is worth noting that the first stage was added to the legislation late in the process, in the House of Lords, and this might be an indication that what the first stage actually involved was not thought through sufficiently.

Interestingly Roth J in *Stainer v Lee*[43] said that a court is able to revise its view as to a prima facie case at the second stage, once it has received evidence and argument from the respondents. If that is the case then it would seem that a court could decline to consider the factors that must be considered at the second stage (and discussed later), if the court believes, at the second stage, that in fact there is not a prima facie case after all.[44]

It is submitted that the first stage should be limited to making sure that a claim is not bogus and should involve the court ensuring that the applicant is a member of the company and the application relates to derivative proceedings, as required by the court in *Wishart*.

Finally, it is to be noted that in practice the courts are willing to permit the telescoping of the two stages if the parties are in agreement with the result that there is just the one hearing.[45] This is sensible in some cases.[46]

---

[43] [2010] EWHC 1539 (Ch); [2011] BCC 134 at [29].

[44] Ibid.

[45] *Wishart* [2009] CSIH 65; 2009 SLT 812 at [9]. For examples, see *Mission Capital Plc v Sinclair* [2008] EWHC 1339 (Ch); [2008] BCC 866; *Franbar Holdings Ltd v Patel* [2008] EWHC 1534 (Ch); [2008] BCC 885.

[46] However see the court's warning comments in *Langley Ward v Trevor* [2011] EWHC 1893 (Ch) at [62].

III. THE SECOND STAGE[47]

If it appears to the court that the applicant does not have a prima facie case then the second stage becomes live. At the second stage the court *must* refuse permission, according to s.263(2), if it considers that a person under a duty to promote the success of the company would not continue the action or if the act forming the basis of the claim has been authorized or ratified. If neither of these applies then the court has a discretion as to whether to allow the claim to proceed. According to the judge in *Iesini v Westrip Holdings Ltd*,[48] at this stage more than a prima facie case must be demonstrated. However, Newey J noted in *Kleanthous v Paphitis*[49] that Part 11 of the 2006 Act does not say that a claim must attain a specific threshold before it is to be allowed to continue. Further, in *Stainer v Lee*[50] Roth J said that there was no particular standard of proof that has to be satisfied. In the former case the judge said that a court can potentially grant permission even if it is not satisfied that there is a strong case. While the merits of the claim will be relevant to whether permission should be given, they will not be decisive as there is no set threshold.[51] Nevertheless, in the same case the judge recognized that the merits will have a bearing on some matters, such as that found in s.263(2)(a), namely whether a director acting in accordance with s.172 would seek to continue the action.[52]

The legislation sets out several factors that a court must take into account in determining how to exercise this discretion, but they are not to be seen as exhaustive. The factors are set out in s.263(3)(4). In exercising this discretion the courts must take account of the following: whether the shareholder is acting in good faith; the importance which a person under a duty to promote the success of the company would attach to continuing the action; whether the wrong could be ratified or authorized; whether the company has decided not to bring a claim; the availability of an

---

[47] For some interesting observations and suggestions on procedure, particularly from a Scottish perspective, see D. Cabrelli, 'Petitioner: Statutory Derivative Proceeding in Scotland – a Procedural Impasse?' (2009) 13 *Edinburgh Law Review* 511.

[48] [2009] EWHC 2526; [2010] BCC 420 at [79].

[49] [2011] EWHC 2287 (Ch) at [40].

[50] [2010] EWHC 1539 (Ch); [2011] BCC 134 at [29].

[51] [2011] EWHC 2287 (Ch) at [42].

[52] Ibid at [45].

alternative remedy; and the views of the independent members of the company.[53] Not all of these factors may be relevant in any given case.[54]

Proudman J in *Kiani v Cooper*[55] acknowledged the fact that where, as in the case before her, there are many factual disputes:

> 'it is difficult to form a sensible provisional view as to the strength of the evidence on each side. The court is well aware that at trial with proper cross-examination a very different picture may well emerge from that appearing on documentary evidence alone. However ... the court must do the best it can on the material before it.'[56]

It should be noted that a court might take the view that permission might only be granted up to a particular point, such as to the time of disclosure. Proudman J made this order in the case just referred to.[57]

The following touches on some of the matters raised in the foregoing provisions.

(a)   The Duty under Section 172

Under the Companies Act 2006 one of the leading duties that a director has in managing a company is to act in what he considers, in good faith, would be most likely to promote the success of the company for the benefit of the members as a whole.[58] The derivative proceedings regime refers to this duty on two occasions. First, it provides in s.263(2)(a) that permission to continue derivative proceedings must be refused if the court is satisfied that a person acting in accordance with s.172 would not seek to continue the claim. The second time that s.172 is mentioned is in the list of factors that the court must take into account in making its

---

[53]   Companies Act 2006 s.263(3) and (4).

[54]   *Franbar Holdings Ltd v Patel* [2008] EWHC 1534 (Ch); [2008] BCC 885 at [31].

[55]   [2010] EWHC 577 (Ch); [2010] BCC 463.

[56]   Ibid at [14].

[57]   It is also something favoured by Roth J in *Stainer v Lee* [2010] EWHC1539 (Ch); [2011] BCC 134 at [37], [55] where a company has what appears to be a very strong case of breach of duty, but it is unclear whether all the resulting loss has now been repaid.

[58]   For a consideration of the duty, see S. Kiarie, 'At the Crossroads: Shareholder Value, Stakeholder Value and Enlightened Shareholder Value: Which Road Should the United Kingdom Take?' (2006) 17 329; P. Beale, 'Directors Beware' (2007) 157 *New Law Journal* 1033; A. Keay, *Directors' Duties* (Bristol, Jordan Publishing, 2009) at Ch 6; A. Keay, 'The Duty to Promote the Success of the Company: Is It Fit for Purpose in a Post Financial Crisis World' Ch 2 here.

decision. With respect to this second occasion, it is provided in s.263(3)(b) that the court is to consider the importance a person acting in accordance with s.172 would attach to continuing the claim. While the common law had no equivalent to s.263(2)(a) or s.263(3)(b), the test for the grant of leave at common law was articulated on the basis of whether an independent board would sanction proceedings.[59] In one case, *Airey v Cordell*, Warren J stated that 'there is a range of reasonable decisions' that a board might make, so that a reasonable board could take a decision either way.[60] He went on to say that shareholders would fail this test only if the court took the view that no board acting reasonably would sanction the action. Provided that the applicant shareholder's decision to take proceedings was one which a reasonable board could take, the court should give permission to proceed even though another board could reasonably refuse to prosecute the action.[61] This was because it would not be 'right to shut out the minority shareholder on the basis of the court's, perhaps inadequate, assessment of what it would do rather than a test which is easier to apply, which is whether any reasonable board could take that decision.'[62]

One of the problems for the implementation of this factor is that the meaning of s.172 has been the subject of interesting, but diverse, commentary from academics and practitioners,[63] and we have very little judicial guidance at present[64] as to the scope and interpretation of the provision, despite the fact that the provision has been in force for over two years. We can probably say that the s.172 duty is connected with the

---

[59]   *Mumbray v Lapper* [2005] EWHC 1152 (Ch); [2005] BCC 990; *Airey v Cordell* [2006] EWHC 2728 (Ch) at [56].

[60]   [2006] EWHC 2728 (Ch); [2007] BCC 785 at [69].

[61]   Ibid.

[62]   Ibid at [75].

[63]   For instance, see A. Keay, 'Enlightened Shareholder Value, the Reform of the Duties of Company Directors and the Corporate Objective' [2006] *Lloyds Maritime and Commercial Law Quarterly* 335; S. Kiarie, 'At the Crossroads: Shareholder Value, Stakeholder Value and Enlightened Shareholder Value: Which Road Should the United Kingdom Take?' (2006) 17 *International Company and Commercial Law Review* 329; D. Fisher 'The Enlightened Shareholder – Leaving Stakeholders in the Dark: Will Section 172(1) of the Companies Act 2006 Make Directors Consider the Impact of Their Decisions on Third Parties?' (2009) 20 *International Company and Commercial Law Review* 10; A. Alcock, 'An Accidental Change to Directors' Duties? (2009) 30 *Company Lawyer* 362.

[64]   The only case outside of the cases dealing with derivative actions that has referred to the section is the Scottish case of *Re West Coast Capital (LIOS) Ltd* [2008] CSOH 72.

idea of acting in the best interests of the company, especially given the fact that the only case that has considered the provision in terms of a breach of duty (but not in detail), *Re West Coast Capital (LIOS) Ltd,*[65] said that the provision effectively sets out the pre-existing law on the subject.

It would seem that it will be a rare case where a court would refuse permission on the basis of s.263(2)(a), namely that a person acting in accordance with s.172 would not seek to continue the action. The reason is that the court in *Iesini,*[66] in accordance with the approach taken by the court in *Airey v Cordell*[67] when dealing with the position applying at common law, held that it would only refuse permission where *no* director would seek to continue the claim. The court in *Franbar Holdings Ltd,*[68] while not putting it in this manner, effectively said something similar, as did the Scottish appeal court in *Wishart.*[69] So as mentioned above, one would think that it would be rare that a derivative action was so obviously undesirable that no reasonable decision maker acting in the company's interests would sanction it. Nevertheless, it must be noted that in *Iesini* the judge did find that the case of the applicant was so weak that he was of the view that no director would seek to continue the claim,[70] and this effectively was also the case in *Stimpson.*[71]

However, while an applicant might be able to hurdle the s.263(2)(a) requirement as far as the s.172 duty is concerned, it would appear that he or she will encounter more difficulty when the duty is considered by the judge in terms of the s.263(3) factors.

In *Franbar Holdings Ltd*[72] the deputy judge said that he believed a court would need to consider the following matters in applying the s.172 duty. These were: the prospects for success of the claim; the ability of the company to recover any damages award;[73] the disruption caused to the

---

[65] [2008] CSOH 72; (Outer House, Court of Sessions, Lord Glennie) at [21].

[66] [2009] EWHC 2526; [2010] BCC 420 at [86].

[67] [2007] BCC 785 at 800.

[68] [2008] EWHC 1534 (Ch); [2008] BCC 885 at [29–30]. This approach was approved of and applied subsequently both by Roth J in *Stainer v Lee* [2010] EWHC1539 (Ch); [2011] BCC 134 at [28] and David Donaldson QC (sitting as a deputy High Court judge) in *Langley Ward Ltd v Trevor* [2011] EWHC 1893 (Ch) at [9].

[69] [2009] CSIH 65; 2009 SLT 812 at [32].

[70] [2009] EWHC 2526; [2010] BCC 420 at [102].

[71] [2009] EWHC 2072; [2010] BCC 387.

[72] [2008] EWHC 1534 (Ch); [2008] BCC 885.

[73] Also mentioned in *Langley Ward Ltd v Trevor* [2011] EWHC 1893 (Ch) at [12].

development of the company's business by having to focus on the claim; the costs involved;[74] and any possible damage that might be done to the company's reputation.[75] The appeal court in *Wishart*[76] added other matters, such as: the amount at stake;[77] and the prospects of getting a satisfactory result without litigation. The deputy judge in *Franbar Holdings* also said that he accepted counsel's argument that where a claim for unfair prejudice under s.994 of the Act has been instituted, in addition to the application for permission, and an offer to buy-out the claimant has been made, a hypothetical director would be less likely to attribute importance to the continuation of the derivative proceedings.[78] But with respect it is hard to see why a director might not want to pursue the action that is covered by the applicant's derivative action even if a s.994 claim could be settled, because the type of action that will be pursued in derivative proceedings is designed to benefit the company, while a s.994 claim will only benefit the claimant. Furthermore succeeding with a derivative claim will often mean that the shareholders benefit indirectly, and while the claimant under the s.994 claim would no longer be a shareholder (after the buy-out) other shareholders might want to see a claim against wrongdoers prosecuted. Finally on this point David Donaldson QC in *Langley Ward Ltd v Trevor*[79] said that the potential winding up of the company could influence a hypothetical director in some cases, such as the case before him.

A further problem that might exist for a member wanting to obtain permission is that in *Franbar Holdings* the deputy judge said that he felt that the applicant needed to do more work in formulating a claim for breaches.[80] Yet this comment was made after the judge had said earlier in his judgment that 'a director will often be in the position of having to

---

[74]   Also referred to in *Stainer v Lee* [2010] EWHC 1539 (Ch); [2011] BCC 134 at [48].

[75]   [2008] EWHC 1534 (Ch); [2008] BCC 885 at [36].

[76]   [2009] CSIH 65; 2009 SLT 812 at [37].

[77]   Also mentioned in *Kiani v Cooper* [2010] EWHC 577 (Ch); [2010] BCC 463 at [44]. But in *Stainer v Lee* [2010] EWHC 1539 (Ch); [2011] BCC 134 at [29] Roth J appeared to downplay the fact that the amount of the recovery might be small where the applicant's case was strong as he felt that such a claim might stand a good chance of provoking an early settlement or leading to summary judgment.

[78]   [2008] EWHC 1534 (Ch); [2008] BCC 885 at [37].

[79]   [2011] EWHC 1893 (Ch) at [14]. The facts of this case seemed to require winding up of the company on the just and equitable ground (s.122(1)(g) of the Insolvency Act 1986).

[80]   [2008] EWHC 1534 (Ch); [2008] BCC 885 at [54].

make what is no more than a partially informed decision on continuation without any very clear idea of how the proceedings might turn out'.[81] The court in *Wishart* agreed with this latter view as it said that directors ordinarily have to take decisions concerning whether litigation should or should not be commenced 'on the basis of only partial information, without undertaking a lengthy investigation of the merits of the proposed case'.[82] This appears to produce some uncertainty and it makes it difficult for an applicant to know how far he or she is required to develop a case before seeking permission. Clearly any case put before a court must indicate an arguable case in the applicant's favour,[83] but, as the respective courts above have indicated, when considering the factor in s.263(3)(b) they must take into account the fact that directors would not necessarily expect an 'iron-clad' case before instituting proceedings. If the courts expect shareholders to make an application only when they have a substantial case then the ambit of the derivative claim will be severely circumscribed, particularly since much of the information needed to frame a detailed case will be in the hands of the directors, and will not be accessible to the shareholders until much later in the proceedings, at the disclosure stage of litigation.

Finally, and perhaps of most concern to a member, is that in *Iesini*,[84] after referring to *Franbar Holdings*[85] and the factors which had been set out there as those which a hypothetical director might take into account in determining whether to proceed with the claim, Lewison J said that 'the weighing of these considerations is essentially a commercial decision, which the court is ill-equipped to take, except in a clear case.' There is no indication as to what would be a clear case. Worryingly, Lewison J's remarks suggest that judges will defer to the decisions of the directors. The remarks are in the same vein as those of judges of the past who have resolutely refrained from passing judgment on what directors have done, on the basis that directors have to make business decisions and judges are not qualified to second guess them on such matters.[86] While the

---

[81]   Ibid at [36].

[82]   [2009] CSIH 65; 2009 SLT 812 at [37].

[83]   Ibid at [38].

[84]   [2009] EWHC 2526 (Ch); [2010] BCC 420 at [86].

[85]   [2008] EWHC 1534 (Ch); [2008] BCC 885 at [30].

[86]   For arguments along these lines, see D. Wishart, 'Models and Theories of Directors' Duties to Creditors' (1991) 14 *New Zealand University Law Review* 323 at 340; M. Whincop, 'Overcoming Corporate Law: Instrumentalism, Pragmatism and the Separate Legal Entity Concept' (1997) 15 *Company & Securities Law Journal* 411 at 426; D. Oesterle, 'Corporate Directors' Personal

Law Commission intended the courts to show deference to directors' commercial decisions,[87] if this approach is applied widely then it is going to be a rare case when permission will be given. The judge can surely reach his or her own view about whether a director is likely to proceed or not proceed. This does not require the judge to become an expert on the company's business. The judge can hear evidence from those who are conversant with the company and its business and then make an independent judgment based on the evidence which he or she believes is credible. This is what is done in a host of cases. Surely many decisions about whether a director has breached his or her duty under s.172 will involve making determinations about commercial matters, and this was envisaged by the Parliament in passing the section as drafted.[88] If judges do apply the approach suggested in *Iesini,* namely refusing to make a judgment in relation to commercial decisions made by directors, the derivative proceedings regime, and s.172 itself, might become virtually redundant.[89]

(b) Ratification

Just as at common law, the question of whether a wrong has, or could be, ratified remains central to the question of whether permission will be given to bring a derivative claim.[90] It is relevant at two points: first

Liability for "Insolvent Trading" in Australia, "Reckless Trading" in New Zealand and "Wrongful Trading" in England: A Recipe for Timid Directors, Hamstrung Controlling Shareholders and Skittish Lenders' in I. M. Ramsay (ed.), *Company Directors' Liability for Insolvent Trading* (Melbourne, Centre for Corporate Law and Securities Regulation and CCH Australia, 2000).

[87] Law Commission, *Shareholder Remedies: Report on a Reference under section 3(1)(e) of the Law Commissions Act 1965* (Law Com, No 246, Cm 3769) (London, Stationery Office, 1997) at para 1.9.

[88] For an argument that judges should be able to make judgments concerning commercial decisions made by directors see A. Keay, 'The Ultimate Objective of the Public Company and the Enforcement of the Entity Maximisation and Sustainability Model' (2010) 10 *Journal of Corporate Law Studies* 35.

[89] See the discussion in A. Reisberg, 'Shadows of the Past and Back to the Future: Part 11 of the UK Companies Act 2006 (in)action' [2009] 6 *European Company and Financial Law Review* 219 at 234–235 where the learned commentator states, inter alia, that the approach in *Franbar Holdings* in relation to this factor is likely to lead to a restrictive approach being adopted.

[90] In addition even where the wrong is ratifiable, the court will need to determine whether the conditions for ratification are met and in particular where the purported ratification is by the general meeting and whether the shareholders were properly informed: see *Stainer v Lee* [2011] EWHC 2287 (Ch) at [45]–[46].

s.263(2)(c) provides that a court must refuse permission if the cause of action arises from an act or omission that has been ratified by the company. If this has not occurred, the court proceeds to the next stage (s.263(3)(c)(ii)), and in considering whether to exercise its discretion the court must have regard to whether the act or omission is likely to be ratified.

In *Parry v Bartlett*, the court considered an argument that while ratification was practically impossible as the company was deadlocked, the court should still refuse permission on the basis that the wrong was ratifiable. The court applied the common law and held that the case fell within the exception to the rule in *Foss v Harbottle*,[91] namely that the company was subject to wrongdoer control. As a result the conduct was not ratifiable.[92] This case was subject to transitional arrangements and permission could only be granted if the claim could have continued as a derivative claim at common law.[93] At common law permission would have been refused if the wrong was ratifiable. However it was confirmed in *Franbar Holdings* that the Act does not alter the common law position that certain wrongs are unratifiable.[94] Such a conclusion was unavoidable given that s.239(6) of the Act states that any rule of law as to acts that are incapable of being ratified by the company remain unaltered by the Act. However, as Boyle points out, it is regrettable as it may result in leave hearings becoming dominated by arguments over whether the alleged wrongs were ratifiable or not.[95]

In *Franbar Holdings* the issue of ratification was considered in detail. Briefly, the applicant was the minority shareholder in Medicentres (UK) Ltd and the defendants were two directors who had been appointed to the board of Medicentres by the majority shareholder, Casualty Plus Ltd, and Casualty Plus itself. Casualty Plus was named as a defendant because although an action can only be brought in respect of a director's breach of duty, third parties can also be sued.[96] The applicant alleged that the directors had breached their duties by diverting business away from Medicentres to Casualty Plus.

---

[91] (1843) 2 Hare 461; 67 ER 189.

[92] [2011] EWHC 3146 (Ch) at [81].

[93] Ibid at [64]. See Companies Act 2006 (Commencement No. 3, Consequential Amendments, Transitional Provisions and Savings) Order (SI 2007/2194) Sch 3, para 20(3).

[94] [2008] EWHC 1534 (Ch); [2008] BCC 885 at 894.

[95] A.J. Boyle, 'The New Derivative Action' (1997) 18 *Company Lawyer* 256 at 258.

[96] Companies Act s.260(3).

It was indicated to the court that Casualty Plus was likely to ratify the defendant directors' conduct.[97] In deciding whether to exercise its discretion in favour of granting leave the court therefore had to determine whether such ratification would be effective. Under s.239 of the Act, neither the votes of any wrongdoing directors, nor anyone connected with them, could be counted for the purposes of ratification. As Casualty Plus was a shareholder and not a director, its votes could only be disregarded under s.239 if it was connected to the defendant directors. There was however no evidence before the court that Casualty Plus was connected within the meaning of s.254 of the Act.[98] The defendants argued that the provisions of the Act dealing with connected persons had replaced the rule that certain wrongs were not ratifiable: provided that the votes of the alleged wrongdoers and those connected to them were discounted, all wrongs could be ratified. It was then argued that, as it was not a connected person, Casualty Plus could ratify the wrong.[99]

William Trower QC (sitting as a deputy judge) rejected these contentions and stated that the connected person provisions in s.239 of the Act were not intended to replace the concept of non-ratifiable wrongs. Rather they imposed more restrictive rules than the common law regarding when ratification would be effective.[100] At common law, a ratifiable wrong could be ratified by the alleged wrongdoers and others connected with them.[101] As a result of s.239 even ratifiable wrongs cannot be ratified by the wrongdoers.

Unfortunately the deputy judge's comments on what constituted an unratifiable wrong reflected the common law position in all its uncertainty. He indicated that Sir Richard Baggalay's statements in *North West Transportation Co Ltd v Beattie*[102] remained good law, namely that ratification was effective provided that 'such affirmance or adoption is not brought about by unfair or improper means, and is not illegal or

---

[97]   [2008] EWHC 1534 (Ch); [2008] BCC 885 at 895.

[98]   Companies Act 2006 s.254(2) provides that a director is connected with a company if he and the persons connected with him together (a) are interested in shares comprising at least 20 per cent of the nominal value of the equity share capital of that company or (b) are entitled to exercise or control the exercise of more than 20 per cent of the voting power.

[99]   [2008] EWHC 1534 (Ch); [2008] BCC 885 at 897.

[100]   Ibid.

[101]   *North West Transportation Co Ltd v Beatty* (1887) LR 12 App Cas 589; *Regal v Hastings* [1967] 2 AC 134 at 149.

[102]   (1887) LR 12 App Cas 589.

fraudulent or oppressive towards those shareholders who oppose it'.[103] These comments seem to be directed at the act of ratification itself, rather than at the wrongs which preceded it. They would be apposite where ratification had been achieved through wrongdoer control of the general meeting and seems to reintroduce the concept of wrongdoer control into the derivative action, although the Act itself makes no reference to this. Nevertheless, it is clear that the deputy judge did have wrongdoer control in mind because he stated that the issue was whether ratification had the effect of improperly preventing the claimant from bringing the claim, which would be the case where the new connected person provisions were not satisfied but there was actual wrongdoer control of the company.[104]

The deputy judge's linking of ratification with wrongdoer control revives a debate which was never completely resolved at common law. To explain, there were two views as to when ratification would be effective or not. The first was that this turned on the nature of the wrong. This was termed the transaction based theory of ratification. The second was that wrongs were not ratifiable because the wrongdoers were seeking to ratify their own default in order to oppress the minority, termed the voting based theory.[105] The weight of the case-law and academic commentary weighed in favour of the former.[106]

However William Trower QC's approach suggests that he tended towards the second view. He accepted that some of the acts complained of might be incapable of ratification, which initially suggests that he was adopting the transaction-based approach, but he then said that these acts were incapable of ratification 'on the votes of Casualty Plus more

---

[103]   Ibid at 594 cited by William Trower QC [2008] EWHC 1534 (Ch); [2008] BCC 885 at 897.

[104]   [2008] EWHC 1534 (Ch); [2008] BCC 885 at 898.

[105]   J. Payne, 'A Re-Examination of Ratification' (1999) *Cambridge Law Journal* 604 at 612; H.C. Hirt, 'Ratification of Breaches of Directors' Duties: the Implications of the Reform Proposal Regarding the Availability of Derivative Actions' (2004) 25 *Company Lawyer* 197 at 202.

[106]   K. Wedderburn 'Shareholders Rights and the Rule in *Foss v Harbottle*' (1958) *Cambridge Law Journal* 93 at 96; J. Payne, 'A Re-Examination of Ratification' (1999) *Cambridge Law Journal* 604 at 614; H.C. Hirt, 'Ratification of Breaches of Directors' Duties: the Implications of the Reform Proposal Regarding the Availability of Derivative Actions' (2004) 25 *Company Lawyer* 197 at 203. See however Vinelot J in *Prudential Assurance Co Ltd v Newman Industries Ltd (No 2)*[1981] Ch 257 at 307 whose view on this point has been described as 'novel' by Payne ibid at 613.

particularly if it was done with the intention of driving down Medicentres' earnings and reducing the amount payable to Franbar (by
Casualty Plus) on the exercise of any option'.[107] This suggests that
ratification might have been effective if it could have been achieved
through the votes of shareholders other than Casualty Plus, and thus
suggests that he adopted the voting based approach. Similarly in *Parry v
Bartlett*, the only other case to consider the matter so far, HH Judge
Behrens commented that he did not think that it was open to the
company to ratify conduct of the nature alleged,[108] but he then went on to
find that the conduct was not ratifiable because the company was subject
to wrongdoer control.[109]

The problem with this view is that it raises the question of what
amounts to wrongdoer control of the general meeting, an issue which
gives rise to substantial difficulties, as discussed below. However the
alternative approach is also fraught with difficulty and has been subject to
extensive criticism, both because it is not clear what kinds of wrongs are
inherently unratifiable[110] and because it disenfranchises innocent shareholders who should be able to ratify all wrongs if they see fit.[111]
However, even if it was accepted that independent shareholders were able
to ratify all misconduct, this would only lead to extensive argument over
whether the facts indicated that the shareholders were truly independent
of the wrongdoers. Although Professor Hannigan points out that this is
the type of judgment that the courts make on the facts every day,[112] the
issue is not whether the courts have the capacity to make findings on this
matter, but the adverse impact raising it would have on the length and
complexity of the leave application. On balance it may be preferable for
the courts to adopt the transaction-based view of ratification and to focus
on classifying what kinds of wrongs are non-ratifiable. At common law
these included expropriation of corporate property such as the diversion
of a corporate opportunity, and wrongs involving dishonesty.[113] The
relevant wrongs in *Parry v Bartlett* and *Franbar Holdings* fell into these

---

[107]   [2008] EWHC 1534 (Ch); [2008] BCC 885 at [47].

[108]   [2011] EWHC 3146 (Ch) at [79].

[109]   Ibid at [81].

[110]   See for example, K. Wedderburn, 'Shareholders Rights and the Rule in
Foss v Harbottle' (1958) 93 *Cambridge Law Journal* at 105; J. Payne, 'A
Re-Examination of Ratification' (1999) *Cambridge Law Journal* 604 at 614.

[111]   H.C. Hirt, 'Ratification of Breaches of Directors' Duties: the Implications
of the Reform Proposal Regarding the Availability of Derivative Actions' (2004)
25 *Company Lawyer* 197 at 201, 205.

[112]   B. Hannigan, 'Limitations on a Shareholder's Right to Vote-Effective
Ratification Revisited' (2000) *Journal of Business Law* 493 at 504.

[113]   *Cook v Deeks* [1916] 1 AC 554.

established categories, although in the latter the beneficiaries of the wrong were not, it appeared, the defendant directors, but Casualty Plus, a company with which they were associated. Admittedly uncertainty will remain over which wrongs are ratifiable and which are not, but this is a question of law, not fact, and so could be resolved by the courts without the need for extensive evidence on the point from the litigants. Some uncertainty is unavoidable given that the Act makes ratification a major battleground in derivative claims by providing that actual ratification will bar a claim, while at the same time failing to clarify the issue of unratifiable wrongs. This position was wisely not adopted in other jurisdictions.[114]

(c) Good Faith

Although the common law requirement that an applicant had to be acting in good faith in bringing a derivative claim had been criticized as uncertain and unworkable,[115] it was carried into the Act by s.263(3)(a). At common law particular uncertainty surrounded the questions of whether permission would be refused where the company had a good claim but the applicant had a collateral purpose in pursuing the litigation, and what role the equitable doctrine of clean hands should play, if any.[116]

The good faith requirement has been raised in most of the recent applications.[117] This is perhaps unsurprising. Given the level of animosity between litigating parties it is tempting to allege that one's opponent lacks good faith. At the same time it is notable that a lack of good faith has, so far, only been established in one of the recent cases.[118]

Turning to the relevance of the shareholder having a collateral motive for bringing the claim, the case law indicates that this need not lead to a

---

[114] Corporations Act 2001 (Aust) s.239: ratification not a bar to derivative claim but to be taken into account by the court; see also A. Reisberg, *Derivative Actions and Corporate Governance* (Oxford, Oxford University Press, 2007) at 154.

[115] A. Reisberg 'Theoretical Reflections on Derivative Actions in English Law: The Representative Problem' (2006) 3 *European Company and Financial Law Review* 69 at 101, 103.

[116] J. Payne, '"Clean Hands" in Derivative Actions' (2002) 61 *Cambridge Law Journal* 76.

[117] But not in *Fanmailuk.com v Cooper* [2008] EWHC 2198 (Ch); [2008] BCC 877, *Langley Ward Ltd v Trevor* [2011] EWHC 1893 (Ch) or *Kleanthous v Paphitis* [2011] EWHC 2287 (Ch).

[118] *Stimpson v Southern Landlords Association* [2009] EWHC 2072; [2010] BCC 387.

finding that good faith is absent, provided the claim can benefit the company. Thus in *Mission Capital Plc v Sinclair*[119] it was argued that the applicants were seeking to bring a derivative claim simply to obtain the benefit of a costs indemnity;[120] while in *Iesini* the shareholders were funded by a third party who would benefit if the claim succeeded and so, it was argued, the action was brought for the benefit of the third party, not the company.[121] In *Parry v Bartlett* the shareholder was seeking to put the company in funds partly so that the company could repay him his contribution under a guarantee of its debts and the expenses he had incurred on its behalf.[122] In none of these cases were these ulterior motives considered relevant since the claim had also been brought for the benefit of the company. In *Wishart* Lord Glennie at first instance commented that it was unclear why a claim which could benefit the company should not proceed simply because the shareholder had other motives for bringing it.[123]

In *Franbar Holdings*[124] the defendants asserted a lack of good faith. This was on the basis that the applicant had failed to accept an offer from the defendants to buy out its shares and had commenced a range of proceedings including a claim for breach of the shareholders' agreement and a s.994 petition. The defendants' view was that only the s.994 petition was necessary, and there was nothing to be gained by an award of damages to the company as opposed to an order to buy out the applicant's shares.[125] They also alleged that a want of good faith was demonstrated by the applicant having made an array of serious allegations which had not been backed up, and by the fact that not all of the directors had been joined as defendants to the derivative claim. The implication, presumably, was that the litigation was vexatious, and motivated by a grudge against the defendant directors. The fact that the defendants cited *Barrett v Duckett*[126] supports this inference: in *Barrett* leave was refused because the action had been brought for an ulterior motive, namely as part of a personal vendetta against the defendant. In making this finding the court had regard not only to the personal history

---

[119]   [2008] EWHC 1339 (Ch); [2008] BCC 866.
[120]   Ibid at 875.
[121]   [2009] EWHC 2526; [2010] BCC 420 at [114] and [120].
[122]   [2011] EWHC 3146 (Ch) at [86].
[123]   [2009] CSOH 20; 2009 SLT 376 at [33].
[124]   [2008] EWHC 1534; [2008] BCC 885 at [30].
[125]   See also *Stainer v Lee* [2010] EWHC 1539 (Ch) at [49] in which the defendants made very similar arguments which were rejected.
[126]   [1995] BCC 362.

between the applicant and the defendant, but also to the fact that the applicant had failed to sue another director (her daughter) who was also involved in the wrongdoing, and had initiated the litigation even though there was little hope of recovery for the company.[127]

In *Franbar Holdings* William Trower QC rejected the defendants' contentions. He did not accept that the applicant had any motive other than a desire to return value to the company through an award of damages to ensure that the value it obtained for its shares on a buy-out was full and fair. He accepted that using the derivative claim to extract value through a buy-out of shares might, in some circumstances, be illegitimate, but in *Franbar* this did not go to the issue of good faith, but to s.263(3)(f), and the question of an alternative remedy.[128] While this confirms that a shareholder who has a collateral motive does not necessarily lack good faith, he did not rule directly on the *Barrett v Duckett* point, that is, on whether permission should be granted when the litigation was malicious. However, provided the action is capable of benefiting the company, and the shareholder can be trusted to conduct it properly, the shareholder's collateral motive should be disregarded. As Palmer J stated in the Australian case of *Swansson v Pratt*, 'it is not the law that only a plaintiff who feels goodwill towards a defendant is entitled to sue.'[129]

It is clear that the issue of whether the shareholder is acting in good faith on the company's behalf is closely connected to the s.263(3)(b) criterion, that is whether a hypothetical director would proceed with the claim.[130] Thus if the action could benefit the company it is less likely that the court will find that good faith is absent, whereas if it could not be in the company's interests the contrary conclusion is more likely to be drawn. So in *Mission Capital Plc v Sinclair*,[131] in rejecting the argument that the applicant lacked good faith, the judge noted that the derivative claim did not simply duplicate the counterclaim and there was a real purpose in bringing the derivative claim.[132] Again in *Franbar Holdings* the court rejected the defendant's argument that nothing would be gained

---

[127] [1995] BCC 362 at 372–373.
[128] [2008] EWHC 1534 (Ch); [2008] BCC 885 at [30].
[129] [2002] NSWSC 583; (2002) 42 ACSR 313 at [41].
[130] A. Keay and J. Loughrey, 'Something Old, Something New, Something Borrowed: An Analysis of the New Derivative Action Under the Companies Act 2006' (2008) 124 *Law Quarterly Review* 469 at 487.
[131] [2008] EWHC 1339 (Ch); [2008] BCC 866.
[132] Ibid at 875.

by obtaining an award of damages for the company.[133] Meanwhile in *Stainer v Lee* Roth J indicated that the fact that the applicant shareholder had sought and secured the support of other minority shareholders before proceeding, was strong evidence of good faith.[134]

However given the tenor of the cases thus far it is easier to identify what factors do not go to good faith than ones which do. In *Wishart*[135] at first instance Lord Glennie, referring to the Australian cases of *Swansson v Pratt*[136] and *Maher v Honeysett & Maher Electrical Contractors Pty Ltd*,[137] acknowledged that there might be a lack of good faith where the applicant did not honestly believe that a cause of action existed or that it had a reasonable prospect of success, and where the application was an abuse of process. In most cases these criteria would overlap, but this would not always be the case.[138] Thus if a shareholder could not honestly believe that an action would benefit the company, good faith would be absent. As for the second of these criteria, an action will be an abuse of process where the shareholder's dominant motive in bringing the action is to achieve a purpose other than one for which it is designed, such as to oppress the defendant.[139] In assessing whether a claim is abusive the court will therefore have to have regard to the shareholder's motive. This begs the question of when a shareholder's motive will be relevant to the issue of good faith and when it will not. In *Iesini* the court held that the question was whether, but for the shareholder's collateral purpose, the action would not have been brought at all. If the action would not have been brought then good faith would be absent.[140] Nevertheless where the claim could benefit the company (albeit as an incidental consequence), it might as a matter of evidence be difficult to demonstrate that the shareholder's sole, or dominant, purpose in bringing the action was to achieve his own ends rather than benefit the company.

---

[133]   [2008] EWHC 1534 (Ch); [2008] BCC 885 at 894–895.
[134]   [2010] EWHC 1539 (Ch); [2011] BCC 134 at [49].
[135]   [2009] CSOH 20; 2009 SLT 376.
[136]   [2002] NSWSC 583; (2002) 42 ACSR 313.
[137]   [2005] NSWSC 859.
[138]   The appeal court agreed that, in assessing good faith, the view that the petitioner might reasonably hold of the merits of the claim was relevant: *Wishart* [2009] CSIH 65; 2009 SLT 812 at [36]. See also *Iesini v Westrip Holdings Ltd* [2009] EWHC 2526; [2010] BCC 420 at [119].
[139]   *Goldsmith v Sperrings Ltd* [1977] 1 WLR 478 at 490. Though not a derivative claim this case was relied on in *Iesini v Westrip Holdings Ltd* [2009] EWHC 2526; [2010] BCC 420 at [119].
[140]   [2009] EWHC 2526; [2010] BCC 420 at [121].

In *Stimpson v Southern Landlords Association,*[141] a case in which the applicant's motives have formed the basis for refusing permission, HH Judge Pelling QC found that claimant had brought the action in order to retain control of the company and because he did not want it to lose its identity through a merger. At common law, using the derivative claim for the first purpose demonstrated a lack of good faith.[142] Confusingly however the judge was not prepared to rule clearly on whether this motive did go to good faith. He considered this unnecessary since the list of factors contained in s.263(3) were not exhaustive, and it was open to the courts to take account of other factors.

It cannot be helpful to allow the factors which the courts will take into account in deciding whether to grant permission to proliferate unnecessarily. This can only prolong proceedings, create uncertainty and result in the unprincipled development of the jurisdiction. In this case it is submitted that it was unnecessary to treat the issue of motive as an additional factor.

It has been argued elsewhere that when actions are pursued by a competitor of a company, or where the claimant has purchased shares in the company after the wrong complained of has come to light and so the share price paid by the applicant reflects the company's loss, the courts should be more inclined to scrutinize the applicant's good faith, and swifter to bar a claim on grounds of lack of good faith.[143] There is a greater risk that even though the claim could benefit the company, its primary function is oppressive, or contrary to the company's interests, aimed at, for example, gaining access to confidential corporate information through the disclosure process, or otherwise disrupting the company's business.[144] An abuse of process may also be established where the shareholder has little intention of pursuing the claim to conclusion, but rather is bringing it to harass the company's management, and to force them to purchase his shares at a higher price (green-mailing).[145] Again,

---

[141]   [2009] EWHC 2072; [2010] BCC 387.
[142]   *Konamaneni v Rolls-Royce Industrial Power (India) Ltd* [2002] 1 WLR 1269.
[143]   A. Keay and J. Loughrey, 'Something Old, Something New, Something Borrowed: An Analysis of the New Derivative Action Under the Companies Act 2006' (2008) 124 *Law Quarterly Review* 469 at 488 and 491.
[144]   See for example, *Harley Street Capital Ltd v Tchigirinski (No 2)* [2005] EWHC 2471 (Ch); [2006] BCC 209 at 219–220 and 231.
[145]   The Civil Procedure Rules r. 19.9 F provide some safeguard against this in that the claim cannot be discontinued, settled or compromised without permission of the court so allowing the court to supervise the settlement.

good faith may be absent if it appears that the shareholder will conduct the litigation in an abusive or unreasonable manner.[146]

A further matter which the courts may take into account under the good faith criterion is whether the applicant has clean hands. The courts' application of the doctrine of clean hands at common law in derivative actions was criticized.[147] Nevertheless there are early signs that it is re-emerging in the statutory action. In *Iesini* the court held that where a shareholder has participated in the wrong of which he complains on the company's part, and if he brings the action to escape the consequences of his own wrongdoing, permission will be refused on the basis that the shareholder is not the proper claimant.[148] The shareholder in that case was a member of the board which had acted negligently, and so would not have been permitted to bring a derivative claim in respect of that negligence.

Finally, in both *Franbar Holdings*[149] and *Wishart* at first instance, the court placed the burden of proving lack of good faith upon the defendants and in *Wishart* made it clear that an allegation of bad faith would require 'precise averments and cogent evidence'.[150] This should deter speculative allegations of lack of good faith and so reduce the length of the proceedings.

(d)   Alternative Remedy

As was the position at common law, s.263(3)(f) provides effectively that the availability of an alternative remedy is a relevant consideration in determining whether the court should grant permission. But while the Act provides that the court must consider whether there is an alternative cause of action which the member could pursue in his or her own right, the common law was broader, and all remedies were taken into account, including alternative avenues of redress for the company itself.[151]

---

[146]   *Barrett v Duckett* [1995] BCC 362 at 372–373.
[147]   J. Payne, 'Clean Hands' in Derivative Actions' (2002) 61 *Cambridge Law Journal* 76 at 83–85.
[148]   [2009] EWHC 2526; [2010] BCC 420 at 122.
[149]   [2008] EWHC 1534 (Ch); [2008] BCC 885 at 894.
[150]   [2009] CSOH 20; 2009 SLT 376 at [33].
[151]   *Barrett v Duckett* [1995] 1 BCLC 243 at 372. Again, if the company is in liquidation a derivative action cannot be brought: *Fargo v Godfroy* [1986] 3 All ER 279, though this is probably better explained as an absence of wrongdoer control.

The provision states that the court must consider whether the act or omission in respect of which the derivative claim is brought gives rise to a cause of action that the member could pursue in his or her own right. In *Franbar Holdings*[152] the court said that the alternative remedy might in some cases be brought seeking relief against the same defendants as the derivative claim, but it is not limited to such remedies. The only limitation is that the alternative claim must arise from the same act or omission covered by the derivative claim. In many cases there will be overlaps between a derivative claim and a claim under s.994 of the Act.[153]

The fact that an action has not been initiated by the applicant by the time the application for permission to continue derivative proceedings is heard will not prevent a court from denying permission on the basis that the claim argued for by the applicant raises a cause of action that the applicant could pursue in his or her own right. However, it might be prudent, given the cases, for a member to refrain from initiating any separate claim until permission for the right to continue derivative proceedings is dealt with. For instance, as noted above, in *Franbar Holdings*[154] the deputy judge accepted counsel's argument that where a claim for unfair prejudice has been instituted, in addition to the application for permission, and an offer to buy-out the claimant has been made, a hypothetical director would be less likely to attribute importance to the continuation of the derivative proceedings.[155]

A judicial finding that an alternative remedy is possible should not alone necessarily mean that permission should be refused. But the decisions in *Franbar Holdings*,[156] *Iesini*[157] and *Kleanthous v Paphitis*[158] seem to make the availability of an alternative remedy a compelling

---

[152]   [2008] EWHC 1534 (Ch); [2008] BCC 885 at [50].

[153]   For a discussion of this overlap, see, B. Hannigan, 'Drawing Boundaries Between Derivative Claims and Unfairly Prejudicial Petitions' (2009) 6 *Journal of Business Law* 606. In *Langley Ward Ltd v Trevor* [2008] EWHC 1534 (Ch); [2008] BCC 885, the court held that the winding up petition on just and equitable grounds would have been a more suitable remedy than a derivative claim and permission would have been refused on this basis had it not already been refused on other grounds.

[154]   [2008] EWHC 1534 (Ch); [2008] BCC 885 at [30].

[155]   Ibid at [37]. See also *Kleanthous v Paphitis* [2011] EWHC 2287 (Ch) at [80] where the fact that the shareholder had initiated s.994 proceedings counted against the grant of permission.

[156]   [2008] EWHC 1534 (Ch); [2008] BCC 885 at [30].

[157]   [2009] EWHC 2526; [2010] BCC 420 at [86].

[158]   [2011] EWHC 2287 (Ch) at [81].

reason for withholding permission. In *Kleanthous* Newey J considered that it was a 'powerful reason' to refuse permission.[159] This is notwithstanding that in *Iesini,* Lewison J said that the existence of an alternative remedy was not an absolute bar to permission being granted.[160] The view that the availability of an alternative remedy is a compelling reason to refuse permission is not a fresh one for in *Mumbray v Lapper,* heard under the common law, winding up on the just and equitable ground,[161] or a s.459 petition[162] were found to be preferable to a derivative action, and permission was refused. But it is submitted that it seems that the courts at common law were more likely to prefer alternative remedies where the applicant lacked good faith.[163] Under the new regime a judge could find against the applicant on the basis that he or she lacks good faith alone.

A court might take the view that if it sanctioned a derivative action where a member has also initiated s.994 proceedings, it would be seen as approving of 'green-mailing,' the practice mentioned above whereby shareholders bring derivative actions to pressurise company management to buy their shares at above the market price. Also, a court could withhold permission on the basis that when hearing the s.994 petition it is able to make an order that the company institute proceedings against the directors or others.[164] The problem this view would create for the applicant is that there will be a long delay before the hearing of a claim against a director or others for damaging the company is actually heard. The applicant must wait for the s.994 petition to be heard, hope that the court orders the company to bring proceedings against the wrongdoer(s) and then wait for those proceedings to come to trial. The uncertainties and time delay inherent in this process could well see the wrongdoers escaping, for a number of reasons, not least being the fact that the member runs out of funds and/or energy.

The court may also take the view, as in *Kleanthous v Paphitis,* that the shareholder is bringing a derivative action solely to obtain the benefit of a costs indemnity order, in which case the s.994 petition (where the

---

[159]   Ibid.

[160]   [2009] EWHC 2526; [2010] BCC 420 at [123].

[161]   Under the Insolvency Act 1986 s.122(1)(g).

[162]   Under the Companies Act 1985 and now superseded by s.994 of the Companies Act 2006.

[163]   *Barrett v Duckett* [1995] 1 BCLC 243; *Portfolios of Distinction Ltd v Laird* [2004] EWHC 2071 (Ch); [2005] BCC 216.

[164]   See s.996(2)(c).

shareholder bears his own costs) would be more appropriate.[165] However although it is usual for a costs order to be made in the shareholder's favour when permission is granted, it is nevertheless discretionary. Therefore concern over costs need not deter the courts from granting permission if other factors point towards the derivative claim being the appropriate remedy. What is important is the nature of the wrong alleged and the remedy sought.[166] In *Kleanthous* itself the wrong alleged was the diversion of a corporate opportunity.[167] This is misconduct which would properly form the basis of a derivative claim and would be most appropriately addressed by granting a remedy to the company. A further consideration is that channelling these types of claims towards the unfair prejudice remedy and the grant of a personal remedy to the shareholder may prejudice the interests of creditors if the company is of doubtful solvency or in financial difficulties.[168]

However there have been cases in which the availability of an alternative remedy has not been treated as compelling. The appeal court in *Wishart* did not consider it to be grounds for refusing permission because proceedings under s.994 would constitute an indirect means of achieving what could be achieved directly through the use of derivative action.[169] HH Judge Behrens reached a similar conclusion in *Parry v Bartlett*: the company's shares had been rendered worthless and the situation needed to be redressed by the company taking action against the director.[170] Meanwhile in *Stainer v Lee*,[171] Roth J was satisfied that the shareholder did not wish to be bought out and would be content with a restitutionary order in favour of the company.[172] But it must be conceded that the case for derivative action in all three cases was arguably stronger overall than any of the other cases heard thus far under the new regime.

---

[165]   [2011] EWHC 2287 at [81].
[166]   Per Roth J in *Stainer v Lee* [2010] EWHC 1539 (Ch); [2011] BCC 134 at [51] citing Millett J *In Re Charnley Davies Ltd (No 2)* [1990] BCC 605 at 625.
[167]   [2011] EWHC 2287 (Ch) at [32].
[168]   B. Hannigan 'Drawing Boundaries Between Derivative Claims and Unfairly Prejudicial Petitions' (2009) 6 *Journal of Business Law* 606 at 617–620. Hannigan argues that this problem could be addressed within the context of a s.994 petition by the court ordering both a buy out of the petitioner's shares and for the wrongdoers to compensate the company.
[169]   [2009] CSIH 65; 2009 SLT 812 at [46].
[170]   [2011] EWHC 3146 (Ch) at [88]-[92].
[171]   [2010] EWHC 1539 (Ch); [2011] BCC 134.
[172]   [2010] EWHC 1539 (Ch); [2011] BCC 134 at [52].

(e)   Independent Shareholders

Section 263(4) provides that the court is, in deciding whether or not to give permission, to have particular regard to any evidence as to the views of members of the company who have no personal interest, direct or indirect, in the matter. This factor appears to owe its genesis to *Smith v Croft (No 2)*.[173] The decision in that case was something of a controversial move by Knox J when he held that where an independent majority of the minority shareholders did not wish a derivative action to proceed, the action would be barred.[174]

It might seem, at first blush, that the views of the members identified in the subsection are to be given special consideration given the fact that it says that the court is to give 'particular regard' to their views, but in fact the introductory words of s.263(3) also refer to the court taking into account 'in particular' the factors set out in the subsection. Thus the factors in s.263(3) and the one in s.263(4) are of equal strength.

Little has been said in relation to the issue of independent shareholders. It is not clear to whom the subsection is directed.[175] As Lewison J said in *Iesini,*[176] the provision is not easy to understand as all members have an interest in any claim that is taken on behalf of the company because the value of their shares could rise or fall depending on the result of the claim.[177] After considering the provision's various interpretations Lewison J said that he was of the opinion that it was referring to those members who were 'not implicated in the alleged wrongdoing and who did not stand to benefit otherwise than in their capacity as members of the company.'[178] This is probably correct, but it leaves us with the situation that it might not always be possible to determine at the permission hearing whether members are able to benefit in a way that is out of the ordinary and in the way mentioned by Lewison J.

The facts of *Stimpson* were such that consideration of independent shareholders was justified. The judge noted the views of some of the

---

[173]   [1988] Ch 114.

[174]   Ibid at 184–185.

[175]   The Law Commission said that the position at common law was not clear: *Shareholder Remedies: Report on a Reference under section 3(1)(e) of the Law Commissions Act 1965* (Law Com, No 246, Cm 3769) (London, Stationery Office, 1997) at para 6.89.

[176]   [2009] EWHC 2526; [2010] BCC 420 at [86].

[177]   Ibid at [129].

[178]   Ibid.

members[179] and they gave limited support to the applicant. The judge said that he would take this into account. In the end it made little difference to the judge's opinion.

In *Kleanthous v Paphitis*[180] there were three shareholders. These were the claimant, the main respondent (a director and majority shareholder of the company), and the third shareholder, C (a minority shareholder and director). Newey J examined the views of C when he came to consideration of s.263(4) yet, as Newey J acknowledged, C was a named respondent.[181] Notwithstanding this Newey J thought that C's views were relevant.[182] This appears to fly in the face of what Lewison J said in *Iesini,* and discussed above. While Newey J had come to the conclusion that the 'independent' member had not benefited from the actions about which the claimant was complaining, it was surely an issue that should be resolved at a final hearing. In any event, given both the fact that C was a director sitting on the company's board when it approved of the actions of the main respondent and majority shareholder, and the fact that C arguably appeared 'to be close' to the majority shareholder, it is difficult to see why he should be characterized as not having a personal interest, at least one that was indirect, in the outcome.

Finally the court will need to determine whether those shareholders who are independent were properly informed given that the wrongdoing directors may well conceal matters that might result in the shareholder vote going against them.[183] If the shareholders are not properly informed this will reduce the weight that can be attached to their views.

(f) Wrongdoer Control

It is unfortunate that the concept of wrongdoer control has resurfaced via the concept of ratification because it was recognized as problematic at common law. First while it may be easy to show in small private companies that the alleged wrongdoers control the general meeting, in larger companies it would be difficult to identify on whose behalf shares are held.[184] It was also unclear exactly what wrongdoer control meant. In

---

[179] [2009] EWHC 2072; [2010] BCC 387 at [42].
[180] [2011] EWHC 2287 (Ch).
[181] Ibid at [83].
[182] Ibid.
[183] See *Stainer v Lee* [2011] EWHC 2287 (Ch); [2011] BCC 134 at [45]–[46].
[184] Law Commission, *Shareholder Remedies: Consultation Paper* (Law Com, Consultation Paper No 142) (London, Stationery Office, 1997) at para 4.13.

Prudential Assurance Co Ltd v Newman Industries Ltd[185] the Court of Appeal held that control covered 'a broad spectrum extending from an overall absolute majority of votes at one end, to a majority of votes at the other end made up of those likely to be cast by the delinquent himself plus those voting with him as a result of influence or apathy'.[186] This suggests that wrongdoer control is established by de facto control of the general meeting even though the wrongdoers themselves do not have majority voting power. However, even where de facto control exists, as it may well do in larger companies where shareholders are apathetic and so tend to vote with the directors, or not vote at all, it would be very difficult to establish.

In *Franbar Holdings* the court referred to the defendant directors having de facto control of the company.[187] Later the judge referred to 'actual wrongdoer control pursuant to which there has been a diversion of assets to persons associated with the wrongdoer.'[188] This comment is a little puzzling. Given that the allegation was that Medicentres' directors had diverted business to Casualty Plus, the majority shareholder, this dictum suggests that the judge did not define Casualty Plus as a wrongdoer, only a person associated with wrongdoers. It is not at all clear why wrongdoer control was found therefore, as the directors were not shareholders. Applying *Prudential Assurance Co Ltd v Newman Industries Ltd* this may have been because Casualty Plus had appointed the directors and so the relationship between the directors and Casualty Plus was such that it was to be viewed as being in league with the wrongdoers. However more explanation as to why this was so would have been helpful. It is also arguable that Casualty Plus itself should have been classified as a wrongdoer. While it had not breached any duties to Medicentres, it had received and exploited business opportunities which belonged to Medicentres and then sought to suppress the claim against it. The case bears some similarities to *Estmanco (Kilner House) Ltd v Greater London Council*[189] in which the Court of Appeal permitted a derivative claim where the majority shareholder (which was not a director) had sought to stifle a corporate action against it. The concept of wrongdoer was never properly defined at common law and, as *Estmanco (Kilner House) Ltd* demonstrates, included majority shareholders.[190]

---

185   [1982] Ch 204.
186   Ibid at 219.
187   [2008] EWHC 1534 (Ch); [2008] BCC 885 at 889.
188   Ibid at [45].
189   [1982] 1 WLR 2.
190   See also *Menier v Hooper's Telegraph Works* (1874) 9 Ch App 350.

There is no reason why it should now exclude majority shareholders where, for example, they have caused directors to breach their duties to the company for the shareholder's own benefit, or have otherwise been a party to the wrongdoing. However these uncertainties highlight why introducing wrongdoer control is a problematic gloss on the provisions of the Act.

Nevertheless in *Wishart*, at first instance, Lord Glennie also thought wrongdoer control was a relevant factor, though not in the context of ratification. Rather, he held that wrongdoer control should be determined as a preliminary issue at the ex parte stage of proceedings, that is, when the court was considering whether there was no prima facie case. However the Act does not require this. Furthermore it is doubtful whether it would be appropriate to resolve the issue of wrongdoer control at this stage of the litigation.[191] Although Lord Glennie considered that this would be relatively straightforward, involving the application of the law to 'readily ascertainable facts,'[192] establishing de facto control is far from straightforward. The appeal court rejected this approach. The court noted that the Act made no reference to wrongdoer control, that the Law Commission had intended to do away with the 'fraud on the minority' exception to the rule in *Foss v Harbottle,* and at common law the concept of wrongdoer control had created difficulties.[193] However, while the court ruled out wrongdoer control as a necessary pre-requisite to the grant of permission, it is not clear that it considered it completely irrelevant. The court also stated that at both the first and second stage of the leave application the matters it could have regard to were not confined to those set out in the legislation. The presence or absence of wrongdoer control could therefore be something the courts choose to have regard to in determining how to exercise their discretion, particularly when considering whether the company is likely to authorize the relevant act or omission (s.263(3)(c)(i)), and whether the company has decided not to pursue the claim (s.263(3)(e)). Thus in *Kleanthous v Paphitis* the applicant shareholder argued unsuccessfully that a decision by a litigation committee that the company should not pursue an action should not carry weight with the court because the decision was not made independently of the alleged wrongdoer. One director on the committee had been a director of a number of companies associated with the alleged wrongdoer

---

[191]   For a different view, see D. Cabrelli, 'Petitioner: Statutory Derivative Proceedings in Scotland – a Procedural Impasse?' (2009) 13 *Edinburgh Law Review* 511 at 515.

[192]   [2009] CSOH 20; 2009 SLT 376 at [29].

[193]   [2009] CSIH 65; 2009 SLT 812 at [38].

while another had been an employee of the company on whose behalf the litigation was brought.[194] Similar issues can be expected to surface in future cases. It would, however, be unfortunate and unnecessary for wrongdoer control to be treated as an additional stand-alone consideration.

IV. THE ROLE OF THE COMPANY AND THE DEFENDANT DIRECTORS

This section considers another area of uncertainty, namely the part the company should play in the permission process and the extent to which the defendant directors should be involved. Regarding the permission process, the Act clearly anticipates that companies will play an active part in resisting the shareholder's application for permission to proceed. Section 261(3)(a) states that at the second stage of the leave application the court can adjourn the application and 'give directions as to the evidence to be provided by the company', but says nothing about the defendant directors.[195]

The justification for allowing the company's involvement is clear. Derivative litigation can cause great harm to the company, in terms of reputational damage and the consumption of corporate resources, and so it may be contrary to the company's interests for the action to be pursued even if wrongdoing does exist. The detriment to the company may vastly outweigh any benefit.[196] Again a number of the permission criteria relate to the company's position regarding whether the litigation should proceed. The company is therefore the proper person to lead this evidence.[197] Nevertheless, practice has been inconsistent. In *Stimpson* the company was not represented at all in the application: the participants

---

[194]   *Kleanthous v Paphitis* [2011] EWHC 2287 at [30] and [75].

[195]   Companies Act 2006 s.261(3)(a).

[196]   The classic example is *Prudential Assurance Co Ltd v Newman Industries Ltd* [1982] Ch 204 at 221, 224–225. See also *Harley Street Capital Limited v Tchigirinski (No 1)* [2005] EWHC 2471 (Ch) at [28], in which the very fact that serious, though groundless, allegations had been made against the management may have caused a drop in the share price and damaged relations with the company's creditors. For a review of the demerits of derivative litigation see A. Reisberg, *Derivative Actions and Corporate Governance* (Oxford, Oxford University Press, 2007) at 47–50.

[197]   Companies Act 2006 s.263(2) (b) and (c) and s.263 (3)(c)(d) and (e); *Wishart* [2009] CSIH 65; (2009) SLT 812 at [19]-[21].

were the defendant directors.[198] In *Franbar Holdings* the defendant directors and the company were jointly represented and it appears that submissions against the grant of permission were made on behalf of both.[199] In neither case did the court comment on the appropriateness of the directors' involvement.

In contrast in *Wishart* the Court of Session held that only the company should be involved at this stage.[200] It gave several reasons. First, the permission stage of proceedings was fundamentally concerned with whether the court should interfere 'in the management of the company by overriding the decision of those responsible under the company's articles for the management of its affairs.'[201] The resolution of this issue did not affect the rights or obligations of the defendant directors and so it was not a matter in which they had an interest as individuals.[202] Second, the application had to occur prior to the commencement of proceedings, and to allow the defendant directors to advance their case before the substantive action had even begun would be unusual and premature.[203] This consideration does not apply with the same force in England since permission is sought after proceedings have been issued. Third, allowing the defendant directors to be represented at the permission hearing would increase the length and cost of the application.[204] Fourth, in determining whether to grant permission or not, the court would consider any weaknesses in the company's case against the defendants, internal company documents which might undermine it, witness affidavits and so forth. It was not in the company's interests for the defendant directors to be given advance notice of these matters, though the court acknowledged that where the defendants remained directors this would be difficult to avoid. Nevertheless, these considerations made it inappropriate for them to be involved at this point.[205]

The court cited a number of Commonwealth decisions in support of its approach. These differed from *Wishart* in that they concerned whether

---

[198]   [2009] EWHC 2072; [2010] BCC 387.
[199]   [2008] EWHC 1534 (Ch); [2008] BCC 885; see also *Iesini v Westrip Holdings Ltd* [2009] EWHC 2526 (Ch); [2010] BCC 420: although some of the defendant directors had separate representation, the company was represented jointly with two other defendant directors.
[200]   The company and the defendant directors were jointly represented on the application: *Wishart* [2009] CSIH 65; 2009 SLT 812 at [18].
[201]   Ibid at [19].
[202]   Ibid.
[203]   Ibid at [21].
[204]   Ibid at [22].
[205]   Ibid at [23].

company outsiders (such as creditors) who were defendants in the derivative claim could intervene in the application for permission to proceed. The cases were not directed at the position of directors and moreover appeared to assume that directors would be involved in their managerial capacity.[206] Nevertheless, the court's position in *Wishart* seems sound, as directors who are separately represented at the permission stage are not acting in their managerial capacity on the company's behalf but in their personal capacity, to protect their own interests, albeit that these interests may coincide with the company's.

However, in the English decision of *Kleanthous v Paphitis*,[207] Newey J refused to follow the approach in *Wishart*. He pointed out that the wording of s.261 differed from that of s.266 which governed the permission stage in Scotland.[208] The latter referred to the company being entitled to take part,[209] whereas s.261 was silent on who was entitled to take part. This though does not settle the question of whether the directors ought to take part – neither s.266 nor s.261 say anything expressly on this issue.

As to this Newey J held that where the defendant directors were shareholders, and the claimant was seeking a costs indemnity order from the company, the directors had an interest other than as defendants in participating in the application because, as majority shareholders, they would 'in practice' bear most of the costs of even unsuccessful litigation.[210] Arguably this places too little weight on the legal reality that the company is separate from its majority shareholders and it is the company's funds at stake, not the shareholders. Again the judge referred to the practice in *Beddoe* applications[211] to allow claimants on a trust fund to participate as fully as possible in the application. However, unlike companies, trust funds are not separate legal entities and, in contrast to the interest of the beneficiary of a trust fund, the shareholders' interest in corporate assets is indirect. It might be said that defendant directors should have a say as they could find themselves funding both sides of the litigation: their defence being funded from their own pockets while the claimant's costs are indirectly funded by them through the company.

---

[206] *Lederer v 372116 Ontario Limited* 53 OR (3d) 203; 141 OAC 338 (2001); *Carpenter v Pioneer Park Pty Ltd (in liq)* [2004] NSWSC 973; (2004) 186 FLR 104 at [10] and [16]; *Chahwan v Euphoric Pty Ltd* [2006] NSWSC 1002.
[207] [2011] EWHC 2287.
[208] Ibid at [44].
[209] Companies Act 2006 s.266(4)(c).
[210] [2011] EWHC 2287 at [44].
[211] Ibid.

However this need not follow: companies can insure themselves against indemnity costs orders and directors may have insurance against their personal costs and liability.

Newey J also accepted the argument that while the defendant directors might be partisan so would the applicant shareholder, and the involvement of the defendant directors would allow the applicant's case to be more thoroughly tested. This would serve the company's interests in deflecting weak claims.[212] However the company itself, through its representatives, could test the shareholder's case: the involvement of the directors seems unnecessary. Furthermore the shareholder's partisanship cannot be equated with that of the directors. The shareholder is meant to be acting in the company's interests and has no direct interest in the outcome of the litigation. In contrast the defendant directors have a direct interest in the outcome and in suppressing the litigation, particularly where the allegations against them are true. Finally even if the learned judge's arguments did support the involvement of the directors there are, it is suggested, stronger arguments against that involvement. In particular the directors' involvement will increase the length and cost of permission applications. In *Kleanthous v Paphitis*[213] for example, the directors were separately represented so that the applicant had arrayed against him three Queen's Counsel, three juniors and three firms of defendant solicitors. Given that most applications for permission are refused, this places the shareholder at substantial risk of very large adverse costs orders, which is likely to act as a significant deterrent to derivative litigation even in cases of serious wrongdoing.

What if the defendant directors are not separately presented: can they provide instructions on the company's behalf to defend the application? This raises the question of *who* exactly within the company can instruct the company's lawyers to defend the application. It would be problematic for this task to be left to the defendant directors as this could breach s.175(1) of the Act which requires directors to avoid situations in which they have, or can have, a direct or indirect interest that conflicts, or possibly may conflict, with the interests of the company. Even if the other directors authorized the alleged wrongdoers' involvement, as the Act permits,[214] this could create problems.

---

[212]   Ibid.

[213]   [2011] EWHC 2287.

[214]   Companies Act 2006 s.175(4); The Companies (Model Articles) Regulations 2008 (SI 2008/3229) Sch 1, art. 14 (private companies); Sch 3, art 16 (public companies).

In *Iesini* a derivative claim was brought against the directors of Westrip Holdings Ltd.[215] A question arose over whether another company, Rimbal Ltd, held property on trust for Westrip. Two of Westrip's directors were the sole shareholders in Rimbal, and it was therefore in their interest for no trust to exist.[216] Despite this conflict of interest these two directors were entrusted with the task of instructing Westrip's lawyers, Mallesons, to advise on whether such a trust existed. When providing instructions one of the directors vehemently denied that a trust had arisen, and the lawyers concluded that it had not.[217] Although the lawyers stated that their advice had not been influenced by the fact that they had received instructions from directors whose interests conflicted with the company's, Lewison J found that there was a strong argument that a trust had been created in Westrip's favour and indicated that he was surprised that the lawyers had failed to give appropriate weight to the documentary evidence indicating that this was so.[218]

This case illustrates the dangers of permitting directors, against whom allegations of wrongdoing are made, to control the instructions given to the company's lawyers. It may have contributed to Westrip believing that it had no arguable claim and to come close to giving up valuable rights. This would never have come to light but for the minority's derivative claim. Independent directors who permit alleged wrongdoers to instruct lawyers to assess the merits of a company's claim against the wrongdoers and to conduct the company's defence of the derivative claim, could breach their duty of care, skill and diligence.[219] However, for such a claim to be sustainable, the company would have to suffer a loss as a result. This could have occurred in *Iesini*, since a valid claim by the company was almost overlooked.[220] It is less obvious what loss would be caused to a company where the wrongdoers' involvement was confined to instructing the lawyers to defend the application for permission to continue a derivative claim on the company's behalf. However, there is a risk that the directors might cause the company to incur unnecessary costs in defending the application in an attempt to stifle the claim, and that the directors' involvement, even through the company, will increase the length of these applications. It is also possible that the company will not receive disinterested advice on the merits of the claim. Finally, the

---

215   [2009] EWHC 2526; [2010] BCC 420.
216   Ibid at [56].
217   Ibid at [56].
218   Ibid at [107].
219   Companies Act 2006 s.174.
220   [2009] EWHC 2526; [2010] BCC 420 at [105].

court hearing the application may attach less weight to the company's arguments where those arguments are advanced by the alleged wrong-doers. This would be the case irrespective of whether they are advancing arguments on their own behalf, or using the company as a mouthpiece.

Given this, instructions should be provided by independent directors only, and in larger companies from a litigation sub-committee of the board, though some have questioned, with justification, whether directors can ever be truly independent of their fellows.[221] Where there are no independent directors, in theory the general meeting could exercise its residual power to act.[222] However, in large companies this would be impracticable. It is difficult to envisage how a dispersed shareholder body could organize itself to provide instructions to a lawyer on the conduct of on-going litigation. In any event it is far more likely that these kinds of companies would have independent directors from whom instructions could be sought. The problem is most likely to occur in smaller companies. Even there, given that the company must give 14 days notice of a general meeting there will be practical obstacles to obtaining instructions from the general meeting,[223] though swifter decisions may be obtained through the use of the written resolution procedure.[224] Where however those involved in the dispute are the only directors and shareholders in the company, the defendants' involvement in a representative capacity is obviously unavoidable.

---

[221]   H.C. Hirt, 'The Company's Decision to Litigate Against its Directors: Legal Strategies to Deal with the Board of Directors' Conflict of Interest' (2005) *Journal of Business Law* 152 at 162, 168; A. Reisberg, 'Theoretical Reflections on Derivative Actions: The Representative Problem' (2006) 1 *European Company and Financial Law Review* 69 at 76, 88–89. See also *Kleanthous v Paphitis* [2011] EWHC 2287 (Ch) at [75].

[222]   *Barron v Potter* [1914] 1 Ch 895; *Foster v Foster* [1916] 1 Ch 532.

[223]   Companies Act 2006 s.307 (1). Shorter notice can be provided if shareholders holding 90 per cent of the nominal value of the shares agree: s.307(5) and s.307(6).

[224]   Companies Act 2006 s.296(4) allows for written resolutions to be passed as soon as the majority of members entitled to vote have agreed to it.

V. CONCLUSION

So far permission to proceed has only been granted in three cases,[225] thus indicating the fact that the courts have kept a tight rein on the use of the derivative process. Certainly many of the applications brought have rightly failed. However, there are three concerns that should be raised about the cases. First, the courts in two of the cases[226] where permission was granted only granted permission conditionally, namely to a point after disclosure. Second, in these two cases very limited indemnity orders as far as costs were made. These concerns suggest that the courts' priority is to ensure that companies' affairs are not disrupted from the continuation of derivative actions except on rare occasions. Third, the means by which the courts reached their conclusions are problematic. While the reforms were never meant to make it materially easier for shareholders to litigate on the company's behalf, it was intended that the criteria should be clearer than what existed at common law, that the concept of wrongdoer control should be discarded, and that the procedure should become more efficient and less lengthy and costly.[227] There is a real risk that these objectives will not be met. Partly this is due to the flawed nature of the reforms themselves such as, for example, the retention of ratification as a bar to a derivative claim,[228] but partly it is due to the approach the courts have taken to interpreting the statutory criteria.

In the decisions to date the courts have blurred the factors that are required to be considered under the Act, and made the operation of the statutory derivative action regime confusing. Notably there remains significant uncertainty as to what a court has to do and when it has to do it. This might be expected in the early days of any new procedures. One might think that the appeal courts would take a lead, yet in *Wishart* the

---

[225] Since this chapter was completed there have been two further successful applications: *Phillips v Fryer* [2012] EWHC 1611 (Ch), 12 June 2012; *Hughes v Weiss* [2012] EWHC 2363 (Ch) 11 July 2012.

[226] *Kiani v Cooper* [2010] EWHC 577 (Ch); [2010] BCC 463 and *Stainer v Lee* [2010] EWHC1539 (Ch); [2011] BCC 134.

[227] Law Commission, *Shareholder Remedies: Consultation Paper* (Law Com, Consultation Paper No 142) (London, Stationery Office, 1997) at paras 14.1–14.4.

[228] A. Reisberg, 'Derivative Claims under the Companies Act 2006: Much Ado About Nothing?' in J. Armour and J. Payne (eds), *Rationality in Company Law: Essays in Honour of DD Prentice* (Oxford, Hart Publishing, 2009) at 51.

court thought it unwise to attempt to state comprehensively or defini-
tively the approach that should be followed when a court is hearing an
application for leave (permission).[229] Perhaps that is just indicative of the
uncertainty that presently exists.

Furthermore the permission cases that have been heard thus far appear
to have led to mini-trials, something that the Law Commission wanted to
avoid in any statutory derivative process.[230] The courts themselves have
already raised this as an issue: Robert Englehart QC (sitting as a deputy
High Court judge) said in the early case of *Fanmailuk.com v Cooper*[231]
that it would be wrong if applications precipitated mini-trials. The cases
tend to suggest that the hope expressed by the Law Commission
concerning the avoidance of mini-trials will not be attained. For instance
the hearing in the *Iesini* case lasted for four days. In *Langley Ward v
Trevor* the court commented that permission applications were 'set fair to
become another time-consuming and expensive staple in the industry of
satellite litigation'.[232] This is something that any prospective applicants
have to bear in mind and the concern is that they might be deterred from
instituting legitimate derivative actions, as the permission process will be
costly and lengthy.[233] There are a number of factors contributing to this:
the existence of a threshold test on the merits which concerned the Law
Commission because of the risk that it would lead to fine distinctions
being drawn as to whether a particular set of facts fell on one side of a
rigid line or not, and detailed argument on the point;[234] unfocused
allegations about lack of good faith; the involvement of the defendant
directors at the permission stage; the reappearance of the criterion of
wrongdoer control.

The approach of the courts in these early decisions, generally speaking,
seems to lend support to Dr Arad Reisberg's view that the traditional
suspicion of the English courts towards derivative actions will continue
especially now that they are 'armed' with very restrictive legislation to

---

[229] [2009] CSIH 65; 2009 SLT 812 at [30].
[230] Law Commission, *Shareholder Remedies: Report on a Reference under
section 3(1)(e) of the Law Commissions Act 1965* (Law Com No 246, Cm 3769)
(London, Stationery Office, 1997) at para 6.72. This was acknowledged in
Wishart [2009] CSIH 65; 2009 SLT 812 at [39].
[231] [2008] EWHC 2198 (Ch); [2008] BCC 877 at [2].
[232] [2011] EWHC 1893 (Ch) at [61].
[233] See *Wishart* [2009] CSIH 65; 2009 SLT 812 at [22].
[234] Law Commission, *Shareholder Remedies: Report on a Reference under
section 3(1)(e) of the Law Commissions Act 1965* (Law Com No 246, Cm 3769)
(London, Stationery Office, 1997) at para 6.72.

'justify' their attitudes.'[235] What the courts appear to be doing is pushing shareholders in the direction of presenting petitions under s.994 of the Act wherever possible on the basis that they seem to view this as a more appropriate avenue to take. While this opens up the prospect of individual remedies for shareholders, it means that they will have to fund the actions themselves without any possibility of an indemnity order on costs.

The law on the subject at hand is obviously going to develop as time goes by and as more judges have the chance to deal with it in cases before them. It is perhaps unreasonable to expect an approach that provides a good degree of certainty to have developed so early in the life of the statutory regime. Nevertheless it is submitted that the present state of uncertainty cannot last for long, as prospective applicants will in many cases be unable to obtain confident and clear advice as to the merits of an application for permission to continue derivative proceedings, and the likely result will be that all but the valiant will be deterred from proceeding. Such a state of affairs would be unfortunate.

---

[235] 'Shadows of the Past and Back to the Future: Part 11 of the UK Companies Act 2006 (in)action' (2009) 6 *European Company and Financial Law Review* 219 at 225.

8 Directors' duties and shareholder litigation: the practical perspective

Joan Loughrey

I. INTRODUCTION

This chapter assesses the practical implications of s.172 Companies Act 2006 and the role of shareholder litigation. This perspective is critical to an informed understanding of the law, and how it operates in practice. The chapter presents the views both of practitioners who are involved in the practical application of the law, and of academics who have carried out empirical research into the themes addressed in this book.

The material herein is an edited record of a discussion between academics and practitioners which took place at the University of Leeds in September 2010. It addresses the following issues: the significance of s.172 and s.174 Companies Act 2006; the jurisdictional difference between derivative litigation and litigation under s.994 Companies Act 2006; and shareholder litigation and enforcement of directors' duties more generally.

II. ON SECTIONS 172 AND 174

DANIEL ATTENBOROUGH:[1] This is a question for Andrew Keay. I often think that it is very easy to be negative about enlightened shareholder value and to say that it has actually achieved very little, or nothing, in law but is it fair to suggest that the word 'enlighten' is a very subtle, gentle term, particularly if you compare it against the vigour and striking nature of such terms as 'maximization' or 'primacy'. As I said, the word enlightened is a rather delicate or subtle term and it does imply only a modest, rather than wholesale change, so I wonder whether you agree that enlightened shareholder value has in fact precipitated a welcome

---

[1] Lecturer in Law, University of Leicester.

change in emphasis in the corporate objective, particularly in respect to non-shareholder constituencies. Section 172 of the Companies Act 2006 does at least permit for the first time directors to consider other non-shareholder constituencies.[2] The position of the common law was that none of these constituencies were ever even mentioned, so at least now you do have directors being permitted, or made aware of the fact, that they can at least think about or have regard to these other constituencies. Do you agree with this assessment of enlightened shareholder value?

ANDREW KEAY:[3] I obviously agree. I have argued that it sometimes might be seen as a bit of a get out of jail free card section because, as you say, directors are given power to, or rather it is *mandatory* for them to have regard to those particular factors. As I have said, you always have to consider though, that what is decided will ultimately promote the success of the company for the benefit of the shareholders or members as a whole, so that while the directors can certainly take into account other factors, and they are given this right to do so, they have still got to be considering that what they are doing will ultimately benefit the members. I think that Peter Taylor, in correspondence that we had, made the very good point that s.172 doesn't have to mean that what the directors do must be for the *exclusive* benefit of the members. So there can be, if you like, incidental benefits, meaning the other stakeholders get some incidental benefit from the action even though the members will benefit. So it doesn't necessarily have to be exclusively beneficial to the members to the exclusion of all other stakeholders. Is that right Peter?

---

[2] Companies Act 2006 s.172(1) provides that 'A director of a company must act in the way he considers, in good faith, would be most likely to promote the success of the company for the benefit of its members as a whole, and in doing so have regard (amongst other matters) to – (a) the likely consequences of any decision in the long term, (b) the interests of the company's employees, (c) the need to foster the company's business relationships with suppliers, customers and others, (d) the impact of the company's operations on the community and the environment, (e) the desirability of the company maintaining a reputation for high standards of business conduct, and (f) the need to act fairly as between members of the company.'
[3] Professor of Corporate and Commercial Law, Centre for Business Law and Practice, School of Law, University of Leeds and Barrister, Kings Chambers.

PETER TAYLOR:[4] Yes, I have been researching this for a number of years.[5] I was puzzled by the term enlightened shareholder value so I looked into this in some detail. In answer to the previous point I think the fact is of course that directors have always been permitted to look at the interests of customers and employees and other stakeholders, necessarily so, in fact, to see the benefit for the shareholders. That in my view does not change: nothing is being changed by incorporating that approach into s.172(1). The conclusion I came to after talking to companies and theorizing about this, is that what s.172(1) and the monitoring function of s.417[6] does, is to try, from a political point of view, to narrow the range of management strategies which a board might choose so as to prevent market failure. In other words shareholder value is wide open to all sorts of misinterpretation and wrong-doing as we have seen with Enron, Polly Peck and GEC Marconi – you name it, there is long list. You could argue that the activities on the Enron board were wholly framed by the concept of shareholder value. So the objective of s.172(1) is to narrow the range of options which the directors can adopt to fulfil shareholder benefit, by causing directors to compulsorily have regard for certain other issues, in other words, to exclude those policies which might go wrong and result in upset. That was my view after three years of intensive work on the subject.

MR JUSTICE DAVID RICHARDS:[7] I take it that the words 'have regard' were deliberately chosen in s.172 as being, on the one hand, a requirement but on the other, as not dictating the outcome. This was essentially a political debate and that was the compromise reached. And I think that given the sort of economy we have I am not sure anyone would thank company law for producing a string of failures because the board had forgotten the commercial objectives of the business.

---

[4]   Former company director and then a research student, Birkbeck College, University College London.

[5]   P.N. Taylor, Enlightened Shareholder Value and the Companies Act 2006 (unpublished PhD thesis, May 2010), Birkbeck College, University of London.

[6]   Companies Act 2006 s. 417 requires companies to publish a business review, the purpose of which 'is to inform members of the company and help them assess how the directors have performed their duty under s.172' (s 417 (2)). For further discussion see C. Villiers, 'Narrative Reporting and Enlightened Shareholder Value under the Companies Act 2006' Chapter Three of this book.

[7]   High Court Judge (Chancery Division), Vice-Chancellor of the County Palatine, Chairman of the Insolvency Rules Committee.

ANDREW CAMPBELL:[8] My contribution is one of having lived through these issues from a business end and I thought it might be useful just to reflect on this. If I go back to the early 1980s before the aggressive (and I think we can use the word aggressive) shareholder value trends in the 1980s and the 1990s, business people were not taking proper account of the cost of capital, they were using too much capital and using it inefficiently and there weren't good performance measures. So the Boston Consulting Group and others came up with the cost of capital concepts which they borrowed from the finance faculties of university business schools and converted into a sort of shareholder value or economic value added thought, which then proved to be so successful in improving performance that it became a creed in its own right. But if you reflect back to what was going on before that then, in my view, management teams were all about managing for all of the stakeholders. The old ICI, before it got the enlightenment of needing to use its capital a bit better, was focused on a broad range of stakeholder objectives in a self-serving way. So we had a period in the 1980s and 1990s when shareholders said 'hang on a second you can't completely forget us.' There is a danger that we now feel that the shareholders have got too much power. My own opinion is that they have just rebalanced what was slightly out of order in the first place. Managers were paying too much attention to other stakeholders and not enough to shareholder value.

JOAN LOUGHREY:[9] This question is for our practitioners, our barristers and our judge. The academics are talking a great deal about s.172 and I'm wondering what your views are on it and if you are aware of it having changed things in practice. I wondered whether your, or your instructing solicitors', advice to directors has changed in the wake of s.172? What are they telling the clients about s.172?

ROBIN HOLLINGTON QC:[10] So far as I am personally concerned, mentioning s.172 is like waving a red rag at a bull. I can understand how the concept of corporate social responsibility is an eminently good one, one that ought to be kept uppermost in the minds of political leaders, especially when you bear in mind that there are many corporations in the world that have a bigger turnover than states do. So you can see that just as you could expect high standards of politicians, so you should also be

---

[8]   Director, Ashridge Strategic Management.
[9]   Professor of Law, Centre for Business Law and Practice, School of Law, University of Leeds.
[10]   New Square Chambers.

entitled to expect high standards of the controllers of these corporations. But I don't see how that can be achieved as a matter of company law. It seems to me that s.172 will fail and the reason it will fail to achieve anything is because the stakeholders whose interests are to be taken into account (other than shareholders) are people who have no locus to seek to enforce the duty. The fish in the stream, which is being polluted by the local post office that happens to be incorporated has no locus to enforce the s.172 duty. So it seems to me that s.172 is inevitably just hot air which will never achieve anything.

LOUIS DOYLE:[11] No it hasn't altered my advice. I want to endorse what Robin has said and simply add that I'm equally cynical about s.172, because other than in an extreme case, you might well ask what competent board would not take account of the sorts of factors set out in s.172. I'm not sure it's changed anything in terms of advice, and it's the easiest thing in the world, of course, to minute that you took account of certain factors. This has an echo of something in the Companies Act 1985. You might recall that under s.309 of the Companies Act 1985, the board was required to have regard to the interests of employees.[12] That was included because as that bill passed through Parliament, it was politically very fashionable at that time to at least give the appearance of giving effect to employees' interests. And what was the number of reported cases on that provision? Zero.

I agree entirely with what Robin has said in that the problem with s.172 is that it reads as something admirable, but it's rather like apple pie and motherhood: it's a great idea – who could speak out against it? But the practical problem is that it probably adds absolutely nothing meaningful to the way in which companies operate at board level.

PETER TAYLOR: I just want to pick up Robin's point that s.172(1) was a red rag to a bull. Margaret Hodge might be disappointed to hear that, were she still in power. I think one has to differentiate between the

---

[11] Barrister, Kings Chambers, Manchester and Leeds and 13 Old Square, Lincolns Inn.

[12] Companies Act 1985 s.309 provided that: '(1) the matters to which directors of a company are to have regard in the performance of their functions include the interests of the company's employees in general as well as the interests of its members; (2) accordingly, the duty imposed by this section on the directors is owed by them to the company (and the company alone) and is enforceable in the same way as any other fiduciary duty owed to a company by its directors.'

enforceability of a law and its practical effect and I said earlier that the practical effect is tangible in the case of s.172(1), according to my research. Obviously that's limited, but certainly the companies I spoke to indicated some response, not in all cases, but there was some response in terms of changing decision-making procedures. For example, one respondent said it was a wake-up call (presumably to remind the directors of the need to 'have regard' to stakeholder interests) and in other cases, respondents said that it was an opportunity for them to introduce documentary procedures which could verify and demonstrate that the constituent interests as required by s.172(1) were being observed. The need to record decision-making in this way had been recommended by companies' legal advisers and professional organizations. Now, s.172 may be enforceable in law only with difficulty, but the practical effect, I suggest, is tangible.

PARKER HOOD:[13] A question for Mr Justice David Richards. How does the law treat non-executive directors these days compared to executive directors because I think in *Equitable Life*[14] it was Mr Justice Langley who said, 'Well, in theory they're treated the same, in practice they're treated differently,' but the cases seem to go in different directions. Is it just simply the effect of applying the second limb of s.174, that is that the directors are assessed by reference to their own personal knowledge and experience,[15] or do you think there is separate treatment for non-executive directors?

MR JUSTICE DAVID RICHARDS: Well the first limb of s.174,[16] you remember, says that you're required to display the care and skill that would be expected from someone performing your function, so inevitably that produces a difference in result between a non-executive director and an executive director, because their functions are essentially different. I think, though, that's not new. The occasions on which a non-executive

---

[13]   Lecturer, Edinburgh Law School, University of Edinburgh.

[14]   *Equitable Life Assurance Society v Bowley* [2003] EWHC 2263 (Comm); [2003] BCC 829.

[15]   The second limb of s.174, contained in s.174(2)(b), provides that in assessing whether a director has breached their duty of care, skill and diligence the courts will have regard to the general knowledge, skill and experience that the director has. The second limb raises the standard of care above the minimum objective standard contained in s.174(2)(a) and expected of all directors. See J. Loughrey, 'The Director's Duty of Care and Skill and the Financial Crisis', Chapter One of this book.

[16]   Companies Act 2006 s.174(2)(a).

director is required to be involved is necessarily far more limited than that for an executive director. The fundamental duties are the same, subject, I think, to what I have just said, but their practical application is going to be very different.

III. ON SHAREHOLDER LITIGATION

DAVID KERSHAW:[17] This is a question for Louis Doyle and Mr Justice David Richards on s.994 and s.459 and the double derivative action. The law appears to provide that under s.459,[18] or s.994 as it is today, you can use s.994 in effect to bring a derivative action to get corporate relief and that seemed to me wholly consistent with the position prior to the Companies Act 2006. The remedial discretion in the Act basically gives the court carte blanche to allow a s.994 petition to result in relief to the corporation rather than to the individual shareholder. But it strikes me that the Companies Act 2006 changes that, for the following reason, which is you can only bring a derivative action now under the 2006 Act if the court says that you have permission to do so and a court is only going to give permission if the court decides that it is in the company's interest to do so. So if you are now allowed, post the Companies Act 2006, to bring a derivative action through the route of the s.994 petition, you would be able to effectively avoid the requirement for the court to take that into account. So it seems to me that the 2006 Act has changed something and I wondered whether you both agreed?

LOUIS DOYLE: The position, I think, is as you identify it, in that there was never a problem with the s.459 petition being brought for the purpose of obtaining a corporate remedy. The action is brought in the name of the petitioner. What appears to have changed, and I will stand to be corrected, is that there is now under the new provision in s.261 of the

---

[17] Professor of Law, London School of Economics.
[18] Companies Act 1985 s.459 provided 'A member of a company may apply to the court by petition for an order under this Part on the ground – (a) that the company's affairs are being or have been conducted in a manner that is unfairly prejudicial to the interests of members generally or of some part of its members (including at least himself), or (b) that an actual or proposed act or omission of the company (including an act or omission on its behalf) is or would be so prejudicial.' The provision has been re-enacted without alteration in the Companies Act 2006 s.994(1).

Companies Act 2006[19] a filter by which the court effectively involves itself in deciding whether or not it is in the company's interests for the action to go forward. But I can't see why, in theory, in the absence of anything being spelled out to this effect, you couldn't as a shareholder bring a s.994 petition and in effect ask for the relief that has always been there within that provision, that is, permission to bring a derivative claim such that the claim proceeds in the name of the company. But I suspect in reality that if a claim like that was going forward, the court is going to be very slow to allow you, if it allows it at all, to get round and in through the back door so to speak, so as to, in effect, circumvent the court's scrutiny of claims brought on the company's behalf that is envisaged by s.260 and s.261 of the Companies Act 2006.

ROBIN HOLLINGTON QC: I think the point you are getting at is the point that is raised in the Hong Kong case of *Re Chime Corporation*.[20] Because if you look at all the English cases up until *Re Chime Corporation* the courts have said: yes there is no problem about using the unfair prejudice petition to remedy a wrong to a company, you can get relief under the unfair prejudice remedy which is, in effect, relief for the benefit of the company, and we all know that there is no filter stage in a s.994 petition but there is, and always has been, a filter stage in a derivative claim. There was one under the old exception to the rule in the *Foss v Harbottle*[21] and there is now obviously even more so in the Companies Act 2006. And what Lord Scott said in the *Re Chime Corporation*, following what Lord Millett said in *Re Charnley Davis (No 2)*[22] (which wasn't an unfair prejudice case), is that there is a distinction between an unfair prejudice petition and a derivative petition – they are chalk and cheese, they serve different purposes and that the s.994 petition is there to remedy mismanagement and put right mismanagement for the future whereas a derivative claim is there to provide a remedy for the benefit of the company when a wrong is done to the company. But I don't really buy that. I think it all depends on the circumstances. It must in theory be right that you can't use s.994 in order to bring what is in effect a derivative claim in nature but which could not be brought as a derivative claim (as a matter of principle that must be right). However clever

---

[19]   Companies Act 2006 s.261(1) provides that 'A member of a company who brings a derivative claim ... must apply to the court for permission ... to continue it.'

[20]   (2004) 7 HKCFAR 546 (CA (HK)).

[21]   67 ER 189; (1843) 2 Hare 461.

[22]   [1990] BCC 605.

lawyers can dress up an unfair prejudice petition so it does not look too much like a derivative claim and so the courts have a difficult job. So it's a difficult question.

MR JUSTICE DAVID RICHARDS: Well, I agree with that. I think Robin may be right that it is a question of trying, as it were, to get to the guts of what the petition is about. Is it essentially a claim that a present or past director should compensate the company for his own breach of duty? If that is the essence of the claim then it's still within the jurisdiction of s.994 because if a significant amount of money is involved it is likely that the shareholders will have been prejudiced by the director's wrongdoing, and such a claim is certainly within the very wide relief that the court can grant under s.994. But the fact is that Parliament has instituted a filter mechanism for derivative claims – that is shareholders bringing claims for compensation for the company – and I think the courts are likely to be alive to that. What is the point of Parliament enacting a filter mechanism if one can simply circumvent it, as Lord Hoffmann has said. So I would expect, (and this is not a point that I am aware has risen yet under the Companies Act 2006, though it may have done) some thinking along those lines from the courts. There is something of an analogy with judicial review because it used to be possible to bring private law actions for declaratory relief on what were essentially public law issues. That is no longer possible because that was seen as circumventing the need for leave for judicial review. If it is a public law claim it cannot be brought in a private law action. However I think the matter under discussion is a little bit woollier at the edges, so I think it comes back to what Robin says: how clever will the petitioners' lawyers be in dressing up what essentially is a derivative claim as a personal claim which can be brought by way of a s.994 petition.

DAVID GIBBS:[23] I have two questions the first for Louis, and one for John as well. The first one is to do with the actual goals of the derivative action, one of which was to make it more accessible for small private companies, which comprise the majority of UK companies, and the first part of the question concerns the need to establish a prima facie case. I think Andrew Keay has argued that if you can show more than a zero per cent chance then you pass the first stage. So I ask, is it really that important to actually have the barrier of the first stage there when it is so easy to pass? It is an unnecessary expense to companies. I think it was

---

[23] Associate Tutor/PhD Candidate, University of East Anglia, UEA Law School.

Stimpson[24] that said it was unduly elaborate. So that is the first part of my first question. The second part is that the reforms tried to get rid of some of the negative tactics used by the defendants but in another case of *Kiani v Cooper*[25] we have the defendants not producing any evidence despite having six weeks to do so, and the judge was critical of that, but the case had only got down to disclosure stage. The defendants spent six weeks putting it off and putting it off. The shareholder, if he doesn't win, may end up having to pay for this. It is another negative tactic and this situation is not really fulfilling the goals of the derivative action. The reform has got rid of the old problems to some extent but we've got this new problem and I was wondering whether this new procedure has actually done anything for the benefit of small private companies.

LOUIS DOYLE: Can I deal with the first query? The effect of the statutory provision is, as Gower's Company Law puts it now,[26] to consign the old *Foss v Harbottle* to the rubbish bin. But both the old and the new action have a common feature in the sense of a filter system. Now the way that you characterize s.261(2) isn't quite right. What the provision does is, it requires the court to dismiss the claim if there isn't a prima facie case made out.[27] But having got over the more than zero per cent problem – and that requirement is not surprising, it is there to prevent frivolous, troublesome, mischievous litigation and is a mechanism that appears all across procedural requirements in the law – after that, and separate from that, the court then has a discretion as to whether to permit the action to proceed.[28] And I mentioned two cases earlier on, *Franbar Holdings Ltd v Patel*[29] and *Stimpson v Southern Landlords Association*,[30] where the exercise of the discretion did not involve leave being given because the view was taken that it wasn't actually in the interests of the company. So

---

[24]   *Stimpson v Southern Landlords Association* [2009] EWHC 2072 (Ch); [2010] BCC 387.

[25]   [2010] EWHC 577 (Ch); [2010] BCC 463.

[26]   P.L. Davies *Gower and Davies Principles of Modern Company Law* 8th edn, (London, Sweet & Maxwell, 2008) at 610.

[27]   Companies Act 2006 s.261(2) provides that 'if it appears to the court that the application and the evidence filed by the applicant in support of it do not disclose a prima facie case for giving permission (or leave), the court must dismiss the application'. That is, the prima facie case must be made out on the issue as to whether or not leave should be granted as opposed to leave being granted on the substantive merits of the action.

[28]   Companies Act 2006 s. 263.

[29]   [2008] EWHC 1534 (Ch); [2008] BCC 885.

[30]   [2009] EWHC 2072 (Ch).

far as what has changed goes, I think the new action at least probably provides the basis for a more coherent uniform approach as the case law develops. It gives you a platform that the old common law derivative action did not provide, in the sense that the old action was difficult, cumbersome and slow. However, I remain pretty cynical about these things in that even though limited owner managed businesses are, as you say, the backbone of the British economy, it will still cost a lot of money to actually litigate disputes in such companies irrespective of how modest the dispute is. Now what the solution to that is I don't know, but the point is that by its nature litigation in the Chancery division is an expensive process on any view.

MR JUSTICE DAVID RICHARDS: I have not got the legislation in front of me but my recollection of the prima facie case requirement is that the court is required to dismiss the application without bothering the company with it at all if there is not shown a prima facie case for the grant of leave, *not* a prima facie case on the merits of the action but just as to whether leave will be granted.

DAVID GIBBS: The other question was for John. You say that other US states are taking cases that would previously have been litigated in Delaware[31] and their judges are making the wrong decisions. I was wondering if your research has shown whether in these cases the judges just weren't experienced enough and that was why they were setting these bad precedents?

JOHN ARMOUR:[32] That is a very interesting question. First let me reiterate what we know. We present evidence that, since the mid-1990s, corporate law cases involving Delaware companies are less likely to be filed in the Delaware courts and more likely to be filed in courts outside Delaware. This suggests the Delaware courts may be missing opportunities to write precedents in relation to new issues. To give you an example, we have a case study of litigation involving a particular sort of misfeasance that

---

[31]   See J. Armour, B. Black and B. Cheffins, 'Is Delaware Losing Its Cases?' *Northwestern Law and Economics Research Paper* No. 10–03 at SSRN: http://ssrn.com/abstract=1578404 and J. Armour, B. Black and B. Cheffins, 'Delaware's Balancing Act', forthcoming (2012) *Indiana Law Journal*. The authors report that Delaware courts currently only hear a minority of shareholder suits involving Delaware-incorporated companies. These suits are increasingly heard by courts other than those in Delaware.

[32]   Hogan Lovells Professor of Law and Finance, Oxford University.

occurred in the early 2000s, 'options backdating', whereby corporate boards massaged the timing of executive stock option grants in an underhand way. This led to a slew of derivative suits. However of the 127 Delaware companies we found that were sued in this way, 80 per cent were sued exclusively *outside* Delaware, and only 3 per cent were sued exclusively *in* Delaware. Options backdating was a 'novel' form of misconduct that presumably would merit a precedent but this jurisdictional pattern as regards the filing of suits meant that Delaware's ability to produce a precedent was, at best, delayed. Consistently with this, we document a second trend in the production of judicial decisions: in corporate law cases against directors of Delaware companies in which a judicial opinion is made publicly available, the opinion has become more likely since the mid-1990s to be written by a court other than those in Delaware. This then raises the question you are asking, which is whether courts outside Delaware are doing a less effective job of deciding particular cases than would Delaware courts. Given the many dimensions across which cases differ, it's hard to think how we would measure this directly. However we have at least two pieces of indirect evidence. The first is anecdotal, from conversations with practitioners. They say things like, '[J]ust the other week, I was litigating a case in Utah, and the judge had never handled a large corporate takeover dispute before.'

They also tell us that the Delaware precedents are very complicated, and that a typical takeover case litigated in Delaware will involve careful discussion of a large number of very lengthy prior decisions. The Delaware courts know their way around these, but a judge in another state with no prior background is going to have real difficulty getting acquainted with the nuances. Some practitioners believe this raises a greater risk that the judge will get it wrong. Almost all of these cases are settled, but we were told that settlement payouts get distorted by increased uncertainty regarding litigation outcomes: in other words good claims may be settled for too little and bad claims for too much. The second piece of evidence concerns the litigation rate in corporate takeovers. We document a secular increase in the incidence of class action lawsuits in corporate takeovers, typically whereby target shareholders assert their board has breached fiduciary duties regarding obtaining the best price. The likelihood of being sued was about 40–50 per cent in 1995; by 2010 it is approaching 100 per cent. Most of this increase has, for Delaware companies, been in courts outside Delaware. It seems implausible to me that we can argue an increase in the litigation rate to nearly 100 per cent reflects universal wrongdoing in corporate transactions. Rather, and consistently with what the practitioners are telling us, it more likely reflects an increased ability of plaintiffs (and their lawyers) to obtain a settlement in unmeritorious cases.

JOAN LOUGHREY: I would also be interested in Professor Armour's idea that litigation on directors' duties could potentially move offshore to, for example, Germany, that is, we could see litigation move abroad, much as litigation has moved out of Delaware, possibly because the Delaware courts are seen as too management-friendly and hostile to shareholder claims?

JOHN ARMOUR: Since the ECJ's decision in *Centros* in 1999,[33] there has been a well-documented trend by German entrepreneurs to incorporate their businesses using the English private company form rather than the domestic Gesellschaft mit beschränkter Haftung (GmbH), primarily so as to avoid the minimum capital requirements of the GmbH. This however raises issues regarding the venue for litigation of corporate law disputes in relation to these companies. Where all the parties are physically located in Germany, it may be much more convenient to bring litigation in the German courts rather than to travel to London for a hearing in the Companies Court. Of course, under the EU Judgments Regulation (formerly the Brussels Convention),[34] litigation regarding the validity of an English company's constitution and the acts of its organs may only be litigated in England. However this encompasses only a narrow range of issues, not including many aspects of directors' duties for example. Consequently, and depending on whether the articles contain any sort of jurisdiction agreement, there may be quite a lot of scope for German courts to take jurisdiction over matters relating to English company law in such a case. I'm told by my German colleagues that there is already litigation taking place in German courts regarding English companies. I have no idea as to the frequency of this sort of litigation, but I do know of at least one practitioner text that is in the course of being written by German corporate law scholars, in German, on the English Companies Law Act 2006 to meet the needs of German litigators in these kinds of cases. I think the phenomenon is very interesting question for future empirical work.

SIMON GRAHAM:[35] My question is, if a member of the public were here, a non-specialist member of the public, he might feel that the societal

---

[33] *Centros Ltd v Erhvervs-og Selkabssyrelsen* (C212/97) [2000] Ch 446.
[34] EC Council Regulation 44/2001 [2001] OJ L 12/1, Arts 22(2), 23(5).
[35] Wragge & Co Solicitors.

need for revenge, whether it's aimed at culpably negligent directors, or directors who appear to have unduly enriched themselves, is not going to be slaked anytime soon. I don't know how many of us are in the mood for more company law reform, or do we need to be more honest in acknowledging that we are where we are for a good policy reason. Also is that impulse for revenge coming from the wrong part of the brain? At the end of the day is it self-destructive?

PROFESSOR ANDREW KEAY: I can't really answer that but can I raise a point that is related to what you've just said about revenge. What astounds me is that apart from some suggestions by the Lloyds shareholders, who appear to be considering some sort of a class action against directors of the company, there hasn't been any more publicity given to possible actions against directors of the banks and other financial institutions. It surprises me really, given the fact that there has been so much attention given to the possibility in the media, yet we haven't heard anything formal at all. What I find incredible is people, you know, banged on so long about Sir Fred Goodwin's remuneration[36] but that's peanuts compared to what's been lost by the banks and what we've had to pay up as tax-payers. It's the directors' duties, or whether there have been breaches thereof, that really is the big issue here and of course it may all depend upon whether the potential defendants could pay (though of course there is insurance, directors' and officers' insurance).

I don't know if this is an answer to your question at all, but I was just astounded that we've not heard anything. It may be in the pipeline but it's been some time now since we've known about the financial crisis and we've heard nothing whatsoever. There may not be any grounds for any action and legal advice has been given that there aren't any grounds, but I am surprised that we haven't seen anything further.

---

[36] Goodwin was the CEO of RBS at the time of the financial crisis and was thought to be the chief author of the bank's decision to takeover ABN AMRO and to bear much of the responsibility for RBS's disastrous performance. On his departure from RBS following its bail-out by the Government it was revealed that he had been awarded a £16.9 million pension pot by RBS. This caused widespread public and shareholder anger: J. Treanor, 'Fred Goodwin pension row: 90% of RBS shareholders vote against pay report' *The Guardian*, 3 April 2009. He eventually bowed to public pressure and gave up part of his entitlement and was later stripped of his knighthood: P. Inman and C. Tryhorn, 'Sir Fred Goodwin shreds his pension by 200,000 – but will still get 342,500 a year' *The Guardian* 18 June 2009; BBC, 'Former RBS boss Fred Goodwin stripped of knighthood' (31 January 2012).

MR JUSTICE DAVID RICHARDS: The mechanism for redress is the Company Director's Disqualification Act 1986. So there is, unusually in a civil context, a mechanism where money is not the central issue.

LOUIS DOYLE: Why has that not been used?

MR JUSTICE DAVID RICHARDS: I think that in the absence of an insolvency[37] there has to be an enquiry, because s.8 of the Company Directors Disqualification Act 1986[38] enables proceedings to be brought on the back of a report, and though that could be an internal rather than a public report, it might take a long time.

SPEAKER:[39] And some bank directors have been disqualified from working in financial services anyway, as the Financial Services Authority has powers which don't require the criteria under the Company Directors' Disqualification Act 1986 to be satisfied.[40]

DAVID CABRELLI:[41] I would like to pick up on a point in relation to the application for leave. Louis Doyle has identified the fact that more often than not the court seems to shut out the continuation of the derivative claim on the basis that there is some potential for a s.994 application. And I was wondering to what extent that translates into the shareholder's remedies because, if the shareholder is pushed towards a personal route, is it the case that the courts would be prepared to give a corporate type remedy, for example some kind of restoration of property to the

---

[37]   The Company Directors Disqualification Act 1986 s.6 provides for the disqualification of directors of insolvent companies on grounds of lack of fitness.

[38]   The Company Directors Disqualification Act 1986 s.8(1) provides that the Secretary of State may apply for a disqualification order against a director or shadow director where, following an investigation into the company's affairs, it appears to him to be expedient in the public interest. Section 8(2) provides that the court may make the disqualification order where it is satisfied that the person's conduct in relation to the company makes him unfit to be concerned in the management of a company.

[39]   Not all participants identified themselves.

[40]   The FSA could ban directors from operating in senior positions in the financial services industry under the Financial Services and Markets Act 2000 s.56 and s.63: see for example FSA *Final Notice: David Baker* (13 April 2010) (Former Deputy CEO of Northern Rock) FSA *Final Notice: Richard Barclay* (13 April 2010) (former credit director of Northern Rock); FSA *Final Notice David Jones* (27 July 2010) (former finance director of Northern Rock).

[41]   Senior Lecturer in Commercial Law, Edinburgh Law School, University of Edinburgh.

company, bearing in mind that in a personal s.994 type action the remedy is usually a buy-out order? Would the courts be prepared to go down a route of a disgorgement order against the director?

LOUIS DOYLE: One thing I just want to distance myself from is that I wasn't trying to say that there's a sort of hard and fast policy you can identify, but the two cases that I mentioned[42] were just fact-specific cases where permission wasn't given and in one of them, the deputy judge was quite forthright in bringing the availability of the s.994 remedy to the fore. But I think we go back to where we were earlier on, when we talked about the difference between the derivative action and s.994: they're two very different animals and in fact the case Robin mentioned, *Re Charnley Davies*,[43] a 1990 decision that Lord Scott refers to in *Re Chime Corporation*, is a case in point. In *Re Charnley Davis*, which was concerned with very similar wording to s.459 as it appeared in the old s.27 of the Insolvency Act 1986,[44] Millett J, as he then was, made the point that what is useful in distinguishing between the two types of action is that instead of looking at the claim on its face and deciding which procedural route it should go down, the clue or at least most of the answers, is usually found in looking at the remedy. Once you've established what remedy the claimant is seeking you are led back into deciding whether or not it's a s.994 petition or a derivative action. Well that's fine in theory, but you can also see the potential for overlap between the two types of claim, because as has already been said, you can easily have cases where the gravity of what's been done wrong, the wrong conduct on the part of the directors, affects the shareholders in a personal capacity as well, because of a reduction in the value of the shareholders' interests. So you can see how you can conceivably run both

---

[42]   *Franbar Holdings Ltd v Patel* [2008] EWHC 1534 (Ch), [2008] BCC 885; *Stimpson v Southern Landlords Association* [2009] EWHC 2072 (Ch), [2010] BCC 387. See now also *Iesini v Westrip Holdings Ltd* [2009] EWHC 2526 (Ch), [2010] BCC 420; *Kiani v Cooper* [2010] EWHC 577 (Ch), [2010] BCC 463; *Stainer v Lee* [2010] EWHC 1539 (Ch); [2011] BCC 134 and *Kleanthous v Paphitis* [2011] EWHC 2287 (Ch).

[43]   [1990] BCC 605.

[44]   Insolvency Act 1986 s.27(1) provides that at any time when an administration order is in force, a creditor or member of the company may apply to the court by petition for an order on the ground that the company's affairs, business and property are being or have been managed by the administrator in a manner which is unfairly prejudicial to the interests of its creditors or members generally, or of some part of its creditors or members (including at least himself).

claims. I have just as a final point to make as a footnote: again, as Robin Hollington said, it's not beyond the wit of a lot of lawyers to very cleverly dress up what might be in substance a s.994 petition as a derivative action, and vice versa in fact.

ZHONG ZHANG:[45] I see that there's a fundamental problem with the derivative action, which is that, on the one hand, you need to avoid the permission stage becoming a mini trial. On the other hand, you need to decide whether this action is beneficial to the company. So, in this case, judges are put in a very difficult position. When the full evidence is not available and not verified by cross-examination, but the court needs to decide whether this action is beneficial for the company I'm not sure how one would approach this question. To make life more difficult, the court needs to decide whether the benefit from a proposed course of action (the litigation) would be outweighed by the harm that it would otherwise cause to the company, even before the action has yet to be approved and when the harm has not actually been caused.

ROBIN HOLLINGTON QC: If I may just come back to that on the derivative action point. Often it may turn on whether the claimant shareholder needs or wants a Wallersteiner order,[46] because the advantage of a derivative claim for shareholders is that you can apply for an order that the company funds the action, which is, if you get it, of huge tactical significance. Once you've got your Wallersteiner order, you're up and running, the company is paying for it and you can't lose, because even if you lose the action the company indemnifies you for the cost. So what I don't think comes out of a lot of the cases, is that it makes a huge difference whether the derivative claim is one that requires a Wallersteiner order or one that doesn't. This is because if the claimant is prepared to fund it himself and is good for the money if he loses, then it seems to me that the court is going to be more willing to grant permission to continue, than in a case where the court is also being asked for Wallersteiner order. I think in many cases the really difficult question is not whether permission should be granted, but whether and on what terms the Wallersteiner indemnity order should be given.

I have no recent experience of the matter, but I agree with you that it must be very difficult for the courts to decide on applications for

---

[45]   Academic Research Fellow, School of East Asian Studies, University of Sheffield.
[46]   Named after the leading case: *Wallersteiner v Moir (No 2)* [1975] QB 373.

permission. There may well be cases where it is right for the company to be separately represented and for it to put forward a case from the point of view of the hypothetical independent board.

Conclusion

Joan Loughrey

This book began with the observation that there has been surprisingly little litigation against bank boards in the UK given that, whatever the precise causes of the financial crisis, the troubles suffered by banks such as Northern Rock plc and the Royal Bank of Scotland plc (RBS) were at least in part a result of poor management. Focusing specifically on the law governing directors' duties in the first part of this book and shareholder litigation in the second, and taking account of practitioner views expressed in the third, the contributions in this book have identified a range of reasons why this might be so and why company law has failed to provide an effective means for holding bank directors to account. Although the behaviour in question was governed by the common law, the majority of contributors concluded that the codification of directors' duties and of the derivative action in the Companies Act 2006 is unlikely to improve the law's efficacy in deterring blinkered short-termist behaviour, in penalizing disastrous senior management decisions or in encouraging greater shareholder engagement.

Turning to directors' duties, Loughrey outlined a number of problems in enforcing both the common law duty of care and its codified version in the Companies Act 2006 s.174. These include a reluctance to second-guess commercial judgment that has caused the courts to be very 'hands-off' in assessing directors' conduct. As a result, judges are unlikely to find a breach of duty even in the case of disastrous decisions unless a serious flaw can be found in the directors' decision-making process, or unless directors have failed to exercise any judgment at all. Moreover proving causation is a significant hurdle and would be particularly problematic in the context of the financial crisis. Nevertheless, the inadequate due diligence carried out by RBS prior to the takeover of ABN AMRO would appear to provide RBS's shareholders with a strong claim for breach of management's duty of care and skill, particularly since this is likely to have been a causative factor in the collapse of

RBS.[1] However, it is notable that the FSA concluded that it could not bring enforcement action against any director of RBS for acting without due skill, care and diligence because the board's conduct was not beyond a range of reasonable responses and other market players would have behaved equally badly.[2] The FSA was, of course, concerned with its own enforcement jurisdiction rather than with the director's statutory duty of care. Nevertheless, if the FSA is correct, and if conducting a disastrous takeover on the basis of what the FSA itself found to be insufficient and inappropriate due diligence[3] is not sufficient to establish a failure to act with due care, skill and diligence, this throws into doubt the utility of the duty of care as an accountability mechanism.

In reaching its position the FSA had taken into account both the fact and content of legal advice that the RBS board had sought from Linklaters in May 2007 regarding whether the board had given the takeover proper consideration[4] and on whether, in September 2007, RBS could have withdrawn from the bid in the face of deteriorating market conditions.[5] As this advice was hidden from scrutiny by legal professional privilege which RBS could have waived but chose not to, it is impossible to assess either its merits, the part it played in the directors' decision-making or in the FSA's decision not to take action against the RBS directors. Given the public interest in understanding what occurred in RBS and why the FSA chose not to take enforcement action, this is unfortunate to say the least. It also raises important questions about the role of legal advice and the extent to which it should be possible for directors to rely on such advice to justify their conduct and to shield themselves against litigation or enforcement action.

Turning to the s.172 duty to promote the success of the company for the benefit of its members as a whole, Keay takes the view in Chapter 2 that it may neither succeed in encouraging more responsible decision-making and in guiding directors away from short-termist decisions nor be an effective means by which directors can be held to account for poor decisions. This is, among other things, due to: the need to show that

---

[1] House of Commons Treasury Committee, *Banking Crisis: Dealing with the Failure of the UK Banks,* Seventh Report of Session 2008–09 (21 April 2009) at para 35; FSA, *The Failure of the Royal Bank of Scotland* (December 2011) at paras 195–197.

[2] FSA, *The Failure of the Royal Bank of Scotland* (December 2011) at para 198.

[3] Ibid.

[4] Ibid at 415.

[5] Ibid.

directors have acted in bad faith before a breach can be established; the fact that stakeholders other than shareholders cannot enforce the s.172 duty; and difficulties in assessing the quality of directors' decisions caused both by the lack of clarity over the meaning of the phrase 'success of the company' and by the fact that directors will be able to justify their decisions against more than one set of criteria.

Chapter 8 revealed a division of opinion between the practitioners and academics regarding the likely impact of s.172. While some academics were more optimistic than Keay about its potential impact, the practitioners shared his scepticism. Like Keay they thought that s.172 was weakened by the fact that stakeholders other than shareholders would be unable to enforce it, while shareholders who could, in theory, enforce the section through the derivative action, will not do so. In their opinion it changed nothing.

It is arguable that assessing s.172 in these terms places too much emphasis on the question of its enforceability, and not enough on its potential for altering behaviour in other ways. As Campbell argues in Chapter 4, bad decisions may be explained by unconscious distortions of directors' decision-making processes. Among the safeguards Campbell suggests could be utilized to address these deficiencies are requirements that boards obtain further data and analysis about a decision, hear from a range of viewpoints and engage in a real debate about its merits. Could s.172 go some way towards providing these kinds of checks? It might, if requiring directors to have regard to the list of statutory factors in s.172 means that they think about matters that they might otherwise have overlooked or, if they did previously consider such matters, to think more carefully about them. The requirement to have regard to the statutory factors could also lead to boards seeking further information about those factors including, where appropriate, reports from independent consultants.[6] Thus complying with s.172 could result in boards obtaining the kind of additional information, analysis and range of viewpoints that Campbell advocates. In turn this could provide non-executive directors, who otherwise depend on management for information, with the necessary material to challenge management and to initiate a real debate, something that did not occur on bank boards in the lead-up to the crisis.[7]

---

[6] See also J. Loughrey, A. Keay and L. Cerioni, 'Legal Practitioners, the Corporate Objective and the Shaping of Corporate Governance' (2008) 8 *Journal of Corporate Law Studies* 79 at 102–103.

[7] D. Walker, *A Review of Corporate Governance in Banks and Other Financial Institutions Final Recommendations* (November 2009) at 12; FSA, *The Failure of the Royal Bank of Scotland* (December 2011) at 234.

The view that observing s.172 could alter behaviour is supported by Taylor in his contribution in Chapter 8. He argued that s.172 had made a tangible difference to directors' behaviour by narrowing the range of factors that directors could take into account, in an effort to avoid the types of short-term disastrous decision-making that led to Enron and the financial crisis. He had found that companies had changed their procedures in response to s.172[8] which is significant given Campbell's argument that changes in the way decisions are made could address unconscious distortions of decision-making processes and lead to better decisions.[9]

On the other hand, as Chapter 8 shows, the practitioners considered that the advice lawyers would give boards regarding how directors should fulfil their duty to act in the company's interests would not alter in response to s.172. It would be, in other words, business as usual. It is of course not possible to draw any firm conclusions from this about the attitude of professional advisers more generally. Nevertheless, if the views of these practitioners were typical, this could have significant implications for the manner in which s.172 is applied and its likely impact. Legal advisers' interpretation of s.172 is likely to be a very significant influence on directors' understanding of and response to the section, particularly given that, as Keay has highlighted, there is a lack of judicial authority on its meaning. In the absence of case law, lawyers' interpretation of what the law requires becomes authoritative until overturned by a judicial decision.[10] Yet authority on s.172 is likely to remain scarce given the low levels of shareholder litigation that Tomasic and Akinbami report and the enforcement problems with s.172 that Keay identifies.[11] As a result the interpretation of the section and what it requires will necessarily be based on the views of a company's legal advisers. Moreover the more uncertain the law is, the more scope there is

---

[8]   P. Taylor, 'Enlightened Shareholder Value and the Companies Act 2006' (unpublished PhD thesis, May 2010), Birkbeck College, University of London.

[9]   See also L. Stout, 'In Praise of Procedure: An Economic and Behavioral Defense of Smith v Van Gorkom and the Business Judgment Rule' (2002) 96 *Northwestern University Law Review* 675 at 677.

[10]   E. B. Rock, 'Saints and Sinners: How Does Delaware Corporate Law Work?' 44 *UCLA Law Review* 1009 at 1096.

[11]   In fact the level of shareholder litigation is likely to reduce given the Court of Appeal decision in *Fulham Football Club (1987) Ltd v Richards* [2011] EWCA Civ 855 that where the shareholders' agreement/constitution provides that shareholder disputes should go to arbitration a shareholder will be prevented from litigating.

for interpretation and the more influential will be the lawyers' advice.[12] Consequently, if lawyers are telling boards that s.172 requires no change of approach, the section may well have little impact on board behaviour, no matter what academics perceive to be its potential.

The role of shareholders prior to the crisis also attracted criticism and there have been calls for institutional shareholders in particular to perform a greater monitoring role. However, as Keay points out and as Villiers analyses in detail, shareholders are impaired in their ability to monitor compliance with s.172, which in turn undermines the potential for enforcement of the section and thus for the promotion of more enlightened behaviour by corporate boards. As Villiers discusses, although the Companies Act 2006 s.417 requires companies to provide a business review which is intended 'to inform members of the company and help them assess how the directors have performed their duty under s.172', the quality of the reporting under this section is poor. Business reviews technically comply with the law in a tick box fashion but do not constitute substantive attempts at clear and useful communication with investors.

Concerns over the quality of narrative reporting led the Government to launch consultations on how to improve matters.[13] It proposed replacing the business review with a Strategic Report which, like the business review, is meant to provide 'a fair, balanced and comprehensive review of the business to enable users to assess how directors have performed their duties under section 172 of the Companies Act 2006'.[14] The Strategic Report is to contain concise high quality disclosures thus simplifying disclosures and making them easier for shareholders to assess.[15] It remains to be seen how successful the Government will be in achieving its goal given that its proposals do not yet address key factors identified by Villiers as contributing to poor quality narrative reporting.

These include fear of liability on the part of boards, should forward-looking statements prove to be inaccurate. This fear has been exacerbated as a result of the financial crisis which disproved many assumptions held

---

[12] L. Edelman, S. Abraham and H. Erlanger, 'Professional Construction of the Law: The Inflated Threat of Wrongful Discharge' (1992) 26 *Law and Society Review* 47 at 48.

[13] BIS, *Corporate Law and Corporate Governance: The Future of Narrative Reporting* (August 2010); BIS, *The Future of Narrative Reporting: Consulting on a New Reporting Framework* (September 2011).

[14] BIS, *The Future of Narrative Reporting: Consulting on a New Reporting Framework* (September 2011) at 49.

[15] Ibid at paras 3.16–3.18.

by business and the markets. Villiers found that under the guidance of lawyers, managers, wary of liability, provide guarded and ultimately uninformative forward-looking statements. She argues that lawyers have blocked the voice of senior management, substituting their own voices instead and in doing so defeated the purpose of the business review. As Villiers notes, this defensive attitude suggests that management has little faith in the safe harbour provisions in the Companies Act 2006 which impose liability on directors for false statements only where directors know or are reckless as to their veracity.[16] Given that merely negligent misstatements will not be penalized and most directors do not set out to make fraudulent or reckless statements, the question is why directors are so wary. The Government has also posed this question, asking whether this is due to misunderstanding about the liability regime.[17]

Villiers' research indicates that at least part of the answer is likely to lie with the board's legal advisers who have either communicated the risks of liability but have not succeeded in communicating the significance of the legislative safe harbours or have provided an unduly pessimistic and cautious interpretation of how the safe harbours will be applied. That this might be happening is supported by research that suggests that lawyers have a tendency to exaggerate legal risk.[18] Since the Government's proposals do not yet address the problem of lawyers exaggerating the risk of liability or of boards failing to hear their lawyers correctly, the problem of boilerplate reporting may well survive the introduction of a Strategic Review.

The Government also proposes to do little about another key weakness identified by Villiers. She argues that the system of enforcement mechanisms fails to penalize companies for presenting themselves in a light which does not reflect their real nature. This undermines the legislative goal of enlightened shareholder value by making it less likely that boards

---

[16] Companies Act 2006 s.463 and s.1270, inserting new s.90A into the Financial Services and Markets Act 2000.

[17] BIS, *The Future of Narrative Reporting: Consulting on a New Reporting Framework* (September 2011) at 26.

[18] L. Edelman, S. Abraham and H. Erlanger, 'Professional Construction of the Law: The Inflated Threat of Wrongful Discharge' (1992) 26 *Law and Society Review* 47; D. Langevoort, 'The Epistemology of Corporate-Securities Lawyering: Beliefs, Biases and Organizational Behavior' (1997) 63 *Brooklyn Law Review* 629 at 655–656; D. Langevoort and R. Rasmussen, 'Skewing the Results: The Role of Lawyers in Transmitting Legal Rules' (1997) 5 *Southern California Disciplinary Law Journal* 375 at 375.

will feel the need to take decisions that truly take into account the impact of their actions in the long term and on a broader range of stakeholders.

However, the Government considered the enforcement activity of the Financial Reporting Review Panel ('FRRP') to be appropriate and that an increase in enforcement activity would place an undue administrative burden on companies and the regulator and could be counter-productive by encouraging the kind of defensive poor quality reporting it wishes to eliminate.[19] This concern is misplaced. As Villiers points out, the failure of the FRRP to pursue action for poor reporting means that directors have little incentive to improve the quality of their reports. At the same time directors have incentives to continue to obfuscate due to fear of liability. The upshot is that directors say as little as possible. Given that the Government has not yet come forward with any proposals that could eliminate this problem it could at least rebalance the incentive structure of directors through tougher enforcement activity.

If narrative reporting is improved to facilitate shareholder monitoring, would it lead to greater shareholder engagement? This seems unlikely. As Villiers points out many shareholders still prefer to sell their shares and exit a company rather than monitor and engage with corporate govern-ance issues.

Tomasic and Akinbami examine in more detail why shareholders have not only failed to be effective monitors ex ante but have also proved to be slow to pursue remedial actions against the boards of banks ex post. Their study shows that over a ten-year period most litigation involving shareholders took place in small private companies rather than public companies, that institutional shareholders form a minority of litigants and that very few claims are derivative in nature. They identify several reasons for this: the costs of activism, information asymmetry, free-rider problems and shareholder conservatism. As these problems survive the financial crisis and have not been adequately addressed, Tomasic and Akinbami criticize the Walker Review's continued emphasis on the shareholder role and are pessimistic about the impact of the Stewardship Code in promoting greater shareholder engagement. They also argue that even when shareholders do seek to hold directors to account, company law fails to provide them with effective tools to do so, whether that is because the law on directors' duties is, as Keay and Loughrey have argued, not fit for purpose, or because company law remedies, particu-larly the derivative claim, fail to provide effective recourse.

---

[19] BIS, *The Future of Narrative Reporting: Consulting on a New Reporting Framework* (September 2011) at paras 8.4–8.7.

Like Loughrey and Villiers, Tomasic and Akinbami flag up the role of lawyers in advising against litigation or enforcement action against bank boards. They argue moreover that lawyers have influenced the development of the law both by lobbying when legislative provisions are being developed and when presenting arguments to the courts over the meaning of the law. In doing, they argue, lawyers have shaped the law on directors' duties and shareholder litigation in such a way that successful litigation against bank boards is unlikely.

The lawyer's role is again highlighted when we turn to another critical factor contributing to the law's impotency, namely the attitude of the courts to shareholder litigation. Hollington's discussion of the use by members of open-ended investment funds of winding up petitions on just and equitable grounds illustrates this point nicely. In the Cayman Islands the courts have taken a 'minority investor-friendly' approach and shareholders have succeeded in having funds wound up, thus retrieving their investments. The Cayman Islands courts have been flexible in shaping the winding up petition into an effective shareholder remedy even when the litigation has occurred in the context of commercial companies run at arm's length from the shareholders. In contrast, in the British Virgin Islands, the courts have shown more hostility to investor claims. Citing *Foss v Harbottle*[20] and the principle of majority rule, the courts there have denied minority shareholders a remedy and left them to the mercy of the funds' management whose interests, as Hollington points out, could potentially conflict with those of the investors. This divergence between the Cayman Islands and the British Virgin Islands highlights the importance of the role of judicial attitudes in promoting or undermining the efficacy of shareholder remedies.

Unfortunately the approach of the British Virgin Island courts, with their focus on majority rule, more closely mirrors that of the English courts where such arguments have long been used to deny minority shareholders the right to bring litigation in respect of managerial wrongdoing and negligence. In particular the courts have shown a marked reluctance to allow derivative claims to proceed, especially in dispersed share-ownership companies and other companies run at arm's length from the shareholders. This in part explains why, as Tomasic and Akinbami point out, derivative claims form a minority of cases brought by shareholders and are rarely brought in public companies. This is significant because in lieu of action taken by the banks themselves, the derivative action would be the most appropriate remedy for shareholders

---

[20]   (1843) 2 Hare 461; 67 ER 189.

seeking redress on their company's behalf for the disastrous management decisions that wrought havoc on the banks. It is true that, as raised in Chapter 8, 'clever lawyers' can seek to use the unfair prejudice petition to obtain a remedy for the company in respect of a wrong to the company to circumvent the restrictive requirements of the derivative action. However, the scope of the unfair prejudice remedy has been so greatly restricted in public companies[21] that it is highly unlikely such attempts would be successful and, as pointed out in Chapter 8, the courts would be alert to such tactics.

It seems unlikely that the introduction of the statutory derivative action under the Companies Act 2006 will soften judicial attitudes to derivative claims in dispersed share-ownership companies. As Keay and Loughrey discuss in Chapter 7 the codification of the derivative action was never, in fact, intended to encourage an increase in shareholder litigation and such an increase has not materialized. Moreover in those cases which have come before the courts following the Companies Act 2006, permission to proceed has been granted in only three cases so far, and then only up to the disclosure stage of proceedings, following which the issue of permission to proceed further was to be reviewed. The courts have often refused permission on the basis that an alternative remedy, in the form of the unfair prejudice petition, is available to the minority shareholder thus channelling disputes about directors' behaviour towards that form of action. Another common ground for refusing permission is that a hypothetical director would not attach sufficient importance to pursuing the claim because, for example, of the damage to the company's reputation that would ensue. Such a restrictive approach in the context of small and medium sized companies,[22] where the courts have historically been more accepting of shareholder litigation, is likely to deter shareholders contemplating derivative actions against bank directors and does not bode well for any attempt to bring such actions. Derivative litigation would often be commercially disruptive and permission might therefore be refused as a result. On the other hand the disruption might not be so great if the litigation was brought against past, rather than existing,

---

[21] *Re Blue Arrow* (1987) 3 BCC 618; *Re Astec (BSR) plc* [1999] BCC 59.

[22] None of the cases involved large publicly owned dispersed share-ownership companies though in *Mission Capital plc v Sinclair* [2008] EWHC 1339 (Ch); [2008] BCC 866 the company was admitted to AIM. *Stimpson v Southern Private Landlords Association* [2009] EWHC 2072 (Ch); [2010] BCC 387 involved a company limited by guarantee which had over 1700 members. Permission was not granted in either case.

management and many of the authors of the banks' misfortunes have left their posts.

Finally while the discussion in this book focused on directors' duties and shareholder litigation, a sub-theme emerged from a number of the contributions regarding the role of a company's legal advisors. Loughrey, Villiers and Tomasic and Akinbami all draw attention to the role of corporate lawyers in shaping the law, in guiding boards on how to engage with their legal obligations and in advising companies and regulators on enforcement action. The contributions suggest that lawyers can be key players in promoting or subverting effective corporate governance and legislative goals. Despite this the role of the lawyers tends to escape regulatory attention. This is an issue that would benefit from further research and debate and from closer regulatory scrutiny.

To conclude, this book finds that not only are the directors of most banks likely to escape accountability but also that the law on directors duties (at least the duties comprised in s.172 and s.174 of the Companies Act 2006) together with the new derivative action do not provide effective means for holding directors accountable in dispersed share-ownership companies generally. As one of the contributors to the Chapter 8 debate has pointed out elsewhere, the private enforcement of corporate governance in the UK is 'close to nil for listed companies'.[23] The contributions in this book provide an insight into why this is so.

---

[23]   J. Armour, 'Enforcement Strategies in UK Corporate Governance' in J. Armour and J. Payne, *Rationality in Company Law: Essays in Honour of Dan Prentice* (Oxford, Hart Publishing, 2009) at 85.

Index